After #MeToo

After #MeToo

Feminism, Patriarchy, Toxic Masculinity and Sundry Cultural Delights

Gerard Casey

SOCIETAS
essays in political
& cultural criticism

imprint-academic.com

Published in the UK by
Imprint Academic Ltd., PO Box 200, Exeter EX5 5YX, UK

Distributed in the USA by
Ingram Book Company,
One Ingram Blvd., La Vergne, TN 37086, USA

ISBN 9781788360272 paperback

A CIP catalogue record for this book is available from the
British Library and US Library of Congress

To the one who,
in 2017,
challenged me to
persist with my work

My own sex, I hope, will excuse me, if I treat them like rational creatures, instead of flattering their fascinating graces, and viewing them as if they were in a state of perpetual childhood
—Mary Wollstonecraft

Contents

Foreword and Acknowledgements

I must begin by making a confession. When it comes to women, I am biased. 'We knew it!' some of my readers will think, 'we've always suspected as much, and now he's finally come out and owned up to it!' Yes, but wait a minute. I am indeed biased when it comes to women, but I am biased in their favour! All my life I have been more favourably disposed towards women than towards men and indeed, when I was teaching at the university, I was always *instinctively* more accommodating and sympathetic to my female students than I was towards my male students, so much so that I had to be vigilant to ensure I didn't inadvertently relatively disadvantage the male students. Despite the deep suspicions of some of those who do not love me, then, I'm not a misogynist; I just don't happen to believe that all women are, like Mary Poppins, practically perfect in every way. I believe, on the contrary, that they are real human beings, with all the virtues and all the faults that being human brings with it. I shouldn't have to say this but I suppose I must: my criticisms of feminism in this book are *not* criticisms of women in general.

To pre-emptively avoid possible misunderstandings, let me make it clear where I stand on male-female issues. I believe that, subject to the constraints of reality, there should be no *state-imposed* discriminatory legal policies that favour either women or men. However, I also believe that, subject to the zero aggression principle (*No one may initiate physical violence against the person or property of another*), individuals or groups of individuals should be free to do as they wish with their property, including favouring one sex over another when it comes to its disposal, if that is their choice. Such decisions, of course, have their consequences, and those who make them must be prepared to live with negative non-aggressive responses to them, including criticism, shunning or boycotting. I believe that women and men should be free to make the social and career choices that they wish, whether others approve of them or not. As long as such choices involve no violation of the zero aggression principle, others are obliged to tolerate such choices, but there is no obligation on others to facilitate them, nor should they be obliged to approve of them on pain of legal sanctions. This is the libertarian core of *After #MeToo*. That said, many of the views I express and the approach I take in *After #MeToo*, while they are *consistent* with the bedrock principle of libertarianism, the Zero Aggression Principle, are not necessarily *implied* by it, and some libertarians could well, and very likely will, disagree with some of what I've written. If I had to find a label to describe the general tenor of my extra-libertarian approach here, the best one would probably be 'socially conservative'.

When I was polishing the final version of the text, I came across a second-hand copy of David Thomas's 1993 book, *Not Guilty: Men—the Case for the Defence*. This discovery was quite serendipitous as I wasn't looking for this book—I couldn't have been looking for it since I didn't even know it existed! As I read through it, I was alternately exhilarated and depressed—exhilarated to find a book from the last millennium touching on so many (but not all) of the points I wanted to make in my own book, and depressed for exactly the same reason! It really *is* depressing, despite the rampant gynocentrism of the last forty years, to find feminists today still chanting the same dirges of oppression, harassment, rape culture, pay gaps and so on *ad nauseam*. The biggest difference between now and forty years ago is that matters are now much worse, so much so that 1993 begins to look like the good old days. Another excellent book I came across just before finishing the final draft of this book was Steve Moxon's *The Woman Racket*. Once again, I was alternately exhilarated and depressed to find a book, this time from the twenty-preteens, that echoed many of Thomas's points and pre-echoed not a few of my own. Whether the convergence of Thomas, Moxon and Casey is either a case of great minds thinking alike or fools seldom differing, I will leave to the reader to decide.

Some may take exception to the levity displayed at various points in this book in the form of sarcasm, irony and rhetorical exaggeration. I make no apology for such levity and it is not to be taken as an indication that I don't think the issues are serious. However, some kinds of folly are so egregious that rebutting them piously gives them more credit than they deserve. I do, of course, employ arguments in various places in the book but my main weapon throughout is the solvent power of laughter. The Devil, it is said, cannot bear to be mocked, and mockery is what the devils of #MeToo and the other diabolical members of the sorority of sorrowful siblings get in full measure. My mockery is directed primarily at human folly and not, except incidentally, at the humans who perpetrate that folly. My religion demands that I love my enemies (that particular commandment really cramps my style!) and I believe that in this book, I am doing just that by practising one of the spiritual works of mercy, namely, counselling the ignorant. I write what I write not *de haut en bas* but as a fellow sinner among sinners; God only knows (and so do my family and friends!) that I have committed my share of idiocies to the common pool of human folly, perhaps more than my share if some of my severer critics are to be believed.

In a few places, I have made use of some material I have already published but I've kept this to a minimum. The re-used material comes primarily from *Freedom's Progress?* (on the patriarchy) and from *ZAP* (on women and work).

I believe that all the statements made in this book about named or identifiable individuals are substantially true. In almost every such case, these statements are a re-publication, either verbatim or in paraphrase, of reports already available in the public domain. In any event, statements made in this book are my honest opinions and are made in the public interest.

Thanks are due to Peter White and Tim Crowley for their help and support. I am especially grateful to Steve Blendell for his superhuman and supererogatory efforts of proofreading. And a special thanks to Jason Walsh for transforming a shapeless mass of words into something approaching a thing of beauty, if not quite a joy forever.

Readers who would like a quick overview of the themes of the book should read the Coda.

The writing of this book was completed on 4 November 2019.

Fun with Feminism

When women kiss it always reminds one of prizefighters shaking hands
—H. L. Mencken

Western society is obsessed with women to the point of mass neurosis
—David Thomas

The apparently simple question, 'Are you a feminist?', contains a trap for the unwary. If you answer *no*, you'll be depicted as some kind of knuckle-dragging Neanderthal who thinks women should be chained, bare-footed, to the kitchen sink. If you answer *yes*, you'll be taken as committing yourself to supporting the campaign for special privileges and perks for women, just because, and only because, they are women.

During the course of the scramble for leadership of the UK's Conservative Party in May 2019, most of the candidates when asked were willing to describe themselves as feminists, but not Dominick Raab. Shock! Horror! Cue Twitter rants and mass expostulation. Who, even in the Conservative Party, could be so benighted as to reject the idea of treating men and women equally? Well, not Dominick Raab as it happens, who describes himself as being 'passionate about equality', an odd kind of thing to be passionate about, but let's take him at his word. But how can that be? Didn't he deny being a feminist, and isn't feminism precisely the doctrine that holds that men and women should be treated equally? It turns out that Raab is not alone in denying he's a feminist. So do most women! Are *they* rejecting the idea that men and women should be treated equally? In one study carried out by the Fawcett Society, just under 20% of young women aged between eighteen and twenty-five described themselves as feminists, and under 10% of women overall so described themselves. Other studies show a somewhat greater proportion of women describing themselves as feminists but, at its highest, no more than a third. Raab, it would seem, is in good (or perhaps bad) company. But the apparent misogyny of Raab, and the seemingly mysterious self-flagellation of a majority of women, is susceptible of a ready solution. Like many another question of whether one is or isn't an X, the answer should be prefaced by 'It depends on what you mean by X.' The term *feminism*, like charity, covers a multitude

When most women repudiate the label *feminist*, precisely what are they rejecting? Are they saying that women shouldn't have the vote, shouldn't be able to own and dispose of property, and shouldn't be able to stand for public office? That's seems antecedently unlikely and, since female suffrage and the right of women to own and dispose of property are the essence of a certain kind of feminism, I would think that almost every woman who thinks about it at all will happily describe herself as a feminist *in this sense of the term*, as indeed would many men. But there are many varieties of feminism, and what I've just described is the essence or core of what is often termed first-wave feminism, whose remit ran more or less from the end of the 18th century to the 1950s. Feminism has had later 'waves' whose aims and ambitions go well beyond those of feminism in its original remit and, as I've noted, not every woman (or man) is willing to sign up to the endorsement of these aims and ambitions; that's what their rejection of the label *feminist* implies.

Types of feminism

To aid our discussion, here is a brief, schematic typology of feminisms, a typology that ought to be reasonably uncontroversial though it must frankly be admitted that almost nothing in this area is uncontroversial. What is called **first wave feminism** was, as I've just mentioned, a movement extending over about 150 years (1800-1950) that was primarily dedicated to bringing about the removal of legal and social prohibitions on women's political participation and on their ability to own and dispose of property.

Second wave feminism arose in the 1950s and it flourished from then until about the end of the 1980s. Simone de Beauvoir's seminal (or ovular) *The Second Sex* was published in 1949 and the year 1963 saw the publication of Betty Friedan's *The Feminine Mystique*. Second wave feminism focussed its attention primarily on family matters, on perceived inequities in the workplace, and on the removal of all remaining legal inequalities between men and women. Part of the family-matters remit of second wave feminism concerned what is sometimes termed reproductive rights, namely, the right to contraception and abortion which should perhaps, in the interests of accuracy, be called non-reproductive rights. The contraceptive pill was approved by the Food and Drugs Administration in the USA in 1960, and the US Supreme Court case of *Griswold vs Connecticut* [1965], with its ingenious discovery of a constitutional right to privacy cleverly concealed within the 'penumbras' and 'emanations' of other constitutional provisions, paved the way for the eventual US-wide liberalisation of abortion in *Roe vs Wade* some eight years later. Ominously, second wave feminism also brought us the first adumbration of the fateful if not entirely pellucid distinction between sex and gender.

Third wave feminism (sometimes called **radical feminism** or **gender feminism**) extends roughly from the 1990s to the present. It piggybacks on second wave feminism but makes greater play of the still less-than-pellucid distinction between sex and gender, and focuses its energies on attacking what it terms 'rape culture', sexual assault, sexual harassment, domestic violence and generalised misogyny. The term *third wave* was introduced by Rebecca Walker in an article she published in 1992 following the appointment of Clarence Thomas to the US Supreme Court. 'Let Thomas' confirmation serve to remind you, as it did me,' she wrote, 'that the fight is far from over. Let this dismissal of a woman's experience move you to anger. Turn that outrage into political power. Do not vote for them unless they work for us. Do not have sex with them, do not break bread with them, do not nurture them if they don't prioritize our freedom to control our bodies and our lives. I am not a post-feminism feminist. I am the Third Wave.' (Walker) What distinguishes third wave feminism from its second wave predecessor is not an easy question to answer but some would say the difference is marked by the concept of *intersectionality*. Second wave feminism is criticised by feminists of a more radical stripe for what they see as its concentration on the concerns of middle class heterosexual white women to the virtual exclusion of the problems of lesbians, women of colour and working-class women. Third wave feminists tend to see the oppression of women, however broadly conceived, as just one aspect of a more extensive notion of oppression of people by sex, by race and by class, these categories intersecting at various points. If you are a worker, you are oppressed; if you're black you are oppressed; if you are a lesbian you are oppressed. If you are a black lesbian worker, you are intersectionally triply-oppressed.

Where there are the oppressed, there must of necessity be oppressors. So, men oppress women, whites oppress blacks, heterosexuals oppress homosexuals, capitalists oppress workers, the cisgendered oppress the trans-gendered and the able-bodied oppress the disabled or differently-abled. The intersection of these categories gives rise to some seeming anomalies so, for example, if you are a black, lesbian company director you are at once oppressed (black and lesbian) and an oppressor (company director). If you are a man you are an oppressor; if you are white you are an oppressor; if you are unemployed, you are oppressed; if you are a worker, you are oppressed. If you are a white, male, unemployed worker you are at once oppressed (unemployed worker) and an oppressor (white and male). It shouldn't need to be stated that being a man doesn't always put you exclusively on the privileged side of the great victim-divide. One can be simultaneously privileged and oppressed but not in respect of the same category. Thus, a cisgendered white woman is privileged in respect of her whiteness and cisgenderedness but oppressed in respect of her femaleness. An able-bodied attractive homosexual is privileged in respect of his able-bodiedness and attractiveness but oppressed in respect of his homosexuality. How are we to calculate the fine grades of oppression and rank them on a scale where they can be compared? Whose victimhood is superior? The radical idea put forward by many patriarchs (men to you and me) that we should treat people as individuals and not as tokens of various types is, of course, just another reprehensible and devious exercise of patriarchal power designed to suppress the oppressed groups' consciousness of their group identities which is what gives them their superior victim status. Such a reactionary idea can be safely ignored.

The distinction between men and women is rejected by feminists as an artificial binary construct designed to maintain and perpetuate the power of the dominant group—men. This radical feminist attack on the binary distinction between male and female is just one form of a general attack on all kinds of binary distinctions. At around the time of its origin, third-wave feminism allied itself with the burgeoning LGB movement and it was also about this time that the T in LGBT—transgender—made its appearance. The recent emergence of militant transgenderism has strained the relationship between radical feminists and those who put the T in LGBT. Since radical feminists have as one of their objectives the elimination of the very idea of woman as one element in the binary man/woman, it is delightfully ironic that in this second decade of the 21st century, they should find themselves in a life-and-death struggle for supreme victim status with those transgenderists who claim to be women, a claim that, given feminists' deconstructive proclivities, can be rejected by our radical feminist friends only at the risk of intellectual incoherence.

One's identity as a victim logically requires the existence of victimisers, and if such victimisers don't spontaneously appear then they must be uncovered. Victim-homosexuals obsessed with homophobia see it everywhere, victim-feminists complain incessantly of structural patriarchal oppression, and those most virulent of victims, the transactivists, are convinced against all reason that the whole of society, including their rivals in victimology (especially radical feminists) are engaged in a transphobic conspiracy to do them down.

As victimisation is a zero-sum game, there is intense competition among the various victim types for the moral high ground. 'I'm oppressed.' 'I'm more oppressed than you are!' Such claims are reminiscent of the famous Monty Python *Four Yorkshiremen* sketch in which a group of middle-aged champagne-drinking buddies compete to tell the wildest and most extreme story of poverty and deprivation, capped with this gem from Eric Idle: 'Right. I had to get up in 't morning at ten o'clock at night, half an hour before I went to bed, drink a cup of sulphuric acid, work twenty-nine hours a day down 't mill, and pay mill owner for permission to come to work, and when we got home, our Dad and our mother would kill us, and dance about on our graves singing "Hallelujah".' Michael Palin says, 'But you try and tell young people today that ... and they won't believe ya.' So, trans against TERFs (trans-exclusionary radical feminists), homosexuals against bisexuals, black gays against white gays, and victims of Islamophobia against victims of anti-Semitism. In radical feminism, the last vestiges of liberal egalitarianism to be found in second-wave feminism are firmly jettisoned in favour of other more radical claims so that, as Herbert Purdy notes, feminism now 'has nothing to do with equality, and it is not about fairness. Neither is it egalitarianism, nor is it born of the liberalism of the enlightenment. Radical feminists are not interested in equality of opportunity, irrespective of race, colour, creed— or sex—principles that are universally accepted as right. Theirs is the communist-utopian definition of equality qua sameness: parity of numbers disconnected from achievement through merit and ability, and divorced from skills and attributes.' (Purdy, vi)

The relatively neat (and much simplified) division between different forms of feminism that I have just sketched is not necessarily the whole story. In the introduction to their book, *What is Feminism?*, Juliet Mitchell and Ann Oakley note, 'There are radical feminists, Socialist feminists, Marxist feminists, lesbian separatists, women of colour, and so on, each group with its own carefully preserved sense of identity. Each for itself is the only worthwhile feminism; others are ignored except to be criticized.' The list of types of feminism, and the characterisation of each type, varies from writer to writer. There are so many forms of feminism that we have pretty much arrived at a situation in which each woman is her own feminist. Rosalind Delmar argues that there is no '"true" and authentic feminism, unified and consistent over time and in any one place, even if fragmented in its origins and at specific historical periods.' (Mitchell & Oakley, 8-9) It is, rather, that 'The fragmentation of contemporary feminism bears ample witness to the impossibility of constructing modern feminism as a simple unity in the present or of arriving at a shared feminist definition of feminism. Such differing explanations, such a variety of emphases in practical campaigns, such widely varying interpretations of their results have emerged, that it now makes more sense to speak of a plurality of feminisms than of one.' (Mitchell & Oakley, 9) Similarly, Nancy Cott notes that

> Feminism is nothing if not paradoxical. It aims for individual freedoms by mobilizing sex solidarity. It acknowledges diversity among women while positing that women recognize their unity. It requires gender consciousness for its basis, yet calls for the elimination of prescribed gender roles. These paradoxes of feminism are rooted in women's actual situation, being the same (in a species sense) as men; being different, with respect to reproductive biology and gender construction, from men. In another complication, all women may be said to be 'the same', as distinct from all men with respect to reproductive biology, and yet 'not the same', with respect to the variance of gender construction. Both theory and practice in feminism historically have had to deal with the fact that women are the same as and different from men, and the fact that women's gender identity is not separable from the other factors that make up our selves: race, region, Culture, Class, age. (Cott, 49)

Are you confused? Who shall blame you? In an interview with *Spiked*, Christine Hoff Sommers was asked if contemporary feminism hadn't become representative of a certain very limited class of women, notably those in the media. She replied, 'Yes, very much so. The polls show that feminism has always struggled to win the hearts and minds of the majority of people. Most women don't identify as feminists ... I think feminism might alienate as many as it attracts. I think it'll certainly scare away most men, because it seems, in its current form, very male averse.' (Sommers 2017) The interviewer wondered if this had to do with contemporary feminism's focus on women's bodies. 'This year,' she asked, 'feminists have protested with pussy hats, signs of uteruses, bloodstained jeans, tampons, leg hair, body shaming—what do you think of this so-called "gross-out" feminism?' Sommers' response is unequivocal: 'Eurgh. It's all quite absurd. This is not how men came to power. These are antics that reinforce some of the worst stereotypes about women. And it's just going to isolate the movement and not make it more attractive.'

Are we still in the era of third wave feminism or did the explosion in the use of social media mark a significant transition from one kind of feminism to another, from third to fourth wave feminism or perhaps even to fifth? Are the campaigns of the Twentyteens against rape culture and street harassment, body-shaming, and the #MeToo movement enough to mark today's feminism as a distinct form of feminism? Who can tell?

Equality of opportunity or equality of outcome?

The kind of feminism that garners most support among women and men is sometimes called liberal or equity feminism. As the name suggests, the focus of this kind of feminism (broadly first wave and part of second wave) is on promoting the equality of men and women by removing legal inequalities between them in the public sphere. Clear as the goals of this type of feminism may seem, they are not without their own ambiguities. Chief among these is what kind of equality its proponents have in mind—equality of outcome or equality of opportunity. This possible equivocation is a fertile source of confusion and the issue surfaced in the now notorious Cathy Newman interview of controversial psychologist, author and Internet star, Jordan Petersen. (see Channel 4) Newman asked Peterson, 'Is gender equality desirable?' and Peterson responded:

> If it means equality of outcome, then it is almost certainly undesirable. That's already been demonstrated in Scandinavia. Men and women won't sort themselves into the same categories if you leave them to do it of their own accord. It's 20 to 1 female nurses to male, something like that. And approximately the same [ratio of] male engineers to female engineers. That's a consequence of the free choice of men and women in the societies that have gone farther than any other societies to make gender equality the purpose of the law. Those are ineradicable differences––you can eradicate them with tremendous social pressure and tyranny, but if you leave men and women to make their own choices you will not get equal outcomes.

Newman interjected with a few instances of her favourite trope. 'So *you're saying*,' she said, 'that anyone who believes in equality, whether you call them feminists or whatever you want to call them, should basically give up because it ain't going to happen.' To which Peterson responded, 'Only if they're aiming at equality of outcome.' 'So,' Ms Newman persisted, '*you're saying* give people equality of opportunity, that's fine.' This time, her account of what Peterson is saying *is* correct, for even she can't get it wrong all the time. Peterson answered, 'It's not only fine, it's eminently desirable for everyone, for individuals as well as societies.' But, once again, Newman reverted to type: 'But still women aren't going to make it. That's what *you're really saying*.' Which, of course, is not what Peterson's really saying at all.

Focusing on the content of the interview, the really odd thing to notice is that Peterson isn't saying anything that would have seemed extraordinary or controversial even as recently as ten years ago. If Ms Newman never does anything else in her life, she will always be remembered for her spectacular display of intellectual incomprehension. She may not want to be remembered for it, but she will be. It's hard, even if you're a *Guardian* reader, to see that interview as anything but a disaster for Ms Newman. (check it out for yourself at Channel 4.) James Delingpole said the interview marked a 'pivotal victory in the culture wars', and Douglas Murray wrote that he didn't think he had ever witnessed an interview that was 'more catastrophic for the interviewer.' (see Delingpole; Murray) I don't want to be mean-spirited but, well, it *was* funny. Newman, gamely trying to make the best of a bad lot, responded to Murray's comments by saying, 'I thoroughly enjoyed my bout with Jordan Peterson as did hundreds of thousands of our viewers. Viva feminism, viva free speech.' Some months later, in a somewhat more reflective and chastened mode, she opined, 'Was it my finest interview? Probably not. If you're a footballer, you don't always push the ball to the back of the net. You win some, you lose some.' (see Ruddick) Is this a tacit admission by Newman that this interview is one that she lost?

Are men and women different?

Equity feminism takes no specific position on the question of whether there are or there aren't significant differences between the sexes. On the other hand, radical (or gender) feminism takes the position that if there were identifiable systematic differences between the sexes, this could be used to invalidate women's claims for equal social, political and legal treatment, hence their fierce rejection of any findings of such differences, no matter how empirically based these findings may be. They are, however, mistaken in that regard. That there may be discernible systematic biological and psychological differences between the sexes no more necessarily validates different social, political and legal treatment of men and women than would a finding that there are discernible biological and psychological differences between various groups of men validate different social, political and legal treatment of those groups. Whatever the truth of the matter about the existence of systematic cognitive and affective differences between men and women, it doesn't affect the basic normative point on which almost everyone agrees, which is that men and women ought to be treated equally by the law.

So, *are* men and women different? The results are in! A study on affectivity conducted at the University of Cambridge involving almost 700,000 people has shown that women *on average* really are more empathetic than men, and men *on average* are more analytical than women. Women tend to have a greater ability to recognise what other people are thinking intuitively and to respond suitably, whereas men have a stronger drive to interpret the world through rule-based systems and to learn how things work through analysing their constituent parts. It is important to note that these differences, while real, are true in the aggregate and tell us little about any particular man or woman. (see Greenberg *et al.*) What kinds of differences are we talking about? Well, ways of thinking along certain more or less well-defined traits—openness, extraversion, agreeableness, conscientiousness and neuroticism. As with most characteristics measured across male-females differences, there is, of course, substantial overlap, but women tend on average to score higher on all five traits than men. Paradoxically, the overlap is higher in countries such as China (84%) which isn't exactly leading the field in the competition for the Nobel Prize in gender equality, whereas the overlap is significantly lower in the Netherlands (61%), which might very well just be a Nobel Prize contender. Another study, this time from Stanford University, confirmed that there are cognitive differences between men and women that appear very early in life, long before they could be the result of social conditioning. (see Goldman; see also Knoedler & Shah) Women are better with language, have finer motor coordination and have greater perceptual speed. When it comes to memory, they are better at long-term memory retrieval. Men, on the other hand, are better at retrieving material from short-term memory and have superior visuospatial skills. Once again, the differences are real but with a great degree of overlap so that they are most apparent at the extremes of a bell curve. The differences would appear to be primarily the result of hormonal influence in the early developmental stages of the child in the womb, and they persist through adult life.

Men and women different!—what a shock! No one had ever noticed these differences between men and women before. Well, of course, as a matter of fact they had, but our feminist friends browbeat them into believing that these apparent differences were simply the product of patriarchal prejudice. Dr Varun Warrier, from the Cambridge team which conducted the 700,000-person study, said, 'These sex differences in the typical population are very clear.' He went on to say that the study confirmed that females 'on average are more empathic, typical males on average are more systems-oriented.' Men scored an average of 9.87 out of 20 for empathy whereas women scored 10.79. When it came to systems thinking, men scored 6.73 whereas women scored 5.45. The authors of a meta-study entitled, 'Men and Things, Women and People: A Meta-Analysis of Sex Differences in Interests,' conclude that 'Results showed that men prefer working with things and women prefer working with people, producing a large effect size (d=0.93) on the Things-People dimension. Men showed strong Realistic (d=0.84) and Investigative (d=0.26) interests, and women showed strong Artistic (d=-0.35) Social (d=0.84), and Conventional (d=-0.33) Sex differences favoring men were also found for more specific measures of engineering (d=1.11), science (d=0.36) and mathematics (d=0.34) .... The present study suggest that interests may play a critical role in gendered occupational choices and gender disparity in the STEM fields.' (Su *et al.*)

What is the source of these differences? Is it entirely a matter of cultural conditioning? Or is it all a matter of biology? The role of biology in such matters is non-zero, but so too is the role of culture. In many discussions on the 'nature versus nurture' debate, there's a tendency to suggest that human nature is either something wholly or substantially genetically determined and thus unalterable, or else that it's nothing more than a product of our history and cultural environment and thus essentially plastic. Neither of these extremes would seem to be correct. Perhaps unsurprisingly, Dr Warrier concluded that, as related studies have shown, the 'individual differences in empathy and systemizing are partly genetic, partly influenced by our prenatal hormonal exposure, and partly due to environmental experience.' The genetic structure of human beings is largely identical; however, the epigenetic expression of our genes is the function of the dynamic interaction of those genes and their environment, resulting in relatively specific character types that, in turn, make possible the emergence of character traits (such as trust, capacity for hard work, a disposition to be self-restrained and delayed gratification in respect of sex, food and money, and so on) that in their turn, give rise to socio-political institutions such as war, religion, trade and law. Genes hold human culture on a leash but the leash, as E. O. Wilson once remarked, is very long. (see Wilson, 167; see also Penman, Carey, Francis and Wade) Not surprisingly, the traits of empathy and analyticity align closely to the professions that people choose, those with the predominantly masculine traits choosing STEM jobs, and those with the predominantly feminine traits choosing non-STEM jobs. The researchers said that the huge study showed that there really are fundamental differences between the minds of men and women at population level, although individuals can still be 'atypical' for their sex.

What difference does any of this make? This research is germane to the issue of choice, not as determining it, but as inclining men and women towards particular choices. As glass ceilings crack and women become more and more educationally and legally equal with men, one might expect that the psychological differences between men and women should equally tend to disappear. But that's not what happens. In fact, the more so-called gender equal a society becomes, the greater the difference in the ways in which men and women think! Some have called this the patriarchy paradox. Erik MacGiolla and Petri J. Kajonius show that countries with *more* women in the workforce, in parliament and in education are also those in which men and women diverge most on psychological traits. (see MacGiolla and Kajonius) A research paper published in *Plus One* found that in countries ranked as *less gender equal* by the World Economic Forum, women were more likely to choose traditionally male courses such as the sciences. The results obtained by MacGiolla and Kajonius are not singular. Dr Steve Stewart-Williams notes that it's not just in personality traits that we find these surprising results. According to him, we also find it in the choices the sexes make of academic specialties and in their choice of occupations. Dr Stewart-Williams, who is the author of *The Ape that Understood the Universe*, is quoted as suggesting that in more gender-equal societies, individuals have greater freedom to follow their own interests. It's all about choice. (see Whipple)

Stewart-Williams goes on to say that we might like to stop thinking that any visible differences between outcomes for men and women in society are necessarily the result of oppression. On the contrary, they 'may be indicators of the opposite: a relatively free and fair society.' If this contradicted some feminist analyses, he said, it was also a surprise to pretty much everyone else too. It seems plausible to suggest that where men and women are treated in radically different ways and have very different opportunities, they would end up measuring very much differently on assessment scales than would men and women in cultures where men and women are treated more equally. But, Stewart-Williams says, this gets it the wrong way around. 'Treating men and women the same makes them different, and treating them differently makes them the same. I don't think anyone predicted that. It's bizarre.' (see Whipple)

The feminist two-step
So, for feminists, are men and women essentially the same or essentially different? The answer is—whichever answer best suits the feminists' immediate purposes! Declan Mansfield describes the feminist two-step, that *pas de deux* of the perpetrators of the perpetually perplexing, as being distinguished by a simple strategy. Whatever the subject, 'feminists will shift their position to the one where attacking men or defending women gains them an advantage. Principles, which were previously defended with zeal, will be abandoned with alacrity the moment they put feminism at a disadvantage.' It's a variation on the classic strategy of 'heads I win, tails you lose!' A basic version of the feminist two-step which, in the (relatively) innocent days of the early 1990s I called 'the feminists' dilemma', saw the sisterhood veer between asserting that men and women are essentially the same or, when more convenient, that men and women are essentially different. Let's tease this out a little.

We are told that we need more women in politics and in business because they will bring their special complementary skills to bear on the current one-sided situation where politics and business are men-heavy. Of course, this claim is plausible only if there are some real and significant differences between men and women but, in other contexts, the claim that men and women are in any way significantly different is rejected as just so much patriarchal prejudice. (see below, the chapter on 'Women at Work') As Steve Moxon notes,

> We're told that men and women are the same. Or, rather, some of the time we're told this. At other times we're told that men and women are essentially and irrevocably different. We're further told that although men and women are different, this is really just something to do with the way we are at the moment, albeit that we have been that way for a long time, living in the sort of society we do. In time, we keep being reminded, all will revert to how supposedly it should be and how it used to be in times of yore: i.e. men and women are the same after all. Even so, it's then insisted that actually, in the end, no matter what we do, men will never get to be truly the same as women: men and women are forever and totally different (except when it's more convenient to regard them as exactly the same). (Moxon, 1)

Here are two contrary theses. Thesis 1: women are strong and independent and the equals of or even superior to men. Thesis 2: women are weak and fragile and in constant need of protection by the state (the state acting as surrogate father), requiring it to provide a hand up, a hand out, special favours (positive discrimination or quotas) or special legal privileges on demand. Of course, both theses cannot be simultaneously true. To see Thesis 2 in operation, consider the following lachrymose tale.

In January 2018 it was revealed that Nottinghamshire Police were to provide 'crying rooms' for female officers going through the menopause, plus extra desk space and better access to showers. It seems that menopausal women were leaving the force so, to prevent the waste of talent, the then Chief Constable of Nottinghamshire Police, Sue Fish, had the bright idea of introducing the new, menopausal-women-friendly policy. A 'Menopause Manager's Guide' directs that 'private areas/spaces' must be made available for 'women to rest/recover/ make a telephone call to personal or professional support' and that 'Women going through the menopause may need to manage the impact of symptoms, a private space to rest temporarily, cry or talk with a colleague before they can return to their workspace.' (Mansell, 6; see also Christodoulou) Would it be unfeeling to ask who is doing their work while they're hanging out in the crying room?

Menopausal police officers will have desks close to windows to keep them cool and they'll have control of the office thermostat. Oh, and they'll be able to take off that annoying body armour if it should become uncomfortable. What! You're going to send them out after gun-toting criminals without body armour? Oh wait! You're *not* going to send them out, just the men. I see. Women are just as good as men and indistinguishable from them in every way—except when they're not. We are told—I can see no evidence of a tongue-in-cheek at the following claim—that 'when a female feels low self-esteem or not herself, the task of running in front of male colleagues can be daunting.' (Mansell, 7) Well, I am sure that the various malefactors whom our police officers are required to pursue will be understanding and compassionate, and will slow down their escapes to make allowances for their pursuers' low self-esteem and their disinclination to run in front of their male colleagues. It seems, then, that women police officers of a certain age are best kept indoors at their desks, close to their safe crying spaces, as opposed to being out on the beat wearing uncomfortable body armour and, in general, dealing face-to-face with criminals and with crime, which is, unfortunately, a fairly central part of a police officer's job. Some insensitive people have suggested this policy is patronising and a crying shame but we don't need to listen to such retrograde comments.

In the *Simpsons* episode, 'Girls Just Want to have Sums' (S17E19, 2006), Principal Skinner puts his two big feet into the feminist swamp when, in an effort to be genial, he attributes the 'B or two' grades in maths of his guest and former pupil, Julianna, to her being a girl. Cue outrage! Repentant, Skinner does all he can to placate the outraged women, but to no avail. At a subsequent meeting, he begins by saying, 'Today, we celebrate the first of many, many, many, many diversity forums. Why is it that women "appear" to be worse at math than men? What is the source of this "illusion," or, as I call it, the biggest lie ever told?' This effort at pre-emptive placation doesn't go down all that well. A woman in the audience shouts, 'You're a worse version of Hitler!' Then Skinner does the big reveal, stepping out from behind the podium to show that he is wearing a skirt. 'Please believe me,' he says, 'I understand the problems of women. See! Am I wearing women's clothes? I didn't notice. When I look in my closet, I don't see male clothes or female clothes. They're all the same.' Mrs Krabappel interjects, 'Are you saying that men and women are identical?' Wrong-footed once again, Skinner protests: 'Oh, no, of course not! Women are unique in every way.' But this gets him into yet more trouble. A woman in the audience yells 'Now he's saying women and men aren't equal.' Caught in the crosshairs of the feminist two-step—there are no differences between men and women and women are simultaneously unique and wonderful and different from men—Skinner protests, 'No, no, no. It's the differences, of which there are none, that make the sameness exceptional.' Exhausted by his efforts at mental calisthenics, he gives up. 'Just tell me what to say!', he pleads. He is replaced by a new principal, Melanie Upfoot, who segregates the school according to sex. Lisa Simpson is, at first, happy with the new arrangements but soon becomes disillusioned, especially by the way mathematics is being taught to the girls. She asks, 'Are we going to do any actual math problems? 'Problems?', replies the teacher. 'That's how men see math, something to be attacked, to be "figured out."' Lisa is somewhat puzzled by this response. 'But isn't it? I mean, confidence-building can't replace real learning.' The teacher rejects her protest, saying 'Sounds like you're trying to derail our "self-esteem engine." Let's sing it back on the tracks!', and the class all sing, 'The best thing I can ever be is to be okay with me.' In a bizarre case of fact following fiction, California's Department of Education in August 2019 issued a draft Ethnic Studies Model Curriculum which, as well as talking about such transparent concepts as 'positionalities, 'hybridities', 'misogynoir' and 'cis-heteropatriarchy' and describing capitalism as a form of power and oppression, also includes a course entitled 'Math and Social Justice'! (see Evers)

So much for fiction; what of fact? Professor Julia Higgins, President of the Institute of Physics, writing in the *Guardian* in 2018, asserted that stereotyping and unconscious biases meant that girls still grow up being treated differently from boys. (Higgins) Her evidence? Well, four times as many boys as girls take physics as a school subject. One might wonder what is especially problematic about this. Are girls physically restrained from selecting physics as a subject if they wish to do so? Do the schools they attend not offer the subject? No? What then is the problem? According to Professor Higgins, there is nothing to suggest that there is any inherent difference between the genders (only two genders, it seems) in respect of an aptitude for or an interest in the sciences. There may well not be any difference in *aptitude* between boys and girls when it comes to the sciences but in the matter of *interest*, wouldn't the fact that four times as many boys as girls take physics as a subject in school constitute *prima facie* evidence to the contrary? Apparently not! This explanation is, it seems, too crude to be true. The problem lies deeper than this. It's much too simple-minded to conclude that individuals might conceivably have different interests and, being free to choose, choose freely. Who could possibly believe that the cause of their having such interests might lie in their individual personalities, and not be the malign effect of the activity of some sinister and nebulous forms of causality such as gender stereotyping and unconscious bias? Professor Higgins concludes that we all have a part to play in tackling the barriers that girls face, to which the obvious response is—who are *we*, and *what* barriers is she referring to?

Physics, it seems, is a feminist issue! (But then, what topic *isn't* a feminist issue?) Perhaps you didn't think that physics might be problematic from a feminist perspective. Don't worry! Others have done the heavy lifting for you. Professor Dr Monika Bessenrodt-Weberpals, who is Vice-President for Studies and Teaching and Equal Rights and Chair of Physics and Gender (I'm not making this up) at the Hamburg University of Applied Sciences, tells us that 'The science of physics displays a lack of self-reflection by making its object absolute, losing any physical contact between the subject, the scientist, and his or her object, and by instrumentalising physics as an instrument of domination.' And who—if we knew what this statement meant—could disagree with that? Professor Bessenrodt-Weberpals believes that 'Students should be taught the theoretical basis, empirical findings and methodological concepts of Women's and Gender Studies in relation to areas of physics ... In particular, they should apply the approaches and methods of gender justice to their work in physics.' I have to admit that I can't immediately see the relevance of gender justice to physics but that's probably because I'm only a man.

The all-time classic and a front-running candidate for the most sublimely silly paper ever published has to be N. Katherine Hayle's 'Gender Encoding in Fluid Mechanics: Masculine Channels and Feminine Flows.' (Hayles) This was published in a journal called *differences*. The lower case 'd' is deliberate and presumably deeply significant. On its web page, we are informed that *differences* has 'established a critical forum where the problematic of differences is explored in texts ranging from the literary and the visual to the political and social. *differences* highlights theoretical debates across the disciplines that address the ways concepts and categories of difference—notably but not exclusively gender—operate within culture.' Professor Hayles has a background in chemistry but her day job is as a Professor and Director of Graduate Studies in the Literature Program at Duke University. She is exercised about fluid mechanics and its apparent lack of centrality among physicists, which she attributes to the association of fluidity with femininity. You can use your imagination to figure out how the categories of rigidity and fluidity are worked out in this paper or, if you're in a penitential mood, you can read the original for yourself. Bring a packed lunch with you. On second thoughts, better not!

Whatever about physics, surely engineering is exempt from feminist criticism? You might think that if any discipline should concern itself with rigour, that discipline is surely engineering. When my airplane is about to take off, I often have an attack of existential doubt about the principles of aerodynamics, and even greater existential doubts about the structural integrity of the airplane's engines and wings! If I thought the engineers who designed and built my airplane were ambivalent in their approach to rigorous methods and standards, I wouldn't ever get on a plane! Now, however, Professor Donna Riley, who holds the impressive title of Kamyar Haghighi Head of the School of Engineering Education in Purdue University, tells us that the notion of rigour in engineering must be relinquished! According to the abstract of her 2017 article 'Rigor/us: Building Boundaries and Disciplining Diversity with Standards of Merit,' rigour 'accomplishes dirty deeds', one of which is *'demonstrating white male heterosexual privilege.'* [see Riley 2017; emphasis added] The very term 'rigour', according to Professor Riley, 'has a historical lineage of being about hardness, stiffness, and erectness; its sexual connotations—and links to masculinity in particular—are undeniable.' Let's see how an argument might go. Premise 1: 'the male sex organ when aroused is rigorous'; Premise 2: 'engineering is rigorous'; Conclusion; 'engineering is concerned with the aroused male sex organ.' Is that how an argument might run? Or perhaps the even stronger (I was about to say 'more rigorous') conclusion might be that 'engineering *is* the male sex organ.' Whichever way the argument goes, it seems to disappear down the black hole of the fallacy of the undistributed middle but that, of course, is only when it is viewed from the perspective of patriarchal logic.

In any event, rigour is bad, very bad. When we come to understand how rigour reproduces inequality, as Professor Riley thinks we must, we see that 'we cannot reinvent it but rather must relinquish it, looking to alternative conceptualizations for evaluating knowledge, welcoming diverse ways of knowing, doing, and being, and moving from compliance to engagement, from rigor to vigor.' Just how rigour reproduces inequality is not entirely clear, but something of what Professor Riley intends to communicate may be gleaned from her contention that rigour may be a defining tool that reveals how 'structural forces of power and privilege operate to exclude men of color and women, students with disabilities, LGBTQ+ people, first-generation and low-income students, and non-traditionally-aged students.' Once again, who could possibly disagree with that claim? Rigour, rambunctious as it is, is not the only bad boy in the engineering class. No, not by a long way. Scientific knowledge itself comes in for a tongue-lashing from Professor Riley, for being 'gendered, raced, and colonizing.' Research, she believes, documents 'a climate of microaggressions and cultures of whiteness and masculinity in engineering.' You might think, at first, that Professor Riley's screed is just another in a long line of hoax papers sent to journals to demonstrate their editorial standards to be less than, ahem, rigorous. But no, alas, this is meant to be a serious paper, published in what purports to be a respectable academic journal.

As we saw at the start of our discussion, one version of the feminist two-step has to do with the very definition of feminism itself. If feminism is ever criticised, the invariable response is: 'What? You're not in favour of equality before the law for men and for women?' And so the objector is wrong-footed. But almost no one objects to feminism as implying equality before the law. But that's not the feminism that is the staple of Women's Studies Programmes which is, at its crudest, a form of special pleading for special privileges for women just because they're women, more accurately, a plea for special privileges for women-like-*me*. Here's a trivial but illustrative example of feminism as a pre-emptive claim for special privileges.

I am sure that all female chess players were thrilled to hear in 2018 that the London Chess Classic was to offer free admission to women to the tournament, while charging men £60 for the same privilege. (Horton) There is, it seems, a gender (by which is meant sex, of course) gap in chess. I can personally attest to the truth of that statement, having been an active chess player for over fifty years. In that time, I have come across very few female chess players, more's the pity. And why is that, one wonders? Well, according to Jovanka Houska, Britain's leading woman chess player, 'there's a lot of institutionalised sexism going on. Sexism is so ingrained people don't know there's something going on.' I don't wish to be rude to Ms Houska but the reason people don't know that sexism is going on in chess is not because it is ingrained but because it is non-existent. There is no institutionalised ageism in chess; there is no institutionalised racism in chess; and, above all, there is no institutionalised sexism in chess, unless it's the institutionalised sexism of women-only tournaments, women-only titles and women-only funding that exist purely for the sake of women. Apart from some problems created by politics, chess players are happy to play anyone prepared to sit across the board from them. To attribute the paucity of women in chess to institutionalised sexism is to engage in the intellectually lazy accusation of discrimination or bias that is routinely but mindlessly proposed when men outnumber women in any particular activity, but never the other way around, of course.

The action of the organisers of the London Chess Classic shows that women are, if anything, welcomed with open arms (metaphorically speaking, I hasten to add!) if they wish to play chess. There is nothing, absolutely nothing—not sexism, whether institutionalised, ingrained or otherwise, not lack of opportunity, not access to transport, not ability to sit, stand, or walk—nothing whatsoever to stop women and girls from playing chess if they wish to do so, now more than ever when you can play chess online 24 hours a day if you choose. But the brutal fact remains that women, honourable exceptions to one side, do not wish to play chess, at least not in any appreciable numbers. No great upper-body strength is needed to lift the chess pieces, and women and girls are as capable of sitting in a chair for long periods of time as any man or boy but—and I can't say this too strongly—women, for the most part, *do—not—like—chess*! And don't tell me you know plenty of women—well, one or two, anyway—who play chess. This is fascinating but irrelevant. When I say 'Women for the most part do not like chess' I don't mean of course that no woman likes chess but that women in the aggregate, in general, by and large, in the main, for the most part, do not like chess. Not liking chess is not a moral failing and there is no reason why women should be forced, induced or bribed to participate in an activity that they do not like. It is a pity that more women do not play chess but it's not a problem, still less is it a problem that needs to be solved. Peace in the Middle East is a problem; getting Brexit sorted out is, and no doubt will continue to be, a problem; but it is *not* a problem that few women choose to play chess; it is merely a fact, even if a regrettable fact. As it happens, the proportion of female players appears to be increasing worldwide, with the US Chess Federation reporting that almost 14% of its players are female, which is a significant increase on the 1% of 20 years ago, although that relatively high percentage is probably not representative of the proportions of women chess players in other countries. (Robertson) Ms Houska did say one true thing, namely, that the standard in the UK of the women is a lot worse than that of the boys and men, but I suppose she would think that that too is the result of ingrained institutionalised sexism.

Ms Houska has another arrow to her bow to account for the relative paucity of women in chess. She said—and I can't quite believe she said this—that 'clubs are not necessarily making it fun for women to play ... there's too much focus on competition but not enough on social life ... Some of the best nights I had when in a club was almost a party setting. I've seen it done in America, they should have ladies only nights.' Aaaaaaaaagh! If a man said this he would be laughed to scorn and accused of sexism, and rightly so. I can usually take this kind of fatuous nonsense with a modicum of good humour and tolerance, but this is beyond annoying. The point of chess *is* competition, as Ms Houska should know as well as any other chess player if not more so! If you don't like competition, don't play chess which, it seems, is what most women do without discouragement from anyone but themselves. Chess players do socialise with one another but their socialising is incidental to the principal purpose of chess clubs which is, believe it or not, playing chess and which is, I say again in case the point has been missed, a competitive activity! In Jane Austen's *Pride and Prejudice*, Caroline Bingley tries to impress Mr Darcy with her seriousness of mind. When her brother proposes a ball she says, 'I should like balls infinitely better ... if they were carried on in a different manner; but there is something insufferably tedious in the usual process of such a meeting. It would surely be much more rational if conversation instead of dancing made the order of the day.' To which her brother Charles replies, 'Much more rational, my dear Caroline, I dare say, but it would not be near so much like a ball.' Chess clubs as party-venues might be fun, but would not be near so much like chess clubs.

In a related piece on chess, Alisha Matthewson-Grand asks 'Where are the women?' (Matthewson-Grand) Why, she wonders, has the world championship never been won by a woman? Ms Matthewson-Grand breezily dismisses all bio-psychological arguments that might explain, in the aggregate, the relative interests and capacities of men and women in relation to chess, and she simply asserts that the fundamental reason for the different levels of skill is a matter of statistics: 'There have been more men represented at the world championship because more men play chess. This, in turn, means that a higher number are bound to reach the skill level of Carlsen and Caruana.' It needs no ghost come from the grave to tell us this since it is obviously true—more men than women play chess and because more men than women play chess, it is to be expected that more men than women reach the highest ranks of the game. But the question that needs to be answered is *why* the participation rate of women in chess is so low in the first place. Why more men than women play chess isn't explained by telling us in a roundabout way that more men than women play chess. As we have seen, Ms Houska thinks the reason is institutionalised sexism and a lack of party atmosphere in chess clubs. Ms Matthewson-Grand's explanation is different. The reasons are complex, she tells us, but her number one choice is the lack of prominent female chess players. 'There are,' she tells us, 'female players who have been recognised for their outstanding skill, such as the Polgar sisters and the current women's number one, Hou Yifan. Yet these women aren't assigned the same level of importance within chess's historical narrative as men such as José Capablanca, Garry Kasparov, Fischer and Carlsen. As all the "heroes" of chess are men, women are taught from an early age to associate good chess with being male.'

Well, well. So that's it—a lack of assignment. It's as if a Committee on the Assignment of Chess Importance sits periodically and deliberates on whom it will assign importance to this week, this month or this year. But—and I know this will come as a shock to Ms Matthewson-Grand—one's importance in chess isn't a matter of assignment, it's a matter of recognition. At the time of writing, Hou Yifan is ranked a commendable 91st place in the rankings, one of only three women to break into the top 100, yet there are many little-known male chess grandmasters more highly rated than she. Has anyone outside the most dedicated chess groupies ever heard of Xiangzhi Bu or Hao Wang, two other Chinese chess players ranked more highly than Hou? No? What a surprise! Few if any of the world's Grandmasters, male or female, will ever be elevated to the pantheon occupied by the likes of Capablanca, Kasparov, Fischer, Lasker, Alekhine and Carlsen but nothing, repeat *nothing*, stops women chess players from attempting to qualify for a crack at the World Championship. If you're good enough, you'll get to compete, and if you're outstanding, you'll end up winning, and that's whether or not you're male or female or tall or short or a lover of classical music or jazz, or bonhomous or anti-social or any other of a multitude of equally irrelevant characteristics.

It is ironic, and perhaps slightly undermines Ms Matthewson-Grand's thesis, to find that her heroine, Hou Yifan, is on record as saying that she finds it hard to imagine girls competing at the same level as men! 'Theoretically,' she said, 'there should be a possibility that a woman can compete for the title in the future, but practically I think that the chances of this happening in the next few decades are very small .... if you look at any sport, it's hard to imagine girls competing at the same level as men.' When she was asked if she believed whether there were any gender differences in the way men and women play the game, Hou said: 'To me, in all aspects of life, sometimes women and men tend to see the same thing from completely different perspectives, and that also comes into chess ... I suspect that the male perspective on chess favours men, perhaps when it comes to the emotional aspect of the game and making practical and objective decisions ... To put it simplistically, I think male players tend to have a kind of overview or strategy for the whole game, rather than focusing too much attention on one part of the game.' (Watson)

In any event, what is Ms Matthewson-Grand's solution to the non-problem of female 'representation' in chess? It is blinding in its simplicity. We need, she says, 'to raise the public profile of female chess players. Alongside the news features on Carlsen, we need to run one on Hou. We need to cover the Women's World Chess Championship with the same fervour as the "main" [her inverted commas] world championship—or at the very least we need to, you know, actually *cover* it.' It might have escaped Ms Matthewson-Grand's notice but coverage of the Chess World Championship is usually much more muted than it was in 2018. Chess doesn't normally command the attention of the world's sports media as do, say, football or rugby or boxing. Without looking it up, would Ms Matthewson-Grand be able to tell us who competed in the last World Championship match before the contest between Caruana and Carlsen, and where and when it was held? No? I thought not. Oh, and by the way, although Hou Yifan has won the Women's World Championship on four occasions, in recent years she has no longer competed in women's only competitions.

Of course, it goes without saying (if you are a radical feminist, that is) that female composers are yet another group of women who have been the victims of male repression. I recently purchased a CD of late 19th and early 20th century chamber music by five Swedish female composers, music that was, according to the author of the deathless prose on the back of the CD cover, 'relegated to obscurity for reasons anything but musical.' Really? Relegated to obscurity for non-musical reasons, was it? And relegated by whom, pray tell, and how was this relegation effected? Having listened to the Trio, String Quartets and Sonatas on this CD, I can attest that they are well made and, for the most part, reasonably attractive compositions, some worth listening to more than once. The same, however, could be said of much of the music of the legions of forgotten male composers who outnumber the forgotten female composers by several orders of magnitude. Riding high on a morally virtuous bandwagon, the British Broadcasting Corporation (BBC) announced in January 2018 that it would record and broadcast the work of five 'forgotten' women composers. This is being done to redress what is deemed to be an historic imbalance. Alan Davey, controller of BBC Radio 3 and Classical Music, said it was incredibly exciting to shine a light on the composers, remarking that 'It means that we are not only expanding the canon of classical music, but actually helping to redress its historic imbalance when it comes to gender and diversity.' These women composers are Leokadiya Kashperova, Marianna Martines, Florence Price, Augusta Holmès, and Johanna Müller-Hermann. Never heard of them? Don't worry. If the BBC's propaganda piece is to be believed, as the result of the BBC's efforts, they stand to become household names! Perhaps I am being cynical but I very much doubt the veracity of Mr Davey's hyperbolical remark that the BBC's women-composer-friendly policy is set to expand the canon of classical music. Steve Moxon shares my doubts:

Feminists have tried to dig up long-lost female classical composers but struggle to break the duck. Not one who could hold a candle to the ranks of pre-eminent men. Victorian ladies ... had endless spare time and no responsibilities. An average middle-class, let alone upper-class woman had servants galore to relieve her of all work and childcare duties. Never before or since has there been such a large sub-group of people with unlimited time to do as they chose .... These women could spend all day playing the drawing room piano, which they would have been encouraged to do from an early age as part of the usual education to be a lady .... If such a lady became a good pianist and sight reader, then why should she not ... go on to compose? The truth seems to be that she was often quite a good pianist, but had little inclination to put in the enormous effort and discipline and to summon up the inspiration to go beyond good playing to actually create the sort of polyphonic notated music she readily learned how to read and play. (Moxon, 74)

The invention of the compact disc (CD) made it possible to record and distribute the work of many previously unheard composers. Despite the welcome availability of new musical experiences made possible by the CD and the re-discovery of many good composers, the received wisdom as to who does and who does not rank among music's greats has not been substantially disturbed. Very few of the newly heard composers can make a plausible claim to sit at music's top table. The reason is very simple. The top table has a limited seating capacity and very few people *of any kind, sex, ethnicity, age, or nationality* can reasonably claim a seat. Have you ever heard of Robert Ashley, Carlo Arrigoni, Ivor Atkins, Charles-Auguste de Bériot, Hippolyte-André-Baptiste Chelard, Isaak Iosifovich Dunayevsky, Armando Gentilucci, Antonín Kammel, Shaiva Mikhaylovich Mshvelidze, Ernest Pingoud, Johan Helmich Roman, Mazimierz Sikorski, Jenö Takács, and Moyssey Samuilovich Vatnberg? I found these composers by opening my copy of *The Grove Concise Dictionary of Music* at random and sticking my finger somewhere on the page. These composers were all significant and prolific enough to merit a mention in *Grove*, but had you ever heard of any of them before reading their names just now? I hadn't, and I have been an avid music lover for over fifty years. Have you seen their names on any concert programmes? Have you ever heard any of their music? No? What a surprise! Even with the increased availability of recordings of obscure music made possible by the CD and by online streaming services, I wish you good luck trying to find recordings of any of their music. I am not saying it's impossible, just very difficult. You might argue that despite their entries in *Grove*, all these neglected male composers are deservedly neglected, unlike neglected female composers. A large claim and one hard to justify since few if any of us have heard their work. But what then are we to make of such as Louis Théodore Gouvy (1819-1898), the Franco-German composer, with two hundred compositions to his credit, including nine symphonies, a requiem and many large scale religious and choral works, two operas, dozens of lieder and a half ton of solo piano music, quartets and quintets? Gouvy's music was highly regarded (except perhaps in France) during his lifetime and was esteemed by such as Brahms and Berlioz but, despite this, after his death, it disappeared from the concert hall and the recording studio until the end of the 20th century when a partial recovery began.

Here's a radical idea. If you want to avoid the endless repetition in live performance and recording of the classical standards (an idea that I am very much in favour of), why not programme the very best music that can be found without regard to the nationality, age, hair colour, skin colour, ambidexterity, shoe size or sex of the composer? Or is that too radical an idea?

Radical feminism

In the end, the radical feminist's problem isn't with this or that legal anomaly or injustice supposed to affect women adversely, but with nature itself. Shulamith Firestone, for example, in the best Aldous Huxley manner, thought that pregnancy was barbaric. For her, the object (one object at least) of the feminist revolution was the creation of the possibility of reproducing human beings technologically. None of that icky sex and pregnancy nonsense! Of course, that most repressive of institutions, the family, with its sexual exclusivity and its distinctively different roles for mother and father, must also go the way of the dinosaur. Sexual roles of all kinds, indeed, the very idea that there are or even could be different roles for men and for women, must be eliminated. To that end, lesbianism is not just a deviant form of sexuality but also a political statement of the non-necessity of men. In the New Dawn, the sexes (or genders) must themselves disappear, and in their place will arise the new androgynous human being in all its glory.

The displacement of heterosexuality from its traditional central social position, and the elevation of homosexuality as a new norm for sexual relations, as good as, if not better, than heterosexuality, have had significant social consequences and will very likely have more. The stable union of hetero-sexuals is essential to social life; that is why marriage, as it was traditionally understood, with its intrinsic intra-generational dimension, received special legal recognition. Homosexual unions, on the other hand, have no such inter-generational significance. In so far as any such union can have an inter-generational aspect, it is only available through adoption or by means of *in vitro* fertilisation or surrogacy. Such unions require from the state no legal recognition beyond the tolerance of activities properly within the purview of adult human beings. Historically, the acceptance of homosexuality by a society, whether *de facto* or *de jure*, is linked with a decline in population, whether as a cause or consequence or as some form of reciprocal causal relation is not entirely clear. The social, cultural and political consequences of a steep decline in population can be severe. There can be little doubt that the decline in the native Roman population contributed significantly to the eventual collapse of the Western Roman Empire. Already, in the contemporary Western world, we are moving ever more quickly towards a demographic cliff-edge. Births are below replacement levels in many western countries, populations are ageing, and the social welfare systems predicated on a large base of workers relative to a small superstructure of dependents but now rapidly resembling more a triangle balanced precariously on the point of one of its angles, cannot continue for ever.

That radical feminism is an ideology quite distinct from equity feminism, which, at its best, is a variety of classical liberalism, should be evident. It exhibits characteristic ideological markers such as a universal enemy (the patriarchy), a universally oppressed group (women), and it proclaims the higher destiny and moral superiority of the oppressed. Lewis Feuer remarks that ideology is under a compulsion 'to magnify every difference into an irreconcilable antagonism, and every antagonism into a manifestation of the system's contradictions; people's emotions and ideas [are] aligned into mutual opposition. To the ideologist, the ideological experience of dramatic confrontation and denouement is the supreme end in itself. The revolutionary experience itself is the goal of the revolutionist; no one feels less at home in the post-revolutionary world than the ideologist.' (Feuer, 180) A defining trait that singles out radical feminism as an ideology is its imperviousness to disconfirming evidence and its division of people into the saved and the damned, the elect and the reject. Possessed of truth, the whole truth and nothing but the truth, imbued by a consciousness of moral superiority and fired by a vision of the New Dawn, radical feminists are not only a danger to themselves (I could happily live with that!), but to society as a whole. The track record of radical ideologies in the 20th century has not been good, leading, as they have done, to the crematoria of the Nazis, the frozen wastes of the gulags, the Great Leap Backwards of Chinese society under Mao's not-so-benign supervision and the killing fields of Cambodia. My first Head of Department had a maxim to the effect that, in politics, one of the few universal truths is that the peasant always pays. History shows this to be true not only in respect of taxation, but also in the social disasters consequent upon ideological revolutions.

Feminism has been thought of as freeing women from the prison and slavery of the home and leading them to the promised land of paid and fulfilling employment. Not every form of employment, however, can be thought of as essentially liberating and as necessarily an improvement on women's position in the home. For most of human history, the necessity to work for a living was seen as a curse; it is only very recently that paid employment had come to be seen as a source of personal fulfilment instead of a burdensome necessity. Even now, there aren't many such personally fulfilling jobs, though there are more than there used to be, but even these jobs involve a significant element of drudgery. Steve Moxon notes, 'Women have woken up to not just the stress and thorough lack of empowerment that work actually provides, but what is for women the pointlessness of it. Their message will be more and more warmly received, though working-class women have always known the harsh reality of work.' (Moxon, 133)

Feminism has also had the effect, whether it was intended to have that effect or not, of according the economy primacy over the personal, and has led to the removal of a certain element of choice from the lives of many women. The irruption of vast numbers of women into the workforce had the inevitable effect of diminishing the returns to labour, so that those women who would have preferred to work in the home were forced into paid employment, whether they wanted to be there or not. Now, in many parts of the Western world, it is almost impossible for a single salary to support a family in a family home. Outside the media and entertainment super-monied classes, both parties in a marriage *must* work outside the home whether they want to or not.

With the mass movement of women into the workforce, family life has tended to become progressively more and more marginalised and, with women's emerging legal and political equality, the traditional male role of protector of women and children has been significantly downgraded if not rejected outright, in large part, because such a role for men was thought to imply a weakness on women's part which would see them regarded as not equal to men. Women moved from the protection of fathers and husbands to the much more powerful protection (as it might have seemed) of the state— the state functioning, ironically, as surrogate father. A significant agent in the triumph of feminism has been the emergence and expansion of the remit of the welfare state, one of whose functions is to supplant the traditional role of the male as the primary provider for the family unit. In order to permit women to enter the workforce in large numbers, *de facto* if not *de jure* sex-specific laws had to be put in place. While sexual harassment legislation is supposedly sex-neutral, its effect is to permit women to obtain redress for what is perceived to be male aggression or, perhaps even more importantly, to be compensated for failures in hirings or promotions taken to be grounded in discrimination against their sex. Similarly, maternity leave constitutes a huge problem for employers, particularly the owners and directors of small enterprises, and it has had to be entrenched in law. It also had to be supplemented by paternity leave that most men neither need nor want in order to sustain the illusion of equality of treatment of women and men.

Experience so far has shown that substitutes for the family, in particular the welfare state, do no better than the family in socialising the young and, in the estimation of the ideologically unbiased, often do considerably worse. Even smaller communal units such as the kibbutzim have become unstable over time and have tended to return to something approximating the traditional family units. If motherhood and fatherhood disappear as distinct roles, to be replaced with sex-neutral parenting, what will the long-term effects on children be? With the advent of mechanical and chemical contraception, sex has been divorced from conception, and with in vitro fertilisation we are halfway to divorcing conception from sex. If we ever engineer an artificial womb, the final separation of human reproduction from human biology will be complete and women will be, as Simone de Beauvoir desired, released from the bondage and servitude of maternity and cease to be the playthings of nature. What the long-term effects of all this will be, if it ever comes to pass, no one can tell.

Feminism in action: 7 feminist vignettes
Actions speak louder than words, and a handful of concrete examples is worth a bucket load of theoretical disquisitions.

Tennis anyone?
Several of the players at the 2018 Wimbledon championships spoke of the guilt they felt about leaving their children when they train or play in matches. Victoria Azarenka said, 'I feel guilty if I take 15 minutes for myself to stretch. I'm trying to, you know, run back to [my son] and spend every second with him. The balance I think is the tough one.' Serena Williams said that she didn't like being away from her daughter Alexis. 'It's hard', she said, limpidly. (Sawer 2018) Some women players complained that matches that are listed as 'To be arranged' left them struggling to make childcare arrangements. Ladies, in the immortal words of John McEnroe, you can *not* be serious! Hire someone to take care of your children for the duration of the tournament! Spend some of the ridiculous money you earn for whacking a ball over a net to pay for childcare on tap! Women are just as good as men and deserve the same rewards as men, but they also deserve special treatment so they can be with their children. Would I be thought ungallant if I were to point out that tennis is a career that they have chosen, and that they need to make sacrifices for it just like men do? It's not a hobby that they can squeeze in between the demands of family life. To borrow the favourite word of the villain Vizzini from *The Princess Bride*, this particular whinge of the female tennis players is *in-con-ceivable*.

It's all about the clothes
Dr Matt Taylor worked for the European Space Agency's Rosetta Mission, which, in 2014, pulled off the spectacular feat of remotely landing the

Philae lander on a tiny speeding comet. Cue hallelujahs and congratulations and praise for Dr Taylor and his team. A few days later, Dr Taylor was on television, not to take the plaudits he and his team so well deserved, but to apologise. (Meikle) Apologise? What for? For the shirt he was wearing when he broke the news. The shirt! Yes, the shirt. Taylor's shirt depicted scantily-clad cartoon women with firearms which some humour-deprived elements of the feminist Twitterati with their outrage-detectors set on maximum took as a clear indication that women aren't welcome in scientific fields. Quite how they drew that conclusion from the graphic representations on the shirt I'm not sure, but draw it they did. Some people have such thin skins that they can manage to take offence at pretty much anything. It's a wonder they can survive from day to day, so sensitive and susceptible are they.

I can't say that I cared much for Taylor's shirt myself, but that's because I like people in positions of responsibility to dress the way adults do and not like video gamers. If I ruled the world, I would have had Dr Taylor indicted on a charge of sartorial malfeasance but, alas, so powerless am I that I couldn't manage to start the modern equivalent of the Spanish Inquisition, the Twitterstorm, which Dr Taylor would not have expected. ('No one expects the Spanish Inquisition!') Some sobbing sisters, however, did conjure up a Twitterstorm, thus making one of mankind's great technical achievements all about the clothes—way to go, ladies. (see Johnson 2014) As Glenn Reynolds put it pithily, it was 'one small shirt for a man, one giant leap backward for womankind.' (see Hemingway 2014) And as another writer noted, 'The case of Dr. Taylor's shirt ... is a vivid example of what happens when a self-enfranchised politically correct cadre sets about quashing freedom and eccentricity in the name of an always-evolving sensitivity. The goal, as one wag put it, is a testosterone-free society in which everything that is not mandatory is prohibited.' (Anon. 2014)

Mansplaining 'mansplaining'

I'm sure you have always wanted to know what 'mansplaining' is. Let me explain—sorry, let me 'mansplain'—it to you. Mansplaining occurs when a man explains something to a woman that she already knows, often in a condescending tone. You might consider the term to be a little, you know, sexist, unless there is a corresponding term to describe those relatively frequent occasions when a woman explains something to a man that *he* already knows, often in a condescending tone but, according to Erynn Brook, 'femsplain-ing' is *not* sexist. (Brook) You see, 'mansplaining' is only one horse in a stable of similar equine beasts. There's also whitesplaining, cisplaining, hetsplaining and richsplaining. The common factor in all these '—splaining' terms is that they're meant to highlight a power differential: white against black, cisgender against transgender, heterosexual against homosexual and rich against poor. By the very nature of the construction of this stable of terms, you cannot have blacksplaining, transplaining, homsplaining and poorsplaining because the power differential only runs downhill, as it were, never uphill. And so, if a woman explains something to a man that *he* already knows, it's not 'femsplaining' because, as human experience supposedly shows, all women relate to all men as inferior to superior in terms of power; it's simply not possible for a woman to have and to exercise power over a man.

If it's not possible for a woman to have and to exercise power over a man, it's hard to know what to make of the daily experience of relationships between the sexes, but the counter-experiential nature of such an assertion is unlikely to bother a doctrinaire feminist. The only safe course if, like me, you are a male, white, cisgendered, heterosexual human being, is never to try explaining anything to anyone! You could perhaps try explaining things to rich people, but you can never be sure that your target isn't just a poor person who has more money than you. As a strategy, silence has much to recommend it but even here, alas, men can also transgress for, as Ms Brooks informs us men, we should recognise that sometimes our mere presence 'prevents others from expressing themselves due to these power dynamics.' I do hope that in explaining all this to us that Ms Brooks is not 'columnsplaining', which is what happens when a newspaper columnist explains things to the newspaper-reading peasantry that they already know (but do not accept), almost always in a condescending tone

The girls are not happy

Suzanne Moore informs us that fewer girls are happy and confident now than used to be the case, and that the reason for this is male violence. (Moore) In 2009, 41% of girls said they were happy; in 2018, only 25%. (These figures come from a survey of girls' attitudes from the Girlguiding organisation.) Leaving to one side the not-unimportant question of how one measures happiness or confidence and how accurate such measurements can be, it seems a rather large leap to conclude that if girls are indeed less happy and less confident than they used to be ten years ago, that the reason for this is male violence. Moore's assertion that the girls' unhappiness is due to male violence is in some tension with the conclusions of the survey in which the respondents identify the pressure of school examinations and social media as the primary culprits, although it is correct that the survey reports that the percentage of girls and young women who feel unsafe outside their safe spaces is 'alarmingly high'. It should be noted that they say they *feel* unsafe; the survey does not establish that they *are*, in fact, unsafe. It might be worth considering whether it would be reasonable to attribute some of these feelings of fear to the omnipresence of social media in these girls' lives, media replete with moral panics of the kind illustrated by Moore's very report. If girls are constantly hearing about how dangerous the world outside their safe spaces is, it's little wonder they *feel* unsafe when negotiating it. The experience of these girls in the matter of feeling unsafe is similar to that of the wider population and for much the same reasons. The UK's Office for National Statistics (ONS) reports that many more people in England and Wales worry about being a victim of crime than will actually experience it. For example, when it comes to robbery, ONS figures showed that just 0.3% of adults were victims of robbery in the year ending March 2016, whereas 9% of those surveyed were very worried they would experience it in the forthcoming year—30 times higher than the rate of victimisation. Clearly, perception is one thing, reality quite another.

Moore does acknowledge that 'the twin evils of social media and exam pressure are always blamed. Both of these things are spoken about as though nothing can be done about them. Girls simply have to negotiate a world knowing they don't look like a Kardashian, and that without the right grades they will be written off at 16.' Whoa! Hang on just a doggone second! It was the respondents themselves who identified social media and exam pressures as the primary causes of their unhappiness, not some external body. And what is the evidence for the extraordinary assertion that without the right grades, girls will be 'written off' unless they look like a Kardashian?

Women, it appears, are not happy. The cynics among us might say that women are never happy except when they're miserable. Roughly 10% appear to suffer from some form of PTSD! One wonders what they'd be like if they'd actually been in combat! Unhappiness appears to be more characteristic of younger women than of older. Young women seem to be locked in an endless cycle of complaining and invidious comparisons, and those who make most use of social media are the most likely to experience some form of depression. Why is this? As just mentioned, the common villain is the ubiquity of social media in their lives. So what should we do about it? Therapy, it seems, is the answer, not, as you might naïvely think, reducing or eliminating altogether their use of social media, which can be done at the flick of a switch and which costs a lot less than therapy. Or they could just cease to be young—time will take care of this problem. Or they could just stop being women—an option that, in our brave new world, is increasingly open to them.

Feminising Philosophy

Progress! Oxford is going to 'feminise' its philosophy reading lists to appeal more to women. It's well known, apparently, that women are massively put off philosophy because most of it is the work of men. Now all that is set to change. At least 40% of recommended authors will be women and, to make sure that students know this, members of the academic staff have been asked to use writers' first names instead of the more gender-blind initials. (Turner 2018) Elizabeth Anscombe, whom we are told was one of the greatest philosophers of the post-war period, published as 'G.E.M. Anscombe' and, as Professor Edward Harcourt tells us, 'If that's what goes on the reading list, understandably students won't know she was female.' One wonders why they should care! Does Anscombe's being female make her arguments more cogent or her theses more philosophically significant? Moreover, while I have a great respect for Anscombe's work, I find the claim that she was one of the greatest philosophers of the post-war period to be, how shall I put it, hyperbolic. As well as beefing up the proportion of women authors on reading lists, the university is also planning to introduce an undergraduate paper on feminist philosophy and has appointed new academics—female academics it seems—to teach it. Professor Harcourt said he hoped that these changes would 'send the message to our female students that philosophy is for you.' Because, of course, up to now, it clearly hasn't been.

I hope it won't be considered rude to point out that reading off an author's gender from that author's name might be considered a trifle transphobic. The new policy mysteriously seems to assume that there are only two genders rather than, as we now know, a thousand blooming flowers. One might think that this manifestation of gender ideology is fundamentally incoherent or one might simply sigh and remark, as one very prominent and highly esteemed woman philosopher (who shall be nameless) remarked when she was informed of Oxford's new policy: 'Oh, good grief! Oxford, yet! What's *wrong* with them?'

A storm in a crowded lift.

Don't make jokes in a lift! Richard Lebow, who was attending the International Studies Association conference in San Francisco, made two mistakes. His first mistake was getting into a crowded lift without checking for the presence of hypersensitive feminists. You can buy an inexpensive feministometer in any branch of your local Let'skeepwomenundercontrol store which will light up when a feminist comes within 50 feet of you, just as Frodo's sword Sting glows when it detects the presence of Orcs. Lebow's second mistake, when he was asked what floor he wanted, was his replying, 'Ladies' lingerie!' Simona Sharoni, a professor of women's and gender studies at Merrimack College, was, like Queen Victoria, not amused by Lebow's lame attempt at humour, and afterwards filed a complaint with the Association. Anyone from an East-Atlantic anglophone background knows that Lebow's remark was a cultural reference to the TV show 'Are You Being Served?' but, not having the advantage of being British, Sharoni couldn't be expected to have this knowledge. (see Lebow; see also Mangan) Unfortunately for Lebow, the complainant was someone who, in her own words, 'had dedicated her life to confronting sexism (and other forms of discrimination and oppression) in academic spaces,' so goodbye to common sense.

When Lebow came to learn of Sharoni's complaint, he sent her a grovelling email, writing, 'I certainly had no desire to insult women or to make you feel uncomfortable', and he suggested that she might have interpreted his remarks out of context. Eager to establish his woke credentials, he also said, 'Like you, I am strongly opposed to the exploitation, coercion or humiliation of women ... As such evils continue, it seems to me to make sense to direct our attention to real offenses, not those that are imagined or marginal. By making a complaint to ISA that I consider frivolous—and I expect, will be judged this way by the ethics committee—you may be directing time and effort away from the real offenses that trouble us both.' Professor Lebow was doomed to be disappointed, for the Association, instead of suggesting that Lebow get some new and better joke material, duly found that he had violated the Association's code of conduct!

Instead of grovelling to Professor Sharoni, Lebow's proper response should have been a rude phrase consisting of two short words, one of four letters, the other of three. In suggesting that Sharoni's complaint was frivolous (how dare he, how very dare he!), Lebow guilty not only of the original offence of attempting to make amusing remarks in lifts, but of the meta-offence of minimising Sharoni's complaint. Once again, the ISA committee snapped to attention, judging this to be an even more serious violation of the Association's code. They insisted that Lebow should offer an unequivocal apology which Lebow, to give him credit, refused to do. The thought occurs to me—radical, I know, but think about it for a moment—that Sharoni might have said something to Lebow *at the time he made his remark* if she really felt that stronly about it. Her delayed action has all the hallmarks of simulated outrage. On reflection, forget that suggestion. It's clearly crazy to expect a woman, a strong and independent woman, to stand up for her beliefs in public.

Covering up a Cover Up

We can, it seems, always count on official and semi-official examples of stupidity to brighten our otherwise dull days. In 2018, the UK's National Trust organised an exhibition (with the help of taxpayers' money) to promote the role of women and, in particular, to celebrate the life of one Margaret Armstrong, the wife of William, Lord Armstrong, an industrialist who founded the Armstrong Whitworth manufacturing concern on Tyneside. Lord Armstrong was also a scientist, an inventor and a philanthropist of note. The six-week celebratory exhibition entitled 'The Great Cragside Cover-up' was advertised as an installation by the artists Kate Stobbart, Rob Blazey and Harriet Sutcliffe—you'll get the point of the 'Cover-up' portion of the exhibition's title in a moment. The artists had one tiny problem highlighting Lady Armstrong's life—they simply couldn't find enough material to allow them to do so. Stobbart said, 'We wanted to try and bring out Lady Margaret (*sic* Armstrong?) and every time we tried to do that we failed really, because conversations with the experts here, and our own conversations when we were back in Newcastle, inevitably led to Lord Armstrong and not very much on Lady Armstrong.' (Halliday) That might have given normal people the clue that there wasn't much point trying to high-light a life that apparently didn't *have* many highlights. But all is grist to the mill of the ideologically committed. So, what did our enterprising installers do? Instead of filling up Lady Armstrong's countryseat, Cragside, with artefacts about her life, and stirring demonstrations of her contributions to science and culture, which they couldn't find for the very good reason that there weren't many, if any, they covered up their failure to discover what they needed by instead covering up the artworks at Cragside that featured men!

Visitors to the exhibition were understandably puzzled and not a little annoyed when they encountered paintings covered with sheets and statues wrapped in bags, and they expressed their complaints voluminously in the comment boxes helpfully provided by the National Trust. Some of those who had paid up to £49.50 for a family ticket said they were baffled that much of the work produced by men or featuring male subjects was shielded from view, and one visitor remarked, not unreasonably, that he failed to see (probably no pun intended) how concealing exhibits related to males was supposed to encourage the appreciation of female achievement.

The National Trust admitted that their idea had backfired but, with a spectacular lack of self-awareness, said that the exhibition wasn't about censoring art or being politically correct (which, of course, is precisely what it *was* about), but was rather designed to encourage visitors to look at the collection in a different way and to stimulate debate. In a curiously inverted way they achieved their aims. The exhibition certainly forced visitors to look at the collection, the little they could see of it, in a different way, and it certainly stimulated debate, but probably not the kind of debate the National Trust had in mind.

*****

So, where does all this leave us? The feminist revolution is well and truly in progress and men have already lost. In the blink of an historical eye, the social and cultural norms of Western civilisation have been set aside; at least, so says Terry Barnes in the *Spectator*. 'Every day,' he tells us, 'is now International Women's Day.' (Barnes 2018) Feminist issues and values frame public discourse and the #TimesUp and #MeToo movements are the signs of the times in which all men are characterised as predators and all women as actual or potential victims. All over the Western world, men, in particular middle-aged (and older) white, heterosexual men, are being denounced by the feminist Red Guard.

Would any feminist worth her salt agree with Barnes's contention that the feminist revolution is pretty much over and women have won? Would they not contend that while women have come just so far, there's still such a long way to go! Women have only just won the first skirmish in the ongoing war against men and the revolution will continue until men are finally and completely ground beneath their high heels.

Women at Work

It's hard to be a woman!
You must think like a man, act like a lady,
look like Helen of Troy and work like a horse
—Anonymous

Women do not find it difficult nowadays to behave like men,
but they often find it extremely difficult
to behave like gentlemen
—Compton Mackenzie

In April 2019, the UK's Home Secretary, Amber Rudd, urged Britain's biggest companies to get more women into senior positions. The creation of 50%/50% gender (sex) shortlists was a suggested strategy to ensure that women occupy a third of top positions in business by 2020. Male executives at Britain's biggest companies were told they must lead the charge by bringing more women into senior positions. The Home Secretary didn't say *why* she thought companies should do this, so I presume the reason for it is supposed to be obvious. But it's not obvious to me.

Women already run some 20% of Britain's six million businesses but this, it seems, is not enough. In September 2018, Robert Jenrick, Exchequer Secretary to the UK's Treasury, described the paucity of female business founders as 'shocking'. (see Johnson 2018) I can understand that this fact might be surprising or maybe even mildly interesting, but why is it shocking? Are women being prevented by physical violence or legal prohibitions from starting up businesses? In the same complaining vein, a letter was sent to various Secretaries of State from an organisation calling itself 'Women Mean Business', signed by over 200 women business leaders. It listed a number of differences between the experiences of men and women when it comes to starting up businesses. The signatories to the letter admitted there is no doubt that there are complex reasons for the disparities between the experience of men and women, but nevertheless they asserted, for no obvious reason except the bare fact of the disparities, that the existence of such disparities showed that women are being held back unfairly.

The German Chancellor, Angela Merkel, said in a speech in Berlin in November 2018 that politics, science, business and culture need more women. (see Agencies in Berlin) Unfortunately, she omitted to tell us *why* more women were needed in politics, science, business and culture, presumably on the grounds that this is a truth universally acknowledged. She also didn't specify explicitly what she meant by equality in her speech, although the context indicates clearly enough that she meant by it some kind of ratio that mirrors the male/female ratio in the wider society. 'The goal,' she said, 'needs to be equality, equality everywhere.' On the other hand, she expressed the hope that 'no one will be forced into a role or a specific task because of his or her gender,' which I would like to interpret as a rejection of quotas and other forms of positive discrimination, but I suspect that that's not quite what she meant.

Beware the anti-feminist backlash, former Australian Prime Minister Julia Gillard told us in 2018. (see Slawson) Launching the Global Institute for Women's Leadership at King's College London, she remarked that those who think things have gone too far should look at the statistics. Women are underrepresented in leadership positions around the world. Only 23% of national parliamentarians, 26% of news media leaders, 27% of judges and 15% of corporate board members are women. Even worse, only 9% of senior IT leaders in the world are women.

Also in 2018, the Irish Minister for Higher Education, Mary Mitchell O'Connor, announced that she was to set up a taskforce to examine the possibility of imposing gender quotas in universities, after the Higher Education Authority (HEA) found that just 21% of professors were female. 'The latest data regarding the gender gap in our third-level institutions confirms [*sic*] we have a gender problem in this sector,' said Mitchell O'Connor, a former primary school principal. 'If we don't decide to act now, we will be reading the same results next year, and the year after that.' She is personally in favour of gender quotas. 'The current pace of change is too slow,' she said, 'and the stakes are too high to continue to just tinker around the edges, or wait for natural adjustment.' Just what *is* the right speed, Ms Mitchell O'Connor? And how do you know what that is? 'Academia should be leading the way,' she continued, 'but, currently, it is lagging behind. The sector is flawed if the female perspective is missing at all levels. We will, as a society, pay if we do not tackle this issue.'

Jobs for the girls

It will not have escaped your notice that common to the pronouncements of Rudd, Merkel, Jenrick, Gillard and O'Connor is the assertion *that* we need more women in business, law, politics and the higher reaches of academia. You may not have noticed, however, that also common to their pronouncements is the absence of any convincing reason for *why* they believe there is this pressing need. Speaking at an event in March 2019, Baroness Hale, who is Britain's most senior judge, called for at least half of the judiciary to be made up of women. (see Taylor) Her reason for this manifesto is that since women make up half the population, they should make up half the judges at least. Previously, Lady Hale had advocated more diversity in the judiciary so that, as she put it, 'the public feel those on the bench are "our judges" rather than "beings from another planet"'. It must be a great consolation when you are being sent down for a 15-year stretch to have your sentence handed out by someone of the same sex and race as yourself. I presume that, by parity of reasoning, Lady Hale would call for women to make up half of the roof workers, garbage collectors and oil rig workers and, since men constitute half the population, I suppose she would insist that *they* should make up half of nurses, secretaries and teachers. How might we bring about such a desirable state of affairs? Well, forced job swaps would rapidly create equality in respect of employment between the sexes. Perhaps we should insist that bin men swap with primary school teachers, and building workers with nurses. It is a curious fact that diversity-as-equality, which is really jobs for the girls and other victim-privileged groups, always seems to be sought in the more glamorous areas of employment, such as TV, entertainment, politics, the universities and the higher levels of business administration, but never in road-maintenance or garbage collection or coal mining or construction. In the end, it's not equality for women as such, but equality (that is, special privileges) for women-like-me.

Why 50%/50% gender representation? Why not 52.7%/47.3% representation? And why for gender, so-called? (really for sex, since there are very many genders but only two sexes.) Why not for race? (Is there any such thing as race? And if so, how many races are there?) Why not for disability? age? height? hair colour? shoe size? or just about any other difference you might choose to select? Why not have it across the board in *every* form of employment, not just high-end jobs. Why the presumption that anything significantly less than 50%/50% is somehow a bad thing, almost certainly the result of some kind of dastardly discrimination? And what exactly, by the way, is this mysterious female perspective that these various sectors are missing? Is it different from the male perspective? If so, in what way, precisely? And why and in what way, *à la* Ms Mitchell O'Connor, will we pay as a society if this so-called problem is not tackled?

Here's a little dialogue intended to explore the thinking of Rudd, Jenrick, Merkel and the rest of the gynocentric gang. The interlocutors are PjfpW, an advocate of posh jobs for posh women, and S, a sceptical inquirer who would like to see something resembling a reason (other than Mitchell O'Connor's oddly anti-feminist 'women's perspective') offered for the gynocentric gang's admonitions.

PjfpW: Women make up roughly 50% of the population; therefore we should expect that there would be roughly 50% of women in all areas of employment.

S: Really, why should we expect that? Men also make up roughly 50% of the population, but they don't make up 50% or anything approaching that percentage of teachers, social workers or nurses, areas of employment that are effectively dominated by women.

PjfpW: Well, whatever about that, we must remove discriminatory barriers to women occupying high-level posts in politics, higher education and business.

S: Are there such barriers? Is the effective domination by women of teaching, nursing and social work a matter of active discrimination against men, or is it just the outcome of individual choices made by individual people? If the disproportionality between men and women in those areas is the outcome of individual choices, why should we expect proportions of men and women to be equal in other areas of employment?

PjfpW: Well, there must be discrimination, or women would be present in those high-level business and politics posts in the proportion that their presence in the general population warrants.

S: But doesn't your claim about discrimination beg the question, assuming the very thing it is supposed to prove? What's the evidence for anti-female discrimination apart from the relative proportions of men and women in particular types of employment? The proportion of men and women in these posts is the matter to be explained—it cannot itself be its own explanation. You explain it by reference to discrimination and then you justify the postulation of discrimination by reference to the relatively low percentage of women in these posts. Even if it weren't logically invalid to make this circular argument—which it is—how can you make it without being prepared to say that the lack of men in teaching, nursing and social work is also a matter of discrimination?

It is apparent, then, that behind the monotonous assertion that 'We need more women!' lies the tacit assumption that if it weren't for barriers of various kinds, the proportion of men and women (remember, for the purposes of this particular piece of propaganda there are only two sexes/genders) in private or public employment would be roughly equal. But this is merely an assumption and, moreover, it is an assumption that flies in the face both of experience and of logic. Thomas Sowell makes this point, and does so with his customary exemplary clarity.

> Neither in nature nor among human beings are either equal or randomly distributed outcomes automatic. On the contrary, grossly unequal distributions of outcomes are common, both in nature and among people, in circumstances where neither genes nor discrimination are involved .... The idea that [the world] would be a level playing field, if it were not for either genes or discrimination, is a preconception in defiance of both logic and facts. Nothing is easier to find than sins among human beings, but to automatically make those sins the sole, or even primary, cause of different outcomes among different peoples is to ignore many other reasons for those disparities .... At the heart of many discussions of disparities among individuals, groups and nations is the seemingly invincible fallacy that outcomes in human endeavors would be equal, or at least comparable or random, if there were no biased interventions, on the one hand, nor genetic deficiencies, on the other. This preconception, which spans the ideological spectrum is in utter defiance of both logic and empirical evidence from around the world, and over millennia of recorded history .... Nor is discrimination automatically excluded. It is one of many possibilities, each of which has to establish its claims with evidence rather than being an automatic presumption.' (Sowell 2018, 18; 100-101]

In 2017, the EU announced legislation that would require companies whose non-executive directors are over 60% male to, as it put it primly, 'prioritise' women. The paternalism of such legislation is, or should be, patently obvious, and any woman worth her salt should treat such patronising nonsense with the contempt it deserves. Job discrimination based on grounds of sex is illegal, in case anyone hadn't noticed, so that women are not legally disadvantaged vis-à-vis men when it comes to employment, including employment as company directors. 'We are in the midst of an obsession with female representation on panel shows, in politics, at the upper echelons of business,' writes Clare Foges, 'and I, as one of the 50 per cent, am heartily sick of it.' (Foges 2017) Well, you're not the only one sick of it, Ms Foges. Most men are (quietly) annoyed by it, and many women rightly resent it as patronising.

The idea that simply by being of a particular sex you are thereby a representative of that sex is fundamentally flawed. No one is a representative of a group simply by virtue of being a member of that group. When I got my first academic job, I wasn't appointed as a representative of Irish people, 30-year olds, men, white people, English-speakers or any other group to which I might conceivably be deemed to have belonged; I was just me. If you're a man, you're not *ipso facto* a representative of men; if you're a woman, you're not *ipso facto* a representative of women. The demand for special privileges for women (and other supposedly under-represented groups) based on a vacuous concept of representation is deeply patronising. The message that this sends is that individuals of the supposedly under-represented group are incapable of making it on their own without a special leg-up or without receiving hand-outs from the powers that be.

Sometimes, *mirabile dictu,* in the face of patently sexist nonsense, justice manages to prevail. *Newsweek* reported in March 2018, that a court in Austria has ruled that an Austrian man, Peter Franzmayr, was discriminated against when a job he had applied for was given to a woman instead. (see Persio) Of the three candidates for the post, Franzmayr was rated higher than the woman who was appointed. The Federal Administrative Court ordered the State to pay Franzmayr compensation of €317,368, saying that it had found a pattern 'according to which [the woman appointed] was treated more favourably than the other candidates from the beginning.' The Austrian Minister of Transport, Doris Bures, admitted that what she called 'the mass underrepresentation of women' had played a role in her decision. She worried that the Court's decision would call into question 'the principle of encouraging the promotion of women.' It's astonishing to me—it shouldn't be, but it is—that Bures (and others like her, such as Rudd, Merkel, Hale, Jenrick, Gillard and O'Connor) in tilting against the quixotic windmills of the phantom patriarchy, cannot grasp that her and their approach is deeply and explicitly sexist.

The demand for quotas, of course, is just a thinly-disguised form of special pleading. To repeat a point already made, if we are to have quotas, could we have them across the board? In primary education, for example, perhaps we should stop recruiting female candidates so that the balance of male and female teachers can even up. Better still, perhaps we could fire a large cohort of female teachers and employ male teachers in their places. So too with places in psychology, law, social work and medicine courses at university. So too with midwifery and nursing. And let's force women (why not some of those over-represented nurses and teachers) to make up 50% of those who do the unpleasant and strenuous jobs that are done more or less exclusively at the moment by men—bricklaying, tree-felling, mining, rubbish collection, slaughterhouse work, roofing and so on.

But still the cry is heard, 'we need to impose a 50%/50% gender split' in employment (of the right kind) between men and women. Really? Why should women rather than any of the other many supposedly oppressed groups have half the plum jobs? And haven't we all got the memo by now that there are many more than two genders? Just in case you haven't realised it by now, all this guff of 'gender equality' is cover for 'jobs for the girls'. What it means is getting men out of high-paying prestigious jobs or, better still, preventing them from getting in in the first place, and substituting women in their place. At the same time employers will be obliged to institute 'family-friendly' policies (in effect, women-friendly policies), guaranteeing that female high-flyers have generous maternity leave arrangements and that their working hours are suitably flexible to compensate for their gender disadvantage (gender disadvantage is code for their choosing to have children!), regardless of whether this is good for their employers or for their fellow workers who have to cover for them during their absences.

The point I've been trying to make in the last few pages is made succinctly and humorously in a sketch from *Not the Nine O'Clock News*. (YouTube 2012) Scene: A board meeting. Three people present: a Chairman and two committee members whom, in the interests of protecting the guilty, I shall call Tweedledum and Tweedledee. Chairman: 'The next item on the agenda, is the appointment of a new top man to my team. I think it ought to be a woman.' Tweedledum is a little surprised by this: 'A woman?,' he says. 'Aye,' continues the Chairman, 'a woman—equal opportunities and so on—and positive discrimination, so preferably black.' Tweedledum is more than a little surprised by this: 'A black woman?' 'Aye,' continues the Chairman, relentlessly, 'a black woman. And we don't employ any ex-convicts at the moment do we?' Tweedledum, beginning to get on board with the programme, suggests, 'What about a black woman ex-convict?' 'Right!' agrees the Chairman, 'a black woman ex-convict—in her late 50s!' 'Late 50s?,' says an extraordinarily surprised Tweededee. 'A lot of people find it very, very difficult to get jobs when they've been made redundant in their late 50s,' explains the Chairman, 'especially if they're educationally sub-normal.' Tweedledum and Tweedledee look at each other quizzically. 'After all,' the Chairman remarks, 'an educationally sub-normal epileptic with speech defects, partial sight and deafness would find it very, very, very difficult to get a job, even though they have a great deal to contribute.' Tweedledee sums up: 'Right, so. We're looking for a woman ... (Chairman: 'make that a pregnant woman') ... a pregnant woman who is black, blind, deaf ... (Chairman interjects: 'tall') ... tall, epileptic, in her late 50s (Chairman and Tweedledee in unison) and an ex-convict.' Chairman: 'Right! Are we all agreed on that? We'll have that advertised immediately. Thank you very much gentlemen.' (He leaves) Tweedledum and Tweedledee look at each other. Tweedledum: 'Bloody typical of JC, that!' Tweedledee: 'Every good job that comes up goes to one of his family!'

But fact doesn't lag far behind fiction. The winner of the 2017-18 Australian Workplace Gender Equality Agency "Employer of Choice for Gender Equality" award is an institution with an 85% female workforce! I kid you not! You may not have known that there was such a thing as the Workplace Gender Equality Agency (and why indeed should you?), but there is, and it must gladden the hearts of all equalitarians to know the 85%/15% female to male ratio is deemed to be equality. The winner of this prestigious if slightly obscure and evidently irrational award is something called Mercy Health which runs hospitals, homes and community care.

What of actual anti-female bias? A classic piece of research that seemed to demonstrate the existence of such bias was the 2000 paper, 'Orchestrating Impartiality: The Impact of "Blind" Auditions on Female Musicians.' (Goldin & Rouse) The endlessly repeated cautionary tale to emerge from this much-cited paper is that the introduction of auditions for orchestra positions in which the sex of the auditionee was concealed led to a spectacular increase in the hiring of female musicians. That interpretation was justified by the study's conclusion: 'We find that the screen increases—by 50 percent—the probability that a woman will be advanced from certain preliminary rounds and increases by severalfold the likelihood that a woman will be selected in the final round.' The authors of the study themselves warn about the small sample sizes, results that were contradictory and even conceded that their findings weren't statistically significant. How then was the rousing conclusion justified? Short answer: it wasn't. A 2017 study that was inspired by the Goldin & Rouse paper asked over 2,100 managers in Australia's public service to recruit from randomly assigned CVs, some revealing the sex of the applicant, some not. (see Hiscox et al.) Christine Hoff Sommers takes up the story: 'The research team fully expected to find far more female candidates shortlisted when sex was disguised. But, as the stunned team leader told the local media: "We found the opposite, that de-identifying candidates reduced the likelihood of women being selected for the shortlist." It turned out that many senior managers, aware that sexist assumptions had once kept women out of upper-level positions, already practiced a mild form of affirmative action. Anonymized hiring was not only time-consuming and costly, it proved to be an obstacle to women's equality.' (Sommers 2019)

According to the Australian Government's own report on this study, its problematic results 'indicate the need for caution when moving towards "blind" recruitment processes in the APS, as de-identification may frustrate efforts aimed at promoting diversity' and 'The results showed that overall, de-identifying applications at the shortlisting stage does not appear to assist in promoting diversity within the APS in hiring. Overall, APS officers discriminated in favour of female and minority candidates'!

Women, it seems, can never win. Not only do they appear to be discriminated against when it comes to attaining top managerial positions, but when they do manage to attain such positions, it seems that what they get is less attractive to them than it is to men. Why should this be so? Because, we are told, having a senior job increases life satisfaction for men but not for women! Research seems to show that men will take more money in a trade off for free time whereas this may not be the case for women. I quote the abstract of the study in which this finding is reported.

Women with managerial careers are significantly less satisfied with their life (*sic*) than their male counterparts. Why? In a representative German panel dataset (GSOEP) we find biological constraints and substitutive mechanisms determining the subjective well-being of female managers. Women's terminated fertility has a negative impact on women's life satisfaction between the ages of 35 and 45, when managerial careers usually take off. Money and spare time can compensate for this biological difference. But to maintain an equivalent level of happiness, women need to be compensated by much more income for each hour of spare time given up than men do. So, in order to reach better gender equality in leadership positions, women must be either paid higher incomes (on average around 10%) or must be incentivized with more spare time than men. (Brockmann *et al.*)

Goodness gracious me! Surely the authors of this study cannot be suggesting that there are sex-based differences in job aspirations or job satisfaction? But yes! The study estimated that 'it would take an extra €12,000 of pay to boost a woman's life satisfaction by the same amount that a man would gain from an extra €5,000 of pay.' (If ever there was an unknowable statistic, this must surely be one! But let that pass.) Women, it seems, value their free time as against monetary rewards more highly than do men. The Brockmann report notes (sharp intake of breath) that 'leadership positions "require a non-stop lifelong commitment to extra-long working hours and early career path-dependencies" which may repel women ... ' My goodness! My heart bleeds for these poor women who are expected to—wait for it—work like crazy if they expect to get to and stay at the top. What tyranny!

You might think that the proposal made by Brockmann and his fellow researchers is a joke, but if it's funny, the laughter is painful. This is a transparently ludicrous demand for *extra* pay and *extra* time off for women for doing the *same* work as men. Not *equal* pay for *equal* work, but *more* pay and *more* time off for women doing the same work. I'm sure that the authors of the study would not want to suggest this but a reasonable conclusion from their research is that it might be wise to call a halt to the incessant encouragement of women towards careers in which they are, apparently, not going to find satisfaction. It appears to be utterly beyond the comprehension of feminists and their gynocentric fellow travellers that 'job satisfaction' is a notion less than a few generations old. 'Men kept women out of the workplace until the 20th century,' feminists will cry. Women didn't have to be repressed to stay out of the workplace because, for most of human history, work outside the home was generally manual, and gruelling, and required significant upper-body strength, and it wasn't, for the most part, a source of empowerment or personal satisfaction. We are constantly told: 'Women can do anything a man can do!' All right, so be it. But now, it turns out, women aren't always as happy as men are when doing what men do. So, what's the answer? The obvious answer is: *try doing something else*! But the answer suggested by the authors of the study is to pay women more than men and give them more holidays than men. In a highly competitive field, that article may well be unbeatable in any competition for the most idiotic article of 2017. Employers are to give an extra €7,000 to women for doing the same work as men? Where is this extra money supposed to come from? Only a recidivist socialist could have such a pathetically juvenile conception of the point of salaries, as if businesses were arms of the welfare state whose aim is to ensure that their female workers are paid enough to feel content, rather than maximising profit for their shareholders.

An aside: the brave new world of the academy.

As we all know, women are as good as or even better than men except, it seems, when they're not. In 2017, 37% of men at Oxford achieved a First Class honours (a percentage that seems wildly extravagant to me, but let that go) while a mere 32% of women managed a First (still an extravagant percentage, but let that go too.) But we can't have that! How to rectify the gap? By letting history students sit one of their five examinations at home! (Turner 2017) The same geniuses who've come up with this sexist idea because of the small gap between men and women in the matter of Firsts are unconcerned, it would seem, that females outperform males pretty much across the board at GCSE, at A levels, and in raw numbers attending university, particularly in a number of individual academic disciplines. So what does this initiative tell us? Well, if you're a woman, it tells you that you are feeble and need to be helped, otherwise, God forbid, you would have to do things on the same terms as men.

The *Telegraph* reported in February 2018 that Oxford has introduced longer examination times for the benefit of women. In the summer of 2017, candidates taking mathematics and computer science papers were given an extra fifteen minutes to complete their answers because, as the report goes on to tell us, 'dons ruled that "female candidates might be more likely to be adversely affected by time pressure". (Diver) Leaving aside the blatant sexism of this move for a moment (just think of the howls of feminist outrage if Oxford introduced changes to examination policies that were intended to improve the scores of male students), just why did the dons think that female candidates might be more likely to be adversely affected by time pressure than male candidates? Are women somehow unable to divide the time available for the entire examination by the number of questions they are required to answer? Do they occupy a different temporal zone from men in the examination hall, one in which time moves more quickly? Is the passage of time itself now part of a patriarchal conspiracy? What seems to have occasioned this extraordinary move was that, in previous years, the percentage of First Class Honours awarded to male students in these disciplines was double that awarded to female students, so something had to be done to improve women's grades. I feel like a simpleton asking this question but—*why* had something to be done to improve women's grades? Why is improving women's grades an issue? If it's that important, why not just ignore examination results altogether and mark the women candidates in accordance with the impressionistic dictates of social justice?

Readers with some residual sense of real justice will be heartened to know that despite this mini-Machiavellian strategy, the only thing that appears to have resulted from it is an increase in the number of 2:1s overall, hardly a good thing, given the rampant grade inflation already well-embedded in the university system, but better than the gender time-tampering intended by the authorities. Male candidates continued to be awarded more First Class Honours degrees than women in mathematics and computer science, though not by a factor of two. Antonia Siu, Undergraduate Representative of Oxford Women in Computer Science, said that while she was 'uneasy about schemes to favour one gender over another,' she was 'happy when people see gaps between groups of people who should not reasonably have such gaps—such as between genders, races or class—and take that as a starting point to think about the kinds of people they unintentionally are leaving behind.' (Diver) I'm not sure that Ms Siu's sentiments, while undoubtedly kind-hearted, are altogether coherent. She does well to be uneasy about policies that favour one gender (her word) over another, but why does she think that it is unreasonable that there are, as she puts it, 'gaps' between genders, races or class, and why does she regard these gaps as signifying the unintentional 'leaving behind' of particular groups of people? We can ignore the stalking horses of race and class, since the extra-time policy is specifically about improving the results of the members of one sex: women.

To the unbiased eye, this policy looks like a blatant piece of sexism. It is, in fact, doubly sexist: sexist in its attribution of temporal frailty to female students—'Temporal frailty, thy name is woman'—and sexist in its proposal to remedy that frailty. Shouldn't those feminists who trumpet the strong, independent, 'women are just as good as men' line object strenuously to this patronising and sexist policy? Or will they rather, since the policy benefits women, keep schtum? Oh, and by the way, the original headline under which this story was reported was, 'Oxford University extends exam times for women's benefit', but this was later changed to clarify that though this has been done to help women perform better, all students will benefit from the extra time, including the male students who don't need the extra time. I see. That, of course, changes everything. (Diver. See also Griffiths & Henry)

The status of men in the modern academy, particularly in the humanities, is well captured by James Hynes in his campus novel, *The Lecturer's Tale*. He describes his anti-hero, who has the ironically heroic name Nelson, as

> one of the shell-shocked and self-effacing white males who made up the lowest ranks of [the university's] English program. Like Nelson, they'd entered the academy because they loved books and the idea of a comfortable, contemplative life. But now they always looked slightly stunned, as if they'd just heard a very loud noise, and were cringingly uncertain when to expect the next one. The loud noise they kept hearing was the impact of very large volumes of cultural studies, queer theory, and postcolonial interventions thudding into the prairie all around them like artillery. Each concussion was an announcement that their race and gender were the root of all evil. That these young men, heirs to a mingled tradition of Calvinism and liberal guilt, already half-believed this themselves only made them more vulnerable; and it slowly dawned on them that the New Order of … feminists hated mild-mannered liberal pluralists even more than it hated honest-to-god conservatives. These young men lived in terror of saying the wrong thing, and they were increasingly unable to tell the difference between what they actually believed and what they professed to in public. (Hynes, 25)

To lighten the mood, here are some little snippets of comic relief. Have you ever wondered why there were no women in the final of *University Challenge* 2017? Be puzzled no longer. The answer, according to Wolfson College's equality and diversity officer, Azita Chellappoo, who doesn't think all-male teams should be allowed on the show, is—hostility. Well, obviously it has to be hostility;

that's the only possible explanation. Let's not consider the possibility that the four best candidates from each institution were chosen—that's an obviously crazy idea!—and that since teams want to win, any team actively discriminating against a superior female contestant in favour of an inferior male would be handicapping itself. Suppose we were to have sex quotas, *à la* Chellappoo, what then? What of the suspicion that would hang over teams selected in this way that the representatives of one sex—all right, let's not be coy, the woman or women—were selected primarily because of her or their being women.

But it's not all bad news for women on the academic front. Vanessa Thorpe reports that 'the hallowed college quads and courts of Oxford and Cambridge hold many more statues of men than of women; a testament to the long tradition of male dominance at Britain's leading universities. But a bronze sculpture of a vulva to be unveiled later this week at Newnham College, Cambridge, is set to help redress the balance with a flourish.' (Thorpe) The work of art, entitled *Beyond Thinking*, is two-stories tall! I suspect some who hear about this would think that *Beyond Belief* might be an equally suitable title for the sculpture. Of course, with the patriarchy being what it is, I'm sure that we can expect to see a two-story stylised penis somewhere on the Cambridge campus sometime soon.

Zombie-alert!—the gender pay gap

Some supposed facts that aren't in fact facts are seemingly incapable of lying down when they're shown to be dead. Zombie-like, they wander around, sucking the vitality out of sensible and rational discussions. The so-called Gender Pay Gap (GPG) is one such zombie fact that rises effortlessly from the grave whenever there's a discussion on discrimination against women. Everybody knows that women are consistently paid only a proportion of what men are paid for the same work. Everyone may know it but it isn't true, at least, not to any significant degree. Historically, of course, it is true that women were paid less than men but the past is a different country and it is hermeneutically perilous to apply the sensibilities of today to the standards of yesterday. Even when men were paid more than women in those situations, however infrequent, where they did the same work, it doesn't follow that this indicated a brutal and arbitrary act of male oppression against women. A key difference between the past and the present is that it was the household rather than the individual that was regarded as the economic base unit of society. 'To a contemporary way of thinking,' writes Steve Moxon, 'an officially-sanctioned policy of a "pay gap" seems particularly unfair. But not from the perspective of payment according to the different inputs of men and women into the shared household, when the wealth available for distribution was so pitifully small that there had to be in effect some tough-minded rationing. Or looked at the other way: there had to be a system where there was one person at least in each household whose income could allow the household as a whole to subsist.' (Moxon, 95) He goes on to note that 'One of the effects of recent equal-pay policy has been to depress absolute pay levels to the extent that both partners now have to work in order to provide for a standard of living that would have been available from a single wage as recently as two decades ago .... The important issue for women was the total household income not where it came from. The less of it they had to earn themselves, the better able they were to be home-makers and child-carers.' (Moxon, 95)

The so-called marriage-bar that was deployed against the continuation of women in employment after marriage is now regarded as *prima facie* evidence of the social dark ages from which women only recently emerged. However, that policy was designed on the assumption, among others, that married women were financially provided for whereas single women were not and so, given the still largely sex-dichotomous nature of employment, single women should not have to compete with married women for limited employment opportunities. It was thus not a pro-male and anti-female policy but rather a pro-*single*-female policy and a policy that was, hardly surprisingly, supported in the main by single female workers. In any event, that was then; this is now. There may be some women who are paid less for doing the same job that a man does. That's always possible but, if so, it's illegal in most jurisdictions and has been so for quite some time.

The scandal of the GPG is often presented in a dramatic fashion. Sometimes we are told that women have to work some proportion of the year for free as compared to men. We can always rely on the *Guardian*, a very present help in trouble, for scare headlines and it duly obliges, telling us that 'Gender pay gap means women work 67 days a year for free, says TUC.' (Jones 2018; see Smethers) Inasmuch as there is any evidence to support the idea of a GPG, it derives from focusing on aggregates, totalling all that men earn, all that women earn, dividing those totals by the respective numbers of men and women, and coming up with an earnings ratio somewhere between 75% to 95% for women to men's 100%. Now this fact, supposing it to be accurate, indeed tells us something, but quite what it tells us is not immediately clear. The presumption by feminists and their fellow travellers is that this difference is the result of raw sex discrimination but, while this might be true, there are many other factors that need to be taken into account before we can conclude that sex discrimination is the culprit. People whom you might expect to be clued into the reality here seem to be as subject to the GPG fallacy as anyone else. Members of the Conservative government in the UK appear to be firmly in its grip. UK government statistics are supposed to show that about 80% of firms pay men more than women. This, according to the former Prime Minister Theresa May, is a 'burning injustice.' That we are dealing with empty rhetoric and not argument here is becoming more and more evident, not least because the language of 'denier' is now being used to stigmatise those who raise legitimate questions about the nature of the data and the conclusions that are being drawn from them, as well as the policies that are being based on them. Helene Reardon Bond, a diversity and inclusion expert who was Head of Gender Equality Policy and Inclusion at Government Equalities Office, and has been the Interim Director of the UK's Equalities Office since 2016, has denounced 'deniers' who say that 'the gap only exists because of the choices women make.' On the contrary, she believes that 'while everyone makes choices, women make constrained choices.' Do they, indeed? And what kind of constraint would those be? (see Firsht)

Some distinctions might help shed light into the murk. The first distinction that needs to be made is between a gender *pay* gap and a gender *earnings* gap (GEG). Let's take an example. Let's suppose that Tom and Barbara have the same job in the same store, each of them, let's say, working at a till. They receive the same pay per hour for doing this job. So there is no *pay* gap between Tom and Barbara. However, Barbara works more hours than Tom and so she earns more than he does, and thus we have an *earnings* gap. In most western countries, it is illegal to pay men and women at different rates for doing the same job, but it is not illegal (yet) to pay Barbara more for doing more of the same kind of work that she and Tom do. Of course, if men and women are doing *different* jobs, then there is likely to be both a *pay* gap and an *earnings* gap.

In connection with the GPG/GEG distinction, let us recall once again Cathy Newman's infamous interview of Jordan Peterson. Her transparent failure to understand what Peterson was on about, a failure which suggests a spectacular level of ideologically-blinkered and almost wilful misunderstanding, seems to have been closely allied to her eagerness to convict him of intellectual (and possibly moral) wrong-doing, an eagerness encapsulated in her frequent question-leader, ' ... you're saying .... ', a phrase that has now passed into Internet folklore. The procedure is as follows. Peterson says something. Then Newman restates what she thinks he has said so as to make it appear absurd or offensive. Peterson repeatedly denies that he is saying what Newman says he is saying. Here's a sample for your delectation, but you should see the whole interview to get the full effect. (see Channel 4) I've italicised the relevant passages so that you can appreciate Newman's hermeneutical harangue in all its glory.

Newman asserts that the pay gap exists and Peterson agrees. Remember Peterson's agreement on this topic—it comes up a little later. He adds, '*But there's multiple reasons for that. One of them is gender, but that's not the only reason.* If you're a social scientist worth your salt, you never do a univariate analysis. You say women in aggregate are paid less than men. Okay. Well, then, we break it down by age; we break it down by occupation; we break it down by interest; we break it down by personality.' Enter Newman: '*But you're saying, basically, it doesn't matter if women aren't getting to the top*, because *that's* what is skewing that gender pay gap, isn't it? You're saying that's just a fact of life, women aren't necessarily going to get to the top.' Peterson expostulates, '*No, I'm not saying it doesn't matter, either. I'm saying there are multiple reasons for it.*' Newman again, 'Yeah, but *why should women put up with those reasons*?' Peterson, patiently, '*I'm not saying that they should put up with it*! I'm saying that *the claim that the wage gap between men and women is only due to sex is wrong.* And it is wrong. There's no doubt about that. The multivariate analyses have been done.' Peterson grants that 'there is prejudice. There's no doubt about that. But it accounts for a much smaller portion of the variance in the pay gap than the radical feminists claim.' Newman puts it to Peterson that '*rather than denying that the pay gap exists, which is what you did at the beginning of this conversation*, shouldn't you say to women, rather than being agreeable and not asking for a pay raise, go ask for a pay raise. Make yourself disagreeable with your boss.' Once again Peterson has to deny what Newman says he said. '*But I didn't deny it existed, I denied that it existed because of gender.* See, because I'm very, very, very careful with my words.'

What kind of factors other than outright sex discrimination could contribute to a gender earnings gap (GEG)? One's age and experience, of course, the kind of work one chooses and, of course, prejudice and unlawful discrimination. In their twenties, women tend to earn more than men. For women in their thirties, the earnings (not pay) gap is less than 2%. Where there is a significant gap in earnings between men and women, it applies primarily to women in their forties (13%) and fifties (16%). One reason why this tends to be so is that women of this age have taken time out of the work force to have and to rear children, and so have less experience and seniority than men in the comparable age range. Is this the kind of constraint that Ms Reardon-Bond has in mind? Another significant factor relevant to the topic of the pay/earnings gap is whether the work is full-time or part time. The Office for National Statistics (ONS), which analyses the data using full-time and part-time as parameters, finds a median hourly difference in pay of just over 9%, in favour of men in respect of full-time employment, but just over 5% median hourly difference in pay in favour of women in respect of part-time employment.

Many of the male/female earnings statistics touted in relation to this topic are effectively useless. In order to get significant points of comparison, you need to compare male workers and female workers who are doing the same job at the same point of seniority with the same job experience and the same qualifications. If you can't match A and B on all these points, you're not talking about the same job, and the comparisons are even more odious than comparisons normally are. It is always possible that women are paid less than men and that the reason for this is simply prejudicial discrimination, but the reality, as Peterson pointed out in the Newman interview, is multivariate, and it is unlikely that even if prejudicial discrimination were a factor, it would account for the whole difference in the GEG.

Even if we consign the gender pay gap to the nether regions where it belongs, the fact remains that there tends to be an earnings gap between men and women in the aggregate. A study conducted by University College London's Institute for Education gives us some idea of why this might be so. It turns out that when boys and girls were asked about the job they would like to have, the average hourly wage for the jobs that girls wanted (medicine, teacher in a secondary school, law, veterinary medicine, nurse, midwife) was 27% lower than those the boys wanted to have, even when the boys' fantasy high-paying careers (pop star, football player) were discounted. Are there other issues? Perhaps women are being consistently recruited to lower paid jobs? Well, unless they are being compelled to take them, this, presumably, is a matter of their choice. Are there issues of gender stereotyping that subtly guide women towards lower paid employment? Once again, unless women are mindless robots, there's still nothing preventing them from aspiring to higher paid employment if they so choose. This looks like choice rather than the constraint hinted at by Ms Reardon-Bond, but perhaps constraint is lurking around the corner.

An Irish Central Statistics Office Report, 'Women and Men in Ireland,' provides some interesting information about males, females and work that, I suspect, would broadly be replicated in most modern Western societies. (Anon. 2011) Women dominate health and social work, accounting for almost 82% of the workers in that category. Education comes next, still heavily dominated by women, where they account for just over 73% of the workers. The ratio of men to women is closest to 50%/50% in accommodation and food services, financial, insurance and real estate, administrative and support services, and the wholesale and retail trade. It starts to edge towards a male preponderance in professional, scientific and technical areas, where men account for 60% of the workers, and continues moving in that direction for information and communication (70%, 30%), industry (72%, 28%), transportation and storage (82%, 18%), agriculture, forestry and fishing (89%, 11%) and construction (92%, 8%). What are we to make of these figures? Well, unless there's some particularly insidious and undetectable form of coercion going on, women by and large choose to work almost exclusively inside buildings, men choose to work both inside and outside of them; men have a preference for technical, industrial and agricultural work, women for social work, health and education. Incidentally, men worked an average of 39.4 hours a week on aggregate, compared with 30.6 hours per week on aggregate for women, and married men worked longer hours than married women, with nearly half (44.5%) of married men working for 40 hours or more a week compared with only 14.7% of married women. The authors of a meta-study in this area conclude that 'Results showed that men prefer working with things and women prefer working with people, producing a large effect size (d=0.93) on the Things-People dimension. Men showed strong Realistic (d=0.84) and Investigative (d=0.26) interests, and women showed strong Artistic (d=-0.35) Social (d=0.84), and Conventional (d=-0.33) Sex differences favoring men were also found for more specific measures of engineering (d=1.11), science (d=0.36) and mathematics (d=0.34) .... The present study suggest that interests may play a critical role in gendered occupational choices and gender disparity in the STEM fields.' (see Su et al.)

When it comes to advanced apprenticeships, the disparities between males and females are even more evident. Here, 53% of men are in engineering and manufacturing technologies, with another 26% of them working in construction and the built environment. That comes to almost 80%. By comparison, 35% of women choose to take the route of health, public services and care, another 28% take business administration and law, while 23% take the road leading to retail and commerce. The *Telegraph* reported that—will this come as a surprise to anyone?—'Men are more likely to go into engineering or construction apprenticeships which pay well, while women more often choose careers in industries such as child development which give lower wages.' (Wallace) (It's more than a little odd to characterise child development as an industry, but let that pass.) It's also the case that 'Men benefit far more than women financially from apprenticeships as female trainees typically enter lower-paying industries [child development, anyone?] at the very start of their careers.' The result of this choice by individuals is that by the time men who take the apprenticeship route reach the age of 23, they out-earn female apprentices with similar level qualifications by 'an average of between 26% and 31%'—these figures come from the London School of Economics' Centre for Economic Performance and Centre for Vocational Education Research. Choice or constraint?

Are marriage and children the factors that constrain (*à la* Ms Reardon-Bond) women's choices? Perhaps women are discriminated against for having children? I'm not quite sure what discrimination would mean in this context unless a woman is physically forced to have children. If a woman is not so forced, it's a choice she has made, and its effect on her ability to work is something she should have taken into account when making that choice. Perhaps it will be urged that because childcare is so expensive, many women are forced to work part-time from financial necessity rather than choice. But the choice has already been made by the woman to have children. The point is sometimes made that the reason women make up so much of the part-time labour force and therefore earn so much less, on average, than men is because they have more unpaid caring responsibilities than men. I would point out that nobody is holding a gun to their heads to undertake those responsibilities, so that we must assume they are freely chosen. And in this connection, motherhood is obviously an issue as is also potential motherhood, which raises the cost of hiring women in the first place. When one factors in the relative degrees of competitiveness between men and women and time out for bearing children, you can account for quite a bit of the GEG. If the unpalatable truth be told, men and single women without children subsidise married women with children.

One woman was reported in the *Guardian* as saying that she 'understood that the gap wasn't about women being paid less for equal work', but was the outcome of what she called 'a glass ceiling' at middle management level. 'Women,' she said, 'take time off to have children, and they never catch up in terms of career progression. Then they take time out to look after elderly dependants.' (Gentleman) Well, yes, some women do, and we must assume, unless there is evidence to the contrary, that that's their choice. But if that is so, then it's hardly surprising to realise that, as a consequence, such women, apart from suffering from a loss of institutional memory related to their discontinuity in service, are likely to be less experienced and to have less seniority than men of a comparable age. And now we're back not to a gender pay gap but to a gender earnings gap. Choice or constraint? Or, perhaps, constraint as the result of prior choices?

The gap in pay between men and women is often taken to be prima facie evidence of anti-female discrimination on the part of employers. What if we could find an example of sufficient size where such a gap exists, but where there is no discriminating employer to point the fickle finger of blame at? Let's look at some evidence. One study that examined information derived from over a million Uber rideshares found a 7% gap between the earnings of male and female drivers. Since all decisions remain with the drivers, no prejudicial or discriminatory employer can be blamed for the disparity. The authors of the study (Cook et al.) concluded from their analysis that three factors contributed to the disparity in earnings: experience, preferences on where and when to work, and preferences for driving speed. Once again, it's all about choice.

What of prejudice and discrimination? There may, of course, be prejudice and discrimination in employment but, if so, an employer will have to pay for the luxury of being prejudicial and discriminatory, and not just in terms of attracting legal sanctions. There is an *a priori* argument that, apart from any empirical data, shows the absurdity of any systematic so-called GPG. If I have a company with 100 employees and I can find a group of workers (A) with the same levels of skills and competencies as group (B), who will work for a significant percentage less than group B, then, unless I have some strange desire to run to the end of a pier and chuck my money into the sea, I will hire exclusively workers from group A. Think about it.

What stops women from having it all—love, sex, money, success and (if you're really broadminded and a little old-fashioned) children? Reality. There's less talk these days about women having it all and more about work-life balance. The pressure is on for longer and better-paid maternity leave and mandatory state-financed childcare, but it's not obvious why the state or employers should undertake the role of minder of other people's children, either *de facto* or by paying for it. We hear of stories that are meant to be horrific, such as that of Rhiannon Broschat, a single mother, who was fired from her supermarket job in Chicago in 2014 because her son's school was closed during freezing weather and she had to stay off work to look after him. Well, that's tough, but it should be pointed out that her employer isn't a branch of Social Services, and if she can't come to work, it's not obvious why she should retain her employment. The clue is the 'single mother' description. For whatever reason, Ms Broschat has to be both breadwinner and child-minder, except when the school fulfils that role for her. Child-minding, by the way, is one of the basic purposes of state-sponsored schooling and perhaps, given the educational ineffectiveness of primary schooling, *the* basic purpose of state-sponsored schooling.

Employment is not a social service but a cost to an employer of producing his goods or services. It is, in essence, an agreement between two parties: the one to supply services in return for a monetary consideration from the other; the other, to supply money in return for services. From a libertarian point of view, the only legal considerations that should enter into a free contract between employer and employee are those given by the zero aggression principle—no one may initiate or threaten to initiate aggression [coercive physical violence] against the person or property of another. The employee does the work; the employer pays the employee for the work. Any other elements in the contract, for example, holidays or flexi-time, should be a matter of negotiation between employer and employee. Of course, in our world, this is not the case. The state interferes massively in the employer-employee relationship, dictating terms such as minimum wages, mandatory holidays, maximum hours of work and the like and, at the same time, turning employers into unofficial and unpaid tax collectors. A possible consequence of government intervention that requires the same average pay for men and for women is that companies may stop employing women in low-paid roles or will not allow them to work part-time. This is a version of what happens when the minimum wage is arbitrarily hiked: we see those in employment benefit, but what we don't see, however, are those who will not now be employed.

In general, women not only do not face inequality in the workplace, they tend to be handled with kid gloves and to be the recipient of special privileges. Maternity leave is one such special privilege, a large cost to employers, not only in terms of pay but in their having to hold a job open for the returning mother (if she ever does return) and the loss of institutional continuity while, in the interim, other employees, men, and women without children, have to deal with the disruption that her absence generates. In this context, consider a letter written to the *Guardian's* agony aunt, Mariella Frostrup seeking advice. The letter writer tells us that she has a 21-month-old baby and took six month's maternity leave at the time around the birth of her child. She's now back at work, work she likes, which involves managing large projects. She'd like to try for a second baby and her boss is offering her a big project. However, if she becomes pregnant, she says her boss wouldn't give her ownership of the project as she wouldn't be there during project delivery, but would instead find someone else to take the responsibility. What, she asks, should she do? Our advice columnist, having told us how enraged that she is that women still find themselves in these kinds of positions, and having delivered herself of a little rant about sexual abuse, harassment, equal pay and the unfair division of domestic labour, has no qualms about telling her correspondent, 'You have every right to run this new project, no responsibility to inform your boss that you are thinking of having another baby and every reason to forge ahead with energy and enthusiasm on both fronts.' (Frostrup)

The gender pay gap in sport and entertainment

In a piece written by Kate O'Halloran we are presented with a high-octane riff on the theme of the gender pay gap. (O'Halloran) What is Ms O'Halloran's complaint? Sports fail to respect women, she tells us, and to see that this is so, all you have to do is to inspect the *Forbes* list of the top 100 paid athletes in the world. There you will see that not one woman makes the list. What more evidence could you need to recognise the gross disrespect in which women athletes are held? One fact that is particularly galling for Ms O'Halloran is that the Brazilian footballer Neymar was paid more than the 'entire top seven women's football leagues combined'! What kind of world is it, Ms O'Halloran wants to know, in which we value 'a single men's football player more than seven leagues of women?' In the face of such baffled exasperation, I am hesitant to suggest that perhaps the answer is that it is the kind of world in which the contribution of this particular individual man is worth more to *his* employers than the contributions of seven leagues of women are worth to *their* employers. Ms O'Halloran is also scandalised by the remuneration received by others on the list. Lionel Messi, number two on the list with $111 million, is another source of particular irritation to her. But if she's irritated by Messi, the top of her head seems to come off when she considers *numero uno*, the boxer Floyd Mayweather. He not only tops the list—that's bad enough—but he does so while having been convicted twice of violence against women. What this tells Ms O'Halloran is that there aren't 'sufficient consequences for men who perpetrate violence against women (especially in sport)', and that 'women aren't respected in the same way that men are.' While not in any way condoning Mr Mayweather's record in the matter of male-female relations, I can't quite see how Ms O'Halloran reaches her conclusions. But wait, there's more! Serena Williams was on the previous year's Forbes' list but didn't make it on to the 2018 one. Why? Because she was pregnant and lost money (or, somewhat more accurately, didn't gain money) that she might otherwise have done. There! You see. Yet more discrimination against women.

It's hard to keep a straight face while perusing this economically illiterate rant. It's even harder to know where to begin dissecting it. Criticising it is a little unsporting, rather like shooting fish in a barrel, but let's make the attempt. First, in professional sport, pay is not allocated for respect but for value added as judged by those who pay the athlete's wages or provide the prize money. Second, professional sport is *sui generis*. It's going to be difficult, if not impossible, to make a general point about rates of remuneration to the sexes from an examination of this very rarefied situation. *All* these people are paid crazy money, but even the women not making this list (such as Serena Williams) make vastly more money than 99.999999% of men. Third, if we are to take what appears to be Ms O'Halloran's argument seriously, the pay of athletes should reflect their efforts. If that is so, then those who play recreational football at the weekend should be paid the same as Lionel Messi! Anyone who works 8 hours a day surely deserves what every other 8-hour-a-day worker gets. In fact, fairness seems to demand that everyone who works should be put on the same pay scale, regardless of any further attribute or skill that they have which might make the work they do qualitatively more valuable to those who pay their wages. After all, if everyone is truly equal, no one has any quality that differentiates one from another. The reason for the apparently unjust pay discrimination against women in sport is, in fact, quite simple. Sportsmen tend to be paid more than sportswomen because more people are interested in watching them and are willing to pay to do so. On the other hand, clothes models are paid extravagant amounts of money—provided they are female. Male clothes models just have to muddle (bad pun intended) along.

It seems that John McEnroe is paid ten times more than Martina Navratilova for his work as a commentator at the Wimbledon Tennis Tournament. Outrageous! Unfair! Sexism! Well, maybe, maybe not. What each of these former tennis champions is doing is not something that can simply be calibrated by the number of hours worked multiplied by a standard pay rate. The contribution of each commentator is unique, and their value is something that is worked out by negotiations between them (or their agents) and the television companies. If you are a female commentator and you think that you're not paid enough, then you should get your agent on to it and negotiate and see what you're worth to your employer.

But it's not only in sport that this 'same-pay' nonsense is rampant. The producers of the Netflix hit, *The Crown*, apologised when it transpired that the star of the show, Claire Foy, was paid less than her co-star Matt Smith. Why on earth should the producers apologise? Is the fact of their being co-stars meant to suggest that Foy and Smith are doing the same work? I should have thought that acting is simply a matter of contract for services. If Ms Foy thinks she's not being paid enough, shouldn't she get a better agent? If she had been paid *more* than her co-star, would she voluntarily have given up her excess salary in the interests of equality? Bizarre! Would she be happy if her co-star's salary was reduced to the level of her salary? Doesn't all this sound a little like the old-fashioned sin of envy? Julia Roberts was paid $20 million for the instantly forgettable rom-com *Notting Hill*; Hugh Grant wasn't. Was anybody outraged by this? I think not.

Averting our gaze for the rich and famous for a moment, what's the general reason for the GPG, according to our oracle? The GPG is, she says, down to the 'disproportionate share of unpaid caring and domestic work' done by women, and the 'greater time out of the workforce, impacting on career progression and opportunities.' At last, something by way of evidence and argument and not just futile fulmination. In respect of these two factors, could I respectfully suggest (once again) that, unless someone is putting a gun to the heads of the women who undertake the disproportionate share of unpaid caring and domestic work, this is something that they choose to do and if they find it so burdensome, they should simply cease to do it. Furthermore, if women spend a significant amount of time out of the workforce because of childbearing, this too, unless the result of coercion, is a matter of choice so, if they don't want to slip down the employment ladder, the solution is obvious—don't have babies.

And finally, a *pièce de résistance*—equal pay for different work! 'Women launch £4Billion lawsuit against Tesco for equal pay' shouts the headline in the *Mirror*. (Britton; see also Butler) Sounds like the usual gender-pay-gap story, doesn't it? Men who work in Tesco's distribution centres are being paid £5,000 a year more than women who work the same number of hours in Tesco stores. Darn it, those oppressed women are being discriminated against yet again. But when you dig a little deeper into the story, matters aren't quite as egregious as they are made out to be. Here are the facts. First, the distribution centre workers (largely male) and the store workers (largely female) do very different jobs! They're not being paid differently for doing the same job; they're being paid differently for doing different jobs! Second, to describe the distribution centre jobs as being 'male-dominated' suggests that women are somehow legally or physically prevented from doing this job rather than its simply being the case that it is largely men who choose to do these jobs whereas women, for the most part, don't. As the story later reveals, it isn't only men who work in the distribution centres.

Paula Lee from the law firm Leigh Day, which is representing the store workers said, 'We believe an inherent bias has allowed store workers to be underpaid for many years.' Really? What inherent bias would that be? The bias that allows people to choose to apply for particular categories of work? But there's more! Lee went on to say, 'In terms of equal worth to the company there really should be no argument that workers in stores, compared to those working in distribution centres, contribute at least equal value to the vast profits made by Tesco, which last year had group sales of £49.9bn.' Ignore the 'vast profits' bombast—that's just smoke and mirrors (or, as one of our revered leaders once said, 'smoke and daggers'!) The key point here is the claim, the evidentially ungrounded claim, that the in-store workers contribute as least equal value to Tesco's profits as do other kinds of worker. Why should there be no argument about this? How does the representative know this? Does she think Tesco is over-paying its distribution centre staff by £3 an hour just because they like (mostly) men more than women? Let's see the principle at work here. Tom cleans the floor for Quickbucks Incorporated whereas Barbara day-trades for them. Echoing the words of Paula Lee, there really should be no argument that floor cleaners contribute at least equal value to Quickbucks Incorporated as do day-traders. Yes. Precisely.

In an ITV interview, Kim Element, who has worked in store for 23 years and who is taking part in the legal action said, 'I think it's a matter of fairness and it was quoted (*sic*) to me by the CEO of Tesco that they couldn't have two people working alongside each other on different rates of pay. We are now on very different rates of pay.' (ITV) When the interviewer made the obvious rejoinder, 'But you're *not* working alongside each other!', Ms Element replied, without a blush, 'We are metaphorically working alongside each other because we are working for Tesco!' Well, Ms Element, you also metaphorically work alongside the store manager since both of you work for Tesco, so I suppose you expect to receive the same level of pay that she does. Since your working alongside the workers in the distribution centres is metaphorical, I'm sure you'd be happy to settle for a metaphorical pay raise.

It's hard to take this specious nonsense seriously as a demand for equal treatment. It is, rather, a brazen demand for *equal* pay for *different* work. The employer is the same but, despite Ms Element's valiant efforts at linguistic legerdemain, the jobs are very different. There is nothing to stop the (largely) female store workers from applying to work in draughty warehouses, driving forklift trucks and lifting heavy stuff around provided they are prepared to desert their cosy, warm seats at the checkout counters. The solution to this non-problem is obvious. If you want to earn what the workers in the distribution centres earn, get yourself a job in the distribution centre.

The Patriarchy

Equality does not mean treating everyone the same
—Baroness Corston

No mechanism for [the patriarchy] has even been tendered,
let alone tested empirically, for the reason that researchers
well know that nothing of the kind does or could exist
—Steve Moxon

Writing in the *Guardian* in October 2017, soon after the initial eruption of the #MeToo phenomenon, Emine Saner asks, 'Is this the end of the patriarchy?' Naomi Wolf writing in the same newspaper in the same month talks about what she describes as a 'rend [*sic*! rent?] in the fabric of the patriarchy.' Saner quotes Vicky Featherstone, artistic director of the Royal Court, who reflects Wolf's image, saying, 'we have got to the top of a mountain, and a rip has been torn in the patriarchy ... things will never be the same again.' What is this patriarchy, this apparently monstrously malign misogynistic entity that Saner, Wolf and Featherstone all agree has been damaged by recent events but which still somehow manages to survive? The patriarchy, Lisa Tuttle tells us, is 'the universal political structure which privileges men *at the expense of women.*' (Tuttle, 342; emphasis added) Radical feminists would have you believe that to be a woman in the twenty teens is to be subject to constant oppression from this insidious and omnipresent enemy. Women's voices are silenced, women are consistently paid less than men for the same work, women are discriminated against in employment, women are sexually harassed and raped, and all this and much more is the result of the operation of the patriarchy. It is not just individual instances of discrimination or violence or the oppression of individual women that need to be identified and resisted, it is the patriarchal *system* as a whole in all its aspects—political, legal, economic—that is at the root of women's oppression, and which must be dismantled if women are ever to achieve true equality.

What is the patriarchy?

As just mentioned, if Tuttle is to be believed, the patriarchy is a universal political structure, not a human being nor even a group of human beings. I am innately suspicious of abstract objects occupying the place of the subject in sentences with transitive verbs. I am reminded of the classic line from Douglas Adams's *Life, the Universe and Everything*: 'Eddies,' said Ford, 'in the space-time continuum.' 'Ah,' nodded Arthur, 'is he, is he?' It is concrete individuals who act; abstract objects, having no causal force, are intrinsically incapable of acting. 'Isms' and 'ologies' and 'archies' don't do anything; people do. It is perhaps inevitable that we must produce sentences with abstract nouns in them occupying the subject position from time to time (I do so myself occasionally in this book), but our intellectual gears risk spinning freely without traction unless these abstract entities are fleshed out by real concrete examples.

The feminist myth of the Patriarchy derives what little evidential support it has (assuming that its adherents require it to have any evidential support at all) from a selective focusing on the supposed benefits accruing to men in traditional social configurations, while completely ignoring their associated burdens. (see Harari, 161-78) You may have noticed that Tuttle's zero-sum definition of patriarchy—male privilege *at the expense of women*—makes no mention at all of men's burdens or responsibilities, nor of women's corresponding benefits and privileges. It takes a curiously creative capacity, malformed by preconceptions, to see the patriarchy at work in the face of what, to a simple-minded observer, would seem to be a mass of countervailing evidence. For example, in a display of what must seem to third-wave (or later wave) feminists like low and devious cunning, nineteenth-century British parliamentarians, all of them men, attempted to conceal their male dominance by legally prohibiting women from working in coal mines, and reserving those delightfully dirty and dangerous jobs for their brother patriarchs. One might have expected the dominant patriarchal group to send members of the dominated group to do their dirty work—literally their dirty work—for them but, to those in the grip of the latest-wave feminist theory, such an expectation is naïve, and the apparently pro-woman actions of the male parliamentarians are merely cloaking devices that serve to conceal their deep-rooted fear and hatred of women. The same patriarchal deceptive strategy employed by those dim and distant British parliamentarians would appear to have been consistently employed in men's historical domination of the military professions in times when, to the eye of the simple-minded, the military life was degrading and physically demanding, even when not dangerous. The patriarchal deception appears to continue today for, even now, the bulk of physically demanding

and dangerous jobs are dominated by men, resulting in a wildly disproportionate rate of workplace fatalities between the sexes. Occupational fatalities
in the USA in 2013 were 93.1% male, 6.9% female, and this ratio of 13:1 is
broadly consistent over time and in different places. (see Anon. 2011) 'It's still
the case that all of the very worst jobs—in terms of work environment, physical
demands, promotion/redundancy prospects, stress, likelihood of injury or
death and extra hours of work regarded as the norm to make up reasonable
pay—are *man*ned 95-100%. (Moxon, 144)

Suppose Tuttle is right in thinking that there is a structure, the patriarchy,
that systematically benefits men at the expense of women. If a social structure
exists that systematically benefits group A at the expense of group B then,
across the entire range of human activities, especially in respect of the distribution of social goods, we should expect to find members of group A doing
substantially better than members of group B. When it comes to the good
stuff, we should expect to find either all As and no Bs in receipt of them or, at
the very least, systematically more As than Bs. When it comes to the bad stuff,
we should expect to find either all Bs and no As in receipt of them or, at the
very least, systematically more Bs than As. Is that what we find in respect of
men and women when we examine the evidence?

No! When one examines the evidence, it does not support the claim that
men are systematically benefitted at the expense of women; in fact, in some
matters, it would appear rather to support the claim that women are systematically benefitted more than men, whether at the expense of men or not is
another matter, dependent upon the benefits being part of a zero-sum game.
It cannot be denied that women have sometimes been economically exploited
and that some men have treated women in sadistic and aggressive ways, but it
is an unbridgeable gulf from these singular facts to the conclusion that there
is a universal system organised by men for their own benefit to the detriment
of all women, everywhere, at all times, *semper et ubique*. To bridge this gulf
involves one in a leap of faith in defiance of all the evidence.

Recent research has shown that contrary to the received (feminist)
wisdom, in most developed countries, men are in fact more disadvantaged
than women! (see Stoet & Geary) According to the Basic Index of Gender
Inequality (BIGI), men turned out to be more disadvantaged than women
in ninety-one countries, while women were more disadvantaged than men
in forty-three. BIGI focuses on three factors – educational opportunities,
healthy life expectancy and overall life satisfaction. Other ways of measuring
gender inequality are biased to highlight women's issues. The Global Gender
Gap Index (GGGI), for example, doesn't measure issues where men are at

a disadvantage, such as harsher punishments for the same crime, compulsory military service and more occupational deaths. Moreover, the GGGI is so complex that it can be difficult to tell to what extent differences in outcomes related to each sex is a matter of social inequality or personal preference. But why should feminists think about these matters rationally and examine the evidence impartially when their intuitions and emotions tell them that the real reason for the continuing oppression of women is the existence and operation of that persistent mythical beast, the patriarchy. I hope I won't be thought unfeeling if I remark that emotions and intuitions, while they have their place in our lives, are not a substitute for reason and argument, especially when it comes to the evaluation of evidence, the accumulation and weighing of statistics, and argument. But for many feminists, reason and evidence and all their works and pomps, are merely patriarchal power plays designed to overcome the epistemological purity of feminine affectivity. The essential irrationality of the female was a standard item of male prejudice. As expressed by Professor Higgins, 'Women are irrational, that's all there is to that! Their heads are full of cotton, hay, and rags! They're nothing but exasperating, irritating, vacillating, calculating, agitating, maddening and infuriating hags!' (*My Fair Lady*) It is deeply ironic that this once common sexist supposition, a supposition that was rightly resented and rejected by the first generation of feminists, should now be quietly adapted and adopted as a position of superior epistemological purity by their latter-day heirs and assigns.

The feminist subversion of the patriarchy has its lighter side. The Australian city of Melbourne has installed 'female' traffic signals as part of a campaign to combat 'unconscious bias.' (Gray *et al.*) I suppose many women must have been deterred from crossing at the old sexist lights, figuring they didn't apply to them. But have hordes of feminists been waiting at traffic lights for ages, refusing to cross at the order of a 'male figure'? If so, this is hard to comprehend since most feminists look more like the short-haired trousered figure on the old lights than the one in a skirt on the new lights. Besides, how do we know the sex or gender of the new signal figure? Just because it's wearing a dress, why should we assume that it's a female? Aren't those who interpret this image in this way themselves being guilty of unconscious bias? Are dresses exclusive to women; can they not now be worn by everyone? Perhaps the figure on the new light is a Scotsman on holiday or one of the new breed of transgender warriors. But some consistency here would be welcome, for sex isn't the only thing we can be unconsciously biased about. Is the figure on the lights slim? Then, perhaps it's unconsciously body-shaming the obese. Is it able-bodied? Then it may be unconsciously discriminating against those who need wheelchairs or other prosthetic devices. Perhaps we should have a range of lights, applicable to each specific group so that no one is excluded and prevented from crossing? My own mischievous misandrist suggestion is that we have a special one which signals: 'Check your privilege, white heterosexual man! Wait until everyone else has crossed before daring to move!' In the same spirit of diversity, inclusion and equality, I suggest removing statues of Lady Justice from court buildings. Having to walk under a blindfolded female symbol of justice on their way to trial obviously promotes unconscious bias against men which could result in judges passing sentences that are heavier on them than on women for the same offences—oh wait, they already do that!

The oppression of women

A fundamental dogma of radical feminism is the deep-rooted and apparently ineliminable oppression of women. If you are a woman, you are oppressed simply by virtue of being a woman. Despite the high volume of feminist complaints, it seems that some women just haven't got the memo about their being universally oppressed. A survey (admittedly small) of some students at the University of Connecticut revealed that the overwhelming majority of respondents—94 percent of whom were women—do not believe that 'discrimination and subordination' are 'salient issues in women's lives.' How fiendish is that pernicious patriarchy! These women are so oppressed that they don't even realise that they're oppressed! Assistant Professor Mogro-Wilson, who is the Discipline Co-ordinator in Social Work at the University, is deeply worried by these findings because, as she quite reasonably concludes, unless the students have a sense of their own oppression and the oppression of other marginalised groups, such as those based on race, culture, sexuality and class, how can they properly help their oppressed clients?

So, where *is* all this oppression of women by men? Before we take a detailed look at some areas to enable us to make some comparative judgements, let us frankly admit that in some areas of life, men have a clear advantage. When it comes to homelessness, for example, men selfishly keep the doorways pretty much to themselves. A 2017 study from the UK's Ministry of Housing, Communities and Social Affairs found that 86% of rough sleepers were men. The homeless charity Crisis also reports that 84% of hidden homeless people (people who are at risk of eviction, sofa-surfing at friends and family or living in unsatisfactory conditions) are men. Between 2013 and 2017 the amount of homeless people who died on the streets or in temporary accommodation doubled and around 90% of those deaths were men. Other areas in which men selfishly outstrip women are suicide (80%) and occupational deaths

(95%). In cases of divorce, men gain custody of children just 20% of the time but, to make up for this deprivation, they receive 63% longer prison sentences than women for the same offences. (More on this presently.) You have to admit that, in these miscellaneous matters, the patriarchy *is* pretty effective but, from a man's perspective, in entirely the wrong way.

Education

Education is one area where boys consistently fall behind girls. In the UK, girls are 20% more likely to finish secondary school with five C grades or higher at GCSE, according to the UK's Department for Education's statistics. In addition, boys are less likely to be high achievers in school. The statistics show that only 52.5% of boys achieve a minimum of five A*–C grades at GCSE compared to 61.8% of girls.

When it comes to teaching, women vastly outstrip men. In England, men make up just 26.2% of teachers (a mere 15.2% in primary schools), 8.5% of teaching assistants and 18% of support staff. Given the preponderance of female teachers in primary and secondary education, it is hardly surprising that feminine modes of behaviour are unreflectively taken to be the norm, and the behaviour of boys judged to be aggressive and disruptive. Boys benefit from being in a highly structured and well-disciplined environment. Conversely, without such structure and discipline, they become bored and frustrated and misbehave.

A 2014 report also showed that boys are three times more likely than girls to be excluded or expelled from school. A friend of the playwright David Mamet once told him, 'Boys are different.' 'And indeed they are,' Mamet agrees. 'Very like each other, and very different from girls .... Our American school system (public and private) is against them. It is no wonder the boys have developed or been diagnosed (which is to say been marginalized) as possessing a whole alphabet full of acronyms, which may be reduced to "I give up, drug them!".' (Mamet, 130, 131; see Moxon, 55-65; see Sommers 2015, passim).

The educational attainment gap between males and females that emerges at school persists throughout academic life. Young men are 27% less likely to apply to university than young women and 30% more likely to drop out. The legal and medical professions are on course to be dominated by women, just as has happened in teaching, with only one third of law graduates being men and only 40% of graduates in medicine being men. Women, it seems, find final examinations unduly stressful and so an increasing amount of formal assessment in our universities takes place by means of continuous assessment. Final examinations are generally something that young men welcome rather than the drip-feed torture of continuous assessment. Course work tends to favour females who are, generally, more diligent that males. That being so, it is hardly surprising that women are starting to outstrip men in many subjects. According to the UK's Universities and Colleges Admissions Service (UCAS), in 2017, over 71,000 fewer men were accepted to UK universities than women. In the class of 2017, men made up around 43% of new entrants. In the USA, the situation is broadly similar, with women earning most of the advanced degrees.

Health

Health is an area in particular in which the disparities between the positions of men and women is quite striking. (see Moxon, 82-90) Men between the ages of 20 and 40 are half as likely to go to the doctor as women in the same age bracket. According to a report compiled by Men's Health Forum in 2014 and revised in 2017, 19% of men die before their 65th birthday. The biggest cause of death in men is cancer, followed by circulatory diseases. Men are 14% more likely to get cancer than women and they're 37% more likely to die from the disease. The most common type of cancer in men is prostate cancer, which accounts for 25% of all male cancer cases and 13% of deaths from cancer. 'Research into prostate cancer—which is sorely needed so as to get a reliable test and to distinguish between different treatment methods—receives just four percent of the funding that research into breast cancer attracts ...' (Moxon, 82) The list of leading killers in the USA shows the following sex disparity.

Incidence of diseases in men and women

Disease	*Male-Female death ratio*
Heart disease	1.5 to 1.0
Cancer	1.4 to 1.0
Stroke	1.0 to 1.0
Chronic Obstructive Lung disease	1.3 to 1.0
Accidents	2.2 to 1.0
Diabetes	1.4 to 1.0
Alzheimer's disease	0.7 to 1.0
Influenza and pneumonia	1.4 to 1.0
Kidney disease	1.4 to 1.0
Septicæmia	1.2 to 1.0
All causes	1.4 to 1.0

(source: National Center for Health Statistics)

Deaths from strokes are roughly comparable in men and women, and men suffer less from Alzheimer's than women do, but in every other category, men outscore women. That seemingly innocuous 1.4 in the right-hand column at the end of the table tells us that the mortality rate is 40% higher for men than for women. What the information in the column doesn't tell you is that men in the US are more than twice as likely to die from liver disease than women, over four times more likely to commit suicide, and just under four times more likely than women to be murder victims. But health discrimination between men and women is even worse than it may first appear for, even while they're enjoying fewer years of life than women, men are more troubled by health problems. Paradoxically, women rate their health as being worse than that of men and see their doctors and visit hospitals at more than twice the rate of men from early adolescence to late middle age. Men, however, become ill at an earlier age than women and those illnesses tend to be chronic. When it comes to acquiring inguinal hernias or having aortic aneurysms, developing kidney stones or bladder cancer, men outstrip women by factors of between three and ten! When it comes to longevity, the disparities continue. Here are the figures from the United States.

Life expectancy in men and women

Year	Females	Males	Gap (years)
1900	48.3	46.3	2
1950	71.1	65.6	5.5
2000	79.7	74.3	5.4
2007	80.4	75.3	5.1

(source: Harvard Medical School)

The international figures more or less mirror those of the USA, with Bosnia, Italy and Japan having significantly higher sex gaps. Central Statistic Office figures for 2012 show that in Ireland the longevity gender gap at 4.5 years is just under the magic number five (83.2 years for women and 78.7 years for men). For the last seventy years, the gap in life expectancy between men and women has hovered consistently at a figure of five years or slightly higher. This is obviously unjust and something must be done about it. Either we raise men's life expectancy to match that of women or, and I regret having to say this, in the interests of equality, we may just have to kill off women when they reach the age of 75! Joking aside, I think that in matters of health and longevity, it must be conceded that the patriarchy may not be quite as effective at privileging men at the expense of women as it might be.

The Franchise

A standard trope in feminism is the valiant efforts of women to achieve political enfranchisement in the face the unremitting efforts of men to prevent them from so doing. The now unshiftable feminist just-so story attributes the acquisition by women of the right to vote to the heroic and selfless agitation of the suffragettes. However, the agitation of the suffragettes was, like much feminism today, not a matter of the advancement of women as a whole, but the acquisition of special privileges for women-like-us, in this case, the 'us' being women of largely upper-class background. 'The suffragettes wanted first and foremost an elitist enfranchisement of themselves to join the men of their own upper- and upper-middle classes, and only argued for universal female suffrage because it was more politically expedient.' (Moxon, 121)

When placed in historical context, the reality is somewhat more prosaic and significantly less heroic. It is true that when voting first became possible, only men were able to vote. What's not so often noticed, however, is that the vast majority of men were not thus privileged. As Steve Moxon notes, 'the real struggle for the franchise was that of ordinary men' who paid the taxes 'and were drafted into the armed forces to fight the wars their taxes paid for.' (Moxon, 93) In England, from the middle of the 15th century, only those men who owned property worth 40 shillings or more were eligible to vote, the not unreasonable idea being that only those with property should have a hand in electing those with the power legally to interfere with their properties. Towards the end of the English Civil War, the issue of universal (male) enfranchisement was discussed by the victorious Parliamentary Army at the famous Putney debates. Putting it at its simplest, the key issue came to this. The Leveller faction in the Army argued that all men were subject to law and so should be in a position to determine who their lawmakers were. The opposing position was articulated clearly by Cromwell's son-in-law, Henry Ireton. Ireton was willing to concede that all those born in England should be protected from ejection from the kingdom, should have 'air and place and ground and the freedom of the highways and other things to live among us.' (Sharp, 104) But, since Parliament disposes of funds raised by taxes from those with a permanent interest in the kingdom, that is to say, from men holding a certain minimum of property, only such as were liable to be affected by such taxation should be in a position to determine the lawmakers. No representation without taxation! Ireton argued forcefully that the Levellers' demands on representation, if put into effect, could very well result in a situation where no property would be secure, since those who wouldn't bear the burden of taxation would be able to lay that burden on others. If all men have a right to voice in elections simply by nature, then 'by that same right of nature ... by which you can say a man has an equal right with another to the choosing of him that shall govern him, by the same right of nature he has the same right in any goods he sees: meat, drink, clothes, to take and use them for his sustenance; he has a freedom to the land, the ground, to exercise it, till it. He has the freedom to anything that anyone does account himself to have any property in.' (Wootton, 291) One is reminded of Bastiat's aphorism 'Government is that great fiction, through which everybody endeavours to live at the expense of everybody else.' (Bastiat, 99) Anyone who lives in a modern democracy cannot but be aware that one part of the population pays for what another part of the population consumes and that, in general, he who robs Peter to pay Paul may always count on Paul's enthusiastic support.

It is worth noting that well over 200 years after Ireton made these remarks, John Stuart Mill would echo them in a more modern setting, arguing strongly that those who receive or stand to receive more benefits from the state than they contribute to it shouldn't be in a position to elect those who determine the collection and the allocation of public funds. Mill writes,

> It is also important, that the assembly which votes the taxes, either general or local, should be elected exclusively by those who pay something towards the taxes imposed. Those who pay no taxes, disposing by their votes of other people's money, have every motive to be lavish and not to economise. As far as money matters are concerned, any power of voting possessed by them is a violation of the fundamental principle of free government; a severance of the power of control, from the interest in its beneficial exercise. It amounts to allowing them to put their hands into other people's pockets, for any purpose which they think fit to call a public one ... That representation should be coextensive with taxation, not stopping short of it, but also not going beyond it, is in accordance with the theory of British institutions .... I regard it as required by first principles, that the receipt of parish relief should be a peremptory disqualification for the franchise. He who cannot by his labour suffice for his own support, has no claim to the privilege of helping himself to the money of others. By becoming dependent on the remaining members of the community for actual subsistence, he abdicates his claim to equal rights with them in other respects. Those to whom he is indebted for this contin-uance of his very existence, may justly claim the exclusive management of those common concerns, to which he now brings nothing, or less than he takes away. (Mill 1861, 331-32)

It wasn't until the Reform Act of 1832 that adult males in the UK who rented (rather than owned) land of a certain value were allowed to vote. This act gave just under 15% of adult males the vote. Two subsequent Acts of Parliament widened the criteria so that, by the late 19th century, around 60% of adult males were entitled to vote. It is often thought that the expansion of the franchise after World War I was granted in token of the contributions made by the conscripted masses to the War to end all Wars. But in truth, it was a matter of political expediency, the same kind of political expediency that had led to the more gradual widening of the franchise in the nineteenth century. The war *was* a significant factor in the extension of the franchise, but it wasn't the sacrifices of the men on the front that led to the change but the much more mundane matter of paying for the massive destruction of life and property. After the war, the rate of tax went from 6% to 30%. 'With such a dramatic rise,' writes Steve Moxon, 'it was imperative to widen the franchise to avert taxpayers voting out the Government. And widening the franchise would enable the income tax base likewise to be widened, and so reduce the tax rate .... This widening of taxation as the basis of universal male suffrage in turn dissolved any basis for enfranchisement other than simple citizenship, and by default this admitted women.' (Moxon, 114)

By 1918, the last vestiges of property restrictions were lifted for men, and all men over 21 were granted the right to vote. Taxation issues to one side, it seemed not unreasonable that those who had been asked to risk their lives for Britain in the Great War should have a say in electing those who made their life and death decisions. At the same time, women over 30 (who, by and large, hadn't been at risk of losing their lives in the War) also got the vote, subject to certain property restrictions. By 1928, all men and women over 21 (18 by 1969) were entitled to vote and all property restrictions had disappeared. Some voters still had more than one vote because of property or educational qualifications, but plural voting finally disappeared in 1948. This, of course, puts us firmly in the position that Ireton and Mill deprecated, namely, that people who are the net beneficiaries of the taxes paid by others are in a position to elect those who impose and distribute those taxes! Representation without taxation!

The situation in the USA was similar to that in the UK in many respects. To begin with, only white, male property owners had the vote but the property requirement was effectively eliminated by the middle of the 19th century. Even so, some states required a person to be a taxpayer to be eligible to vote, and this requirement survived in a few states until the 20th century. A series of Constitutional Amendments extended the vote to non-whites, to women, and others, until finally we arrived at universal adult suffrage for those aged 18 or over.

Women's demand to own and dispose of property in their own right was granted pretty much as soon as they demanded it. If the patriarchy, that oppressive institution, responded promptly and accommodatingly in this way to this demand, it is a little difficult to see it as the system that privileges men at the expense of women. It is, perhaps, worth mentioning that when married women were not allowed to own property in their own right, they had a right to maintenance from their husbands who were also responsible for their wives' debts, a doctrine known as coverture. Indeed, even when married women were granted the right to own property in their own right, they retained their right to coverture! 'Coverture was the fiercest legal insistence that a man take responsibility for his family, no matter how wronged he may have been, and no matter how capable his wife was of taking full responsibility for her own behaviour. So coverture does not just provide evidence of female disadvantage as against male privilege. It also provides evidence of *male* disadvantage and *fe*male privilege.' (Moxon, 106; emphasis in original) For women benefitting from coverture, what was hers was hers and what was her husband's was hers as well! In 1910, a schoolteacher, Mark Wilks, was imprisoned for failing to pay the taxes of his wife Elizabeth (a doctor), even though he claimed he couldn't afford it and, moreover, that she had failed to provide him with details of her income, which was her right as a married woman who owned her own property and income! So, in the matter of the franchise and the right to own and dispose of property, when it comes to privileging men at the expense of women, we might reasonably judge that, once again, the patriarchy isn't quite up to the job.

Criminal justice

If you want to be a criminal, it will pay you to take out some insurance against conviction and sentencing by making sure you're a woman. If you can manage to be young and attractive, so much the better. Lauren Fowler, a junior doctor, was found by the police, swearing and slurring her speech after she had crashed her car. A couple of months after that incident, she was caught again, having consumed half a bottle of vodka. But, you know, she is a woman and a doctor, and being a doctor is stressful so there was no need to stick her in jail. And then there was a certain 21-year old Rebecca Batchelor who was happy to enrich herself from the proceeds of her boyfriend's cunning wheeze of defrauding pensioners. The sensitive judge thought her naïve and suspended sentence. If you're irritated by a nightclub security guard, go smash a glass into her forehead. That's what Sophia Brogan did, and she received a suspended sentence. Do good-looking young men get the same kind of sympathetic treatment from the law? It seems not. Statistics from 2015 show that men (good-looking or not) are about twice as likely to end up in jail for an indictable offence as women. Car theft? Better be a woman. If you're a man, you're three times as likely to get jail-time. Violence against the person? Same again.

Why this disparity in treatment, I wonder? Well, there is a publication called the Equal Treatment Bench Book that will explain things to you. If you suffer from low blood pressure, reading this treatise is a splendid non-chemical way of treating your condition. It has in it a section, 'Gender', in which Baroness Hale of Richmond is quoted as saying, 'It is now well recognised that a misplaced conception of equality has resulted in some very unequal treatment for the women and girls who appear before the criminal justice system. Simply put, a male-ordered world has applied to them its perceptions of the appropriate treatment for male offenders ....' (see Judicial College, 6-16) What does Lady Hale mean by speaking of 'a misplaced conception of equality'? Is she saying that male and female offenders *shouldn't* be treated in the same way? It seems as if feminists want equality with men until it means getting the same sentence for the same offence, and then equality somehow becomes a misplaced conception. Moreover, I am not sure who, apart from Lady Hale, recognises the misplaced conception of equality of which she speaks or, indeed, how well it is recognised, but let that pass. I may be entirely wrong on this but that passage seems to me to be saying that one's sex *is* a relevant factor in sentencing, and while the passage as it stands is consistent with a policy that women should receive *more* severe sentences than men for the same offence, it in fact turns out—what a surprise—the other way around. You would expect our feminist friends to protest at this egregious example of sexism in the law, insisting that this special treatment is infantilising, and demanding that women, as responsible agents, should receive the *same* treatment as men; no perks or privileges for one sex as against another. But our feminist friends are strangely silent on the matter. You might think, naïvely, that for the same offence, one should receive the same sentence, whether one is male or female, whether one is nicely spoken and well-educated or whether one comes from the wrong side of the tracks. But that's not going to happen. So, as I said, if you're planning a life of crime, begin by ensuring that you are a woman and, if possible, a good-looking young woman, preferably either in or with aspirations to be in a respectable profession. That's your stay-out-of-jail card in this Monopoly version of justice.

The *Telegraph* reported that Victor Parry, a serial drunk driver who, having drunk a bottle of wine, smashed into three cars, was told by Samuel Buckingham, the judge who heard his case, that if he had been a woman, he would have received a custodial sentence. (Sawer 2019) Leading feminists have condemned the decision as blatantly sexist. 'It is unbelievable,' said one feminist spokeswoman, 'that in the 21st century, someone should be treated preferentially simply because he is a man. A more outrageously blatant example of the operation of the patriarchy would be hard to find.' The previous four sentences are correct except in three salient details. First, the driver wasn't Victor Parry but Victoria Parry; second, the judge wasn't Samuel Buckingham but Sarah Buckingham; and third, there has been to date no condemnation by any prominent feminists of the blatant sexism of the judge's decision. In fact, what Judge Birmingham told the court was that 'If Miss Parry was a man, there is no question it would have been straight down the stairs, because this is a shocking case of dangerous driving .... ' She went on to say to Ms Parry, 'You richly deserve an immediate custodial sentence of 18 months.' Despite saying this, the judge imposed a *deferred* sentence of 3 months on Ms Parry, so it appears that her sex must have made her offence a somewhat less shocking case of dangerous driving than it would have been had it been committed by a man. Parry's drunken exploit didn't endanger just herself. Overtaking into oncoming traffic, she ran into a van before her vehicle was eventually brought to a halt by the combined momentum-busting efforts of the wing mirror of one car (Vauxhall Insignia) and the side of another (BMW), whereupon her car then burst into flames. I'm sure that if she had seriously injured or killed another person, that person would have appreciated the diminished gravity of their injuries or deaths because of Ms Parry's sex.

You might think the judge's decision was just a somewhat clumsily phrased example of extending leniency to a first time offender if it weren't that Parry isn't a first-timer. She already had two convictions for drunk driving, so why the spectacular sexist leniency? We can only speculate, but the report contains some pointers towards an answer. It appears that Ms Parry started drinking up to two bottles of wine a day when in an abusive relationship but, according to her lawyer, she is now out of that relationship and so the judge concluded that, given her genuine regret and her good behaviour since May of 2018, she should be given a chance to give up drinking and to get her life in order. I am sure we are all pleased that Ms Parry has been given a second (in reality, a fourth) chance, especially the driver of the van she smashed into and the owners of the mirror-less Vauxhall Insignia and the totalled BMW, and we should ignore the carping of those hard-hearted and sympathy-deficient critics who might be of the opinion that prison was just the place in which Ms Parry might begin her alcohol-free regime. If we had a masculinist movement (we don't), and it had a spokesman (it doesn't), he might have said (he didn't), 'It is unbelievable that in the 21st century someone should be treated in a preferential manner simply because she is a woman. A more outrageously blatant example of the operation of the matriarchy would be hard to find.' I wonder if Victoria Parry's case was the kind of thing Lady Hale had in mind when she remarked that a misplaced conception of equality has resulted in some very unequal treatment for the women and girls who appear before the criminal justice system.'

And then there was the infamous case of Lavinia Woodward. Ms Woodward punched her then-boyfriend in the face, stabbed him in the leg, and threw a laptop, glass and jamjar at him, all while under the influence of drugs and alcohol. Despite this, Ms Woodward, a student at Oxford, did not receive a custodial sentence because it might have damaged her university career. We were told that she had a troubled life and had been abused by a former boyfriend—so that's all right then. It seems that if you are 'that bright' and a woman, and your victim is a man, battery is something that can be overlooked. The judge in her case was investigated over three complaints. The Judicial Conduct Investigations Office (JCIO) which investigated the judge's conduct rejected all the complaints since they related not to conduct (such as falling asleep in court or using inappropriate language) but to a judicial decision. Some critics of the decision have suggested that what gave rise to the leniency extended to Ms Woodward was her being 'posh'. John Azah, the chief executive of the Kingston Race and Inequalities Council said, 'If she [Woodward] wasn't Oxford-educated, if she came from a deprived area, I don't think she would have got the same sentence and been allowed to walk free.' Yes, Mr Azah, and by the same token, if she hadn't been a young woman, it's also very likely that she wouldn't have walked free. Mark Brooks of Mankind Initiative was somewhat more on the ball than Mr Azah, saying, 'In terms of whether the genders were reversed, we would expect any man committing this type of crime to go to prison and rightly so.' In June 2018, the UK's Justice Secretary, David Gauke, revealed that women will be jailed only for serious crimes, thus giving official sanction to what appears to already be the effective policy. But why only women, one wonders? Isn't this clearly a case of sexism? I hope that our radical feminists will protest against this invidious application of unequal standards yet again to men and women. But, as Baroness Corston remarked in her staggeringly tendentious report on women in the criminal justice system, 'Equality does not mean treating everyone the same.' (see Corston)

But it's not only posh women who go to Oxford who seem to receive benign treatment from the bench. Even if you envision a career only in low-level street crime, it still really helps to be a woman. In August 2018, it was reported that Chantelle Craig, who admitted participating in a vicious assault on another woman, an assault that involved punches and kicks, had the charge against her struck out, leaving her without a conviction on her record. Instead, she paid €250 compensation to the victim, wrote her a letter of apology, and completed 10 hours of voluntary work, as well as taking some anger management classes.

I hope the victim felt that the €250 and the letter of apology were adequate compensation for being punched and kicked. The beneficiaries of Ms Craig's voluntary work were, no doubt, duly appreciative of the free labour, and Ms Craig herself may have benefitted from her anger management classes (though one may reasonably doubt that), but it's a little difficult to see how the voluntary work and the anger management classes were of any satisfaction to the victim who, after all, was the one who was punched and kicked. I wonder if the justice system would have been as understanding and as forgiving if the assailant's name had been Peter or Thomas instead of Chantelle.

In Ennis, Co. Clare, in 2018, a two-year *suspended* jail term was imposed on one Shannon Jordan who pleaded guilty to stabbing another girl several times in the eye with the heel of her stiletto shoe. The victim, who was seventeen years old at the time of the assault, suffered a fractured eye socket and lacerations, and required extensive medical attention, including surgery. In his comments, the Judge was remarkably understanding and exceedingly gracious—to the defendant!—telling her that she had made every effort to rehabilitate herself, and consoling her by saying that while he had no doubt that this was a bad experience for her—again, the defendant!—there was no reason why she shouldn't have a bright future. Ah well, girls will be girls! And wasn't there drink involved! What, if anything, the judge said to the victim doesn't appear to have been reported. Well, I think we can all be grateful for the judge's reassurance that there isn't likely to be an outbreak of stiletto violence in Co. Clare in the near future. Just one small point. Would it be insensitive of me to suggest that if the defendant had been a man, the judge might have been somewhat less gracious and understanding? Just a thought, a cynical thought perhaps, but a thought. Justice must not only be seen to be done but sometimes, as in this case, it must be seen to be believed!

Irish women abroad also seem to attract some of the judicial leniency that their sisters at home enjoy. Cathrina Cahill, who pleaded guilty to the manslaughter of her fiancé in Australia, says that she in fact loved him dearly. (Schiller & Schelkowski) Her fiancé, David Walsh, appears to have been a controlling and unpleasant man, but Cahill nevertheless said that she loved and adored him and thought he was going to change. Well, if manslaughter is what love and adoration leads too, I'm glad no one loves and adores me in a Cahill-like way! Her manslaughter plea was based on the claim that she suffered from a substantial impairment due to an abnormality of the mind. We're not told what the evidence for this claim was apart from the fantasy, dear to the hearts of many women, that they can change their menfolk, so we can only speculate. It might be worth noting that the assault that resulted in Mr

Walsh's death was not the first time that he had been physically attacked by the loving Ms Cahill. At the time of the homicide, Ms Cahill was on a good behaviour bond, having been convicted of recklessly wounding Mr Walsh in 2015 with a glass candle holder, and was the subject of an Apprehended Violence Order (AVO) designed to protect the object of her love and adoration from her undesired physical attentions. In what must be characterised as a well-balanced relationship, Mr Walsh too had had an AVO issued against him, to protect Ms Cahill from *his* undesired physical attentions. Their relationship was, in the words of the judge, 'pretty stormy.' Neither party in this affair appears to have been a paragon of self-restraint, but the court heard evidence that the cases of violence from Mr Walsh to Ms Cahill were limited, while her attacks on him had involved a candle and a knife in an incident that occurred before the fatal attack. The homicide occurred when Mr Walsh, who was intoxicated, attacked a man who had been invited into the home shared by him, Cahill and two other female housemates. Trying to stop the attack, Cahill, who had, as the Irish expression goes, 'drink taken', was punched by her Prince Charming, at which time she took out a large, sharp knife from a cutlery drawer and stabbed him. It is perhaps worthy of note that her substantial impairment due to an abnormality of mind didn't prevent her finding and opening a cutlery drawer and abstracting a knife therefrom.

Sally Challen met her estranged husband at the home they used to share as a married couple. She cooked him a meal and, while he ate it, she took out a hammer she had in her bag and bludgeoned him, hitting him more than twenty times. While the contents of a woman's handbag are a thing of mystery to most men, I think it fair to say that carrying a hammer in one is a little out of the ordinary. Hitting someone twenty times is also hard to characterise as an action that is inadvertent or accidental. The whole affair suggests premeditation and the intention to kill or cause serious bodily harm. Why did Ms Challen do what she did? She told those who coaxed her away from the edge of a cliff, 'If I can't have him, no one can', which sounds very much like good old-fashioned jealousy. Her original conviction was quashed. She pleaded guilty to manslaughter and no retrial was ordered, and as she had already served the time she would have been given for manslaughter, she was immediately released. By all accounts, her spouse was a less than ideal husband, but one thing that he conspicuously did *not* do was to hit his wife twenty times on the head with a hammer. Just like Ms Cahill, Ms Challen tells us she regrets killing the man she loved. Challen is just the latest in a lengthening line of women who have killed their spouses in a premeditated fashion but have had a plea of 'diminished responsibility' or its equivalent accepted by the courts, converting what looks to the disinterested eye to be premeditated murder into manslaughter, literally *man*slaughter. (see Newman)

Sara Thornton was convicted of murdering her husband. She didn't deny the killing but claimed that the stabbing was an accident. The stabbing occurred while her husband was lying drunk on a sofa. At her trial in 1990, her counsel put forward the defence of diminished responsibility, but the jury convicted her of murder. The judge remarked, not unreasonably, that she could simply have walked out of the house or gone upstairs. Her first appeal was rejected but, at her second appeal in late 1995, her lawyers put forward the defence of 'battered woman syndrome.' The original murder conviction was quashed and a retrial ordered. At the retrial, the prosecution produced evidence that suggested premeditation on Thornton's part; however, the defence produced psychiatrists to testify that Thornton suffered from dissociation. Convicted this time of manslaughter, Thornton was immediately released in view of the time in prison that she had already served. The parallels between her case and that of Challen are remarkable.

A combination of the hammer motif *à la* Challen and the knife theme *à la* Thornton made its appearance in the case of Carol Peters, who killed her husband by stabbing him twenty eight times *and* also hitting him on the head with a hammer. Her original 1992 conviction of murder was quashed, and upon retrial she was convicted of manslaughter but, as she had already served the sentence that would have been imposed for manslaughter (4 years), she was released. Pamela Sainsbury garrotted her husband as he slept; Zoora Shah poisoned hers with arsenic; Josephine Smith simply shot her husband in the head; and Kiranjit Ahluwalia set her husband alight in his bed, not metaphorically but in reality.

It's always useful before giving vent to righteous indignation to put the boot on the other foot. 'What are we saying here,' asks Brendan O'Neill. Are we saying

> that women are sometimes incapable of controlling their emotions and their behaviour? Some men are treated abominably by their wives. They are put down, mocked, told they are pathetic, prevented from going to the pub, and so on. If one of these men smashed his wife's head in with a hammer, would we say that wasn't true murder? Would we plaster his image on the front pages of newspapers? Would MPs and campaigners offer him solidarity? I should hope not. And yet they have done this with Challen. The implication is that women enjoy less moral autonomy than men, that they are given to rash behaviour, that they cannot be held fully responsible for what they do. This case threatens to infantilise women who commit crimes. (O'Neill 2019)

I suspect that O'Neill is right in his assertion that what is sauce for the goose would most certainly *not* be sauce for the gander. Perhaps I'm wrong. If so, I wait to see the gleeful headlines and hear the cheers of masculinists as a man walks free in similar circumstances to Challen, Peters and the rest of the gang. Like Brendan O'Neill, Belinda Morrissey argues in her study *When Women Kill* that the way in which the actions of such female killers is framed by feminists has the effect of depriving them of genuine human agency.

It's not only Irish women, at home or abroad, who enjoy the favour of the Courts. In 2018, it was reported that a Canadian woman who did not realise she was pregnant and who killed her newborn child by apparently wounding it and placing it in a plastic bag, has been subsequently diagnosed with non-psychotic pregnancy denial and dissociative amnesia. The woman pleaded guilty to infanticide and was sentenced to—wait for it—pregnancy testing twice a year, twenty months' house arrest and three years probation. The prosecution lawyers (note, not the *defence* lawyers!) had argued that sending her to prison would have penalised her three non-killed children by depriving them of their mother. The judge, Linda Despots, described the woman as a gentle and responsible mother! Would I be thought hard-hearted if I suggested that in this instance, the quality of mercy, not to mention the quality of logic and the quality of law, was strained!

And, in what could be a stellar entry in the feminist two-step stakes, consider the following. The phenomenon of premenstrual syndrome (PMS) can be offered as an element in a defence to a criminal charge, if the defendant can show that she was suffering from it at the time the crime was committed and, because of this, either that her act was involuntary or, alternatively, that at the time of the criminal act, she did not possess the mental state required by law for the commission of a crime. Since the 1950s, PMS has been used as a defence or a mitigating factor for offences ranging from shoplifting to murder. In the UK in the 1980s, Sandie Craddock killed a fellow worker. Despite her 45 (!) prior convictions, she was able to argue that PMS had caused her to act out of character! As a result, she was found 'not guilty' of murder but guilty of manslaughter due to diminished responsibility. Christine English, who in a rage killed her lover by crushing him between her car and a utility pole, was given a less harsh sentence on the grounds of diminished criminal liability owing to severe PMS. Christopher Boorse notes that 'most remarkably, neither woman was punished for her killing: Craddock received probation; English, a 12-month conditional discharge with a driving ban. About a year after her conviction, Craddock (now Smith) was re-arrested for an equivocal attempt to murder a policeman. Convicted on three new charges, Smith again argued

PMS to mitigate her sentence and again received probation. These judgments were approved on appeal.' (Boorse)

A hyper-exaggerated form of PMS called premenstrual dysphoric disorder (PMDD) affects between 3-8% of women of reproductive age. (Henderson) During PMDD, hormone fluctuations affect the woman's brain chemistry and the result is severe mood disturbances. Jayashri Kulkarni, who is a psychiatrist and the director of the Monash Alfred Centre at Monash University in Melbourne, says that during instances of PMDD, the symptoms of which include anxiety, rage and hostility, 'All sorts of things can go astray, including work performances and relationships with colleagues.' You might think that an employer, not wishing to hire someone who is subject to anxiety, rage and hostility, and whose work performance and relationships to colleagues goes 'astray' for up to two weeks every month, might be permitted to inquire if a prospective female employee suffers from this condition but no, that would be sex discrimination. So, a woman's hormonal condition becomes relevant when it is to her possible advantage (as a defence in criminal cases), but not when it is to her possible disadvantage (in seeking employment) By the way, you might think that if PMS can be used as a defence for women, men should be allowed to use evidence of fluctuations in testosterone levels as a defence against being convicted of violent crimes such as assault and murder. But that, of course, would just be silly.

Professor Sonja Starr of the University of Michigan Law School found in the US Federal Criminal Cases 'large gender gaps favoring women throughout the sentence length distribution (averaging over 60%), conditional on arrest offense, criminal history, and other pre-charge observables. Female arrestees are also significantly likelier to avoid charges and convictions entirely, and twice as likely to avoid incarceration if convicted.' (Starr) One might conclude from the sample of cases I've mentioned and from Professor Starr's research that the criminal courts subscribe to women's hypoagency, that is, to the doctrine that women have less than complete human agency and so are not completely responsible for their actions, a doctrine to which, one might think, feminists would vociferously object.

If we were to take the feminist doctrine of the widespread under-representation of women seriously, then we might worry that women are underrepresented in prisons. And since diversity is unquestionably a great good in and of itself, it would clearly be beneficial to the women themselves and the other prisoners if we could have more diversity in the incarcerated demographic. We can dismiss objections based on such outdated white male notions as 'desert' or 'merit'. One shouldn't be guaranteed a coveted place in our prison system just because one's actions deserve or merit punishment. When one thinks about it, it becomes evident that there are systemic patriarchal barriers to women's full participation in custodial environments. This is because women are socialised into accepting and reproducing non-violent behaviours and lack clear role models in prisons to emulate; prison too often appears as a male-stereotyped institution. An obvious way to get behind such oppression, therefore, is to get more women into our jails, receiving a fairer share of jail time regardless of the seriousness of their crimes, indeed, regardless of whether or not they have ever committed a crime. 'Crime' or 'criminal acts' are terms defined by a patriarchal society after all, and our commitment to equality demands that these terms be redefined to ensure equal representation everywhere. After we resolve the issue of equal representation in jail, we can go on to consider how to apply the principles of equality and diversity to hospital patients and inhabitants of psychiatric institutions.

It may seem a little difficult in light of the facts to argue that, in the matter of criminal justice, we witness a clear exhibition of male privilege at the expense of women but, since the doctrine of the patriarchy is an ungainsayable transcendental truth, feminists have no doubts that the seemingly inferior position of men vis-à-vis the law cannot be other than an elaborate patriarchal smokescreen, cunningly designed to conceal the reality of female oppression.

Domestic abuse, domestic violence

The UK government published its draft Domestic Abuse Bill in March 2018, which Bill includes a new category of financial abuse. This continues the intrusion of the political (public) into the personal (private), the last movement of which was the Serious Crime Act of 2015. That act criminalised what was termed 'controlling behaviour' in intimate relationships, a category of crime that had already been enlarged to include emotional abuse as a form of domestic violence. When most people think of domestic abuse, the new term for what used to be called domestic violence, they think of actual violent physical contact between the body of person A and the fist, legs, arms of person B, or various implements wielded by person B. The concept of domestic abuse now covers not only actual violence, but has been extended to include emotional abuse, controlling behaviour and, thanks to the 2018 Act, financial abuse. A great leap forward in the fight against crime! The change of nomenclature is not innocent. Abuse can be pretty much anything that any person finds unpleasant or unwelcome, ranging from the trivial to the serious; violence, however, is something that is evident to all and not simply a matter of subjective perception on the part of the person in receipt of it. (see Moxon, 160-78)

If we are to believe what they say, the UK's Conservative government appears to think that the problem of domestic abuse is everyone's business. No, it's not. It's the business of the people involved, the perpetrator and the victim, their families and friends and, if there is actual violence, the law. The point of the new laws with their inflated conception of domestic abuse appears to be that it will help the relevant agencies to prevent the abuse happening in the first place. We should pay no attention to the agencies that are involved with these issues which tell us that such laws rarely work; it's much more important for politicians to send the right signals. Virtue signalling is important to how our public representatives are perceived, and justice, however flakily it is conceived and administered, must be seen to be done, even if there isn't any justice to *be* done.

What needs to be done is to treat domestic violence (violence, note, not abuse) on all fours with any other form of violence, and by that, I mean real smack-in-the-mouth violence, genuine threats-with-a knife violence. The law does not (and should not) concern itself with trifles: *de minimis non curat lex.* If the law is to be brought to bear on what is unpleasant but relatively trivial, its time and energy risks dispersal. Since often what permits violence to occur or to continue to occur in domestic contexts is the inability of the injured party to leave a dysfunctional relationship, the solution is to make departure possible. The new virtue-signalling laws do nothing whatsoever to bring this about.

Of course, it goes without saying that whatever happens in the UK will eventually come to pass in Ireland, just a little later. If the UK extends the notion of domestic abuse to include the psychological and the financial, so too will Ireland. COSC, the Irish Government's National Office for the Prevention of Domestic, Sexual and Gender-based Violence, tells us that while 'we often associate domestic abuse with physical violence ... not all forms of abuse leave a bruise or a mark.' It concedes that such abuse can be harder to spot, even for victims or witnesses—a concession that is, in itself, revealing. How can you be abused if you're not sure that you're being abused? Few people are baffled by the violent nature of a punch in the nose! It's a little like being wrong about your favourite colour! How is it possible?

So what do the good people at COSC have in mind? They are concerned about people who exhibit 'a consistent pattern of manipulative and intimidating behaviour towards their partner.' The perpetrators of such abuse, we are told, use 'emotional or psychological control to dominate, intimidate, threaten or humiliate the other person.' Hold it right there! That's an interesting collection of verbs. The question is whether the actions described by any of them are necessarily linked to physical violence. Intimidation or threatening behaviour would already be criminal if it caused a genuine anticipation of physical violence (battery) and so there is no need for a law specifically to prohibit and punish it. Domination and humiliation, unpleasant as they may be, are not necessarily a prelude to physical violence and so it is difficult to see why they should be criminalised. Enter the Domestic Violence Act 2018, which proudly declares coercive control to be a criminal offence. Speaking at the passage of the legislation, the Minister for Justice informed us that, 'for too long, domestic violence has been seen primarily as physical abuse. The new offence of coercive control sends a clear, consistent message that non-violent control in an intimate relation is criminal.' He was eager to tell us that those whose actions fall under the act are criminals because the effect of such behaviour 'can be as harmful to victims as physical abuse because it is an abuse of the unique trust associated with an intimate relationship.' (Department of Justice and Equality) I'm not quite sure how he knows that it *can* be as harmful as physical abuse or, indeed, how our legislators generally are competent to concern themselves with breaches of trust in intimate contexts, but I am sure we are all glad to know that nothing escapes their eagle eyes. You won't be surprised—if you are, you shouldn't be—to find that two out of three cases of domestic abuse involve the shiny new offences of coercive control or emotional abuse. What that means, of course, is that defining domestic abuse in this way effectively *triples* the number of cases! Of 15,833 cases of domestic abuse against women reported to Women's Aid in 2017, 10,281 were cases of so-called emotional abuse. Assuming that when we subtract the cases of emotional abuse, we're left with cases of actual physical abuse, this means the number of cases of physical abuse is just 5,552, which is 5,552 cases too many, but significantly less than 15,833.

Typically, how do emotional abusers or exponents of coercive control set about achieving their goals? COSC tells us: 'Abusers use threats to control such as threatening to kill or hurt the victim or threaten to kill or hurt pets or the victim's children.' I hesitate to point this out again but such threats, if causing a genuine apprehension of physical violence (using the objective 'reasonable person' standard) are already forms of criminal behaviour and do not require special legislation. Emotional abusers, we are told, can also 'threaten to make false charges against the victim in order to control access to children.' That, apart from being a tactic typically employed by women against men, should be covered by the provisions against perverting the course of justice. If behaviour that genuinely threatens physical violence against a domestic partner is already covered by the provisions of the criminal code, what need have we of this legislation? 'None' is the answer I'm fishing for unless, like our legislators, you want to signal your virtue loudly and clearly and continue the process of criminalising the unpleasant.

So much for things in Ireland. What of the UK? In the *Mail Online*, Sarah Vine cannot resist a little gentle satire, recommending that you should

think carefully before you have that post-festive ding-dong about whose fault it was the turkey resembled a relic from Chernobyl and the roast potatoes were raw. Choose your words wisely when suggesting that next year's Christmas dinner might be more relaxed without the presence of her father and his helpful carving advice. And if like me you're the sort of spouse who is inclined to chip in with the occasional domestic encouragement—the washing machine is in the downstairs loo, dear, in case you were wondering—then beware. You could be committing a criminal offence. But far from being just another piece of seasonal silliness, this new law has all the hallmarks of being yet another piece of knee-jerk legislation—barely thought through, dreamt up to spin a few positive headlines—that ends up having disastrous unintended consequences such as criminalising healthy marital discourse. What it won't do is tackle real domestic violence, of the kind that puts women in hospital or in fear of their lives. And yet it is so typical of the age we live in. We see it over and over again: a terrible thing—in this case, domestic violence—goes ignored for a long time and then politicians suddenly get all wound up about it and over-compensate with clumsy laws. (Vine)

Until 2017, the UK's domestic abuse figures were moving downwards. In that year, the number of domestic abuse offences reached a 10-year low of 1.9 million. Of these, 1.2 million victims (63%) were female, and 713,000 victims (37%) were male, a ratio of roughly two to one. But, as we have seen, the definition of domestic abuse has been expanding inexorably and the figures for 2017 don't take into account the new offences of coercive and controlling behaviour. The Office of National Statistics said that, 'New survey questions to better estimate experiences of this type of abuse have been introduced into the survey from April 2017 and estimates from these questions will be available in 2018.' The director of the Durham University Centre for Research into Violence and Abuse, Professor Nicole Westmarland, said the changes in the definition of domestic abuse could lead to the downward trend being reversed. She commented, 'The ways in which domestic abuse is perpetrated may be changing, with physical abuse becoming more and more socially unaccept-able, and new opportunities for abuse opening up with the development of new technologies and forms of social media.' She went on, 'Excluding sexual violence by partners and ex-partners and not properly measuring coercive and controlling behaviours means that a large proportion of domestic abuse is being hidden ... If these were included we would see an increase, particularly in terms of the abuse of women.' (Rudgard 2017) The Office of National Statistics agrees with the estimate that the inclusion of coercive and controlling experi-ence would widen the gap between men and women.

Ah yes, now I see. *That's* why the new offence is included, because if it weren't, domestic abuse, as reported, would be largely but still very far from exclusively a male-on-female offence. The chief executive of Women's Aid says that the change in the law would 'better reflect survivors' experience of domestic abuse, especially the gendered nature of abuse, which is that women are overwhelmingly the victims and men overwhelmingly perpetrate domestic abuse. Perhaps it would be overwhelming in the new dispensation, but the pre-coercive-and-controlling domestic abuse ratio of two women to one man, while significant, is hardly overwhelming.

Just over 13% of men say they've been a victim of domestic abuse at some point in their lives but, in fact, in every three reports of domestic abuse, one victim is male. Despite this, you would sometimes get the impression that women, and only women, are victims of domestic abuse and the reason for this, it seems, is that boys and men are inherently violent and misogynistic. On a recent trip to London, while travelling from London City Airport to the City, I saw a billboard with the following legend, 'When men have power, they abuse it.' Men are supposed to be intrinsically violent and misogynistic, women weak and defenceless as the result of gender inequality. Like Sarah Vine, I can't wait to see nagging and scolding women caught in the net of these new emotional and controlling behaviour abuse laws as they used to be in the Middle Ages, so that the number of desperate female criminals who can expect to be leniently treated by our criminal law system will skyrocket.

Though it is often tacitly ignored, when not denied, men are also affected by domestic abuse. In Ireland, the organisation Amen received 5,196 reports of domestic abuse against men in 2016, 3,730 of them involving psychological or verbal abuse. That leaves 1,466 cases of genuine physical abuse. COSC, the Irish National Office for the Prevention of Domestic, Sexual and Gender-based Violence, concedes that 'it is now widely accepted in Ireland that both men and women can be victims and perpetrators of violence in the home', but they are eager to emphasise that the 'impact and severity of abuse experienced by women is much greater than that by men particularly for more severe behaviours.' (COSC)

Domestic violence, then, is not an exclusively female issue when it comes to victims. Both men and women are involved in such violence, and women are often the initiators of such violence. Anywhere from one quarter to one third of domestic violence victims are men. Men, however, are also significantly less likely to tell anyone if they've suffered domestic abuse. Some 10% will tell the police (compared to 26% of women), 11% will tell a health professional (compared to 23% of women), and 23% will tell someone else in a position of authority (compared to 46% of women). When they do call in the police, the results are not especially encouraging. In a survey, a quarter of the male respondents said they themselves 'had been arrested despite being the victim, half were threatened with arrest despite being the victim, and most of the remainder reported that the police had totally ignored what they had to say.' (Moxon, 177) There is also a significant dearth of support for men suffering from domestic abuse. In the UK there are 93 safe spaces offering refuge or safe houses for male victims of domestic violence, and only 22 of these are male only. For women, there are around 4,000 of these refuges. There is no refuge for men in London. Domestic violence—*real* domestic violence— isn't an instrument of patriarchal control but it is a crime that troubled male and female partners commit against one another. Men do more damage than women do, but women conduct and initiate violence as often as men do, and one of three killings by partners is by a woman.

In the foregoing discussion, I have been taking the figures for the relative proportions of male and female victims of domestic abuse as given. But, as Steve Moxon tells us, they are not unproblematic:

> The root of the popular misapprehension that DV [domestic violence] is a women's issue is very simple. If you only look at those in (women's) refuges or in criminal proceedings; or if you only ask women, or both men and women but only about DV as a crime; then unsurprisingly you will find that there are few male victims compared to female. It can appear to be 'gender neutral' to ask men whether they have themselves been on the receiving end of the crime of DV, but they will often or usually answer 'no', even if they have been persistently and seriously assaulted by their women partners. This is because men don't usually regard physical assault against them by their partner as criminal, no matter how serious. (Moxon, 160-61)

So much for domestic violence in either its old-fashioned or new-fangled varieties. What about even more serious crimes against women? Julie Bindel had a piece published in the *Guardian* under the attention grabbing if hyperbolic headline: 'A war on women is raging in the UK—the femicide statistics prove it.' (Bindel 2018) She tells us that last year [2017], 139 women died misogynistically in the UK as a result of male violence. The reason for the death of these women is, according to Bindel, what she sees as a misogynistic culture in the UK that is, in turn, part of a global pandemic. She omits to mention— perhaps it's of no interest to her or perhaps it just slipped her mind—that in the year ending March 2017 the majority of homicide victims were male (433, 71%) whereas female victims were a minority (180, 29%). If we were to look at these numbers without filtering them through the lens of feminist prejudices, we should conclude from this that what we have here is not a war on women but a war on men. It *is* true that there are significant differences between men and women when it comes to the relationship between victims and their killers or suspected killers. Figures from the National Office for Statistics tell us that 50% of female adult homicide victims aged 16 and over were killed by their partners or ex-partners (82) in the year ending March 2017, whereas only 3% of male victims aged 16 and over were killed by their partners or ex-partners (13). (In these statistics, the terms 'partner' or 'ex-partner' are taken widely to include an adulterous relationship, a boyfriend or girlfriend, a common-law spouse or cohabiting partner, an ex-spouse, an ex-common-law spouse or an ex-cohabiting partner, an ex-boyfriend or an ex-girlfriend, or a spouse, including civil partners.) On the other hand, male adults were most likely to be killed by a friend or acquaintance, around one-quarter (112, 24%) being killed by such people in the year ending March 2017. Female victims were less likely to be killed by a friend or acquaintance (16, 10%). Around one-fifth of adult male victims (104, 22%) were killed by strangers, compared with around one in eleven female victims (14, 9%).

Ms Bindel is bravely prepared to speculate on the reason why women are killed by men. It is, she thinks, the result of a sense of male entitlement, ownership and access to women. If, she writes, 'men continue to see women and children as their property, and believe that women exist to satisfy them sexually, then the rape and murder of women will never end.' (Bindel) It's not entirely clear where this idea comes from. To which men do their wives and children present themselves as their property? Interesting as the homicide figures are, they don't tell us *why* these women were killed by their partners or ex-partners, still less, as Bindel speculates, does it tell us that 'These men cannot bear the thought that a woman has rejected them—because after all, in the violent, controlling mind of the perpetrator, she belonged to him. This is misogyny in its clearest form.' (Bindel) If one were to be uncharitable (and why not!), one might say that Bindel's assertions are baseless speculation in its clearest form.

Let's step back from Ms Bindel's lurid speculations and take a detached look at the statistics. (see Office for National Statistics) Excluding the 96 cases of manslaughter determined to result from the event at Hillsborough in 1989, there were 613 homicides in total in the UK in the year ending in March 2017—up 8% on the preceding year. (For statistical purposes, homicide is taken to be either murder, manslaughter or infanticide, where infanticide is defined as the killing of a baby under one year old by its mother while the balance of her mind was disturbed as a result of giving birth.) It is perhaps worth noting that 'the number of male victims has increased at a faster rate than females in recent years, with male victims of homicide increasing by 33% to 433 from 325 in the year ending March 2015, ending a generally downward trend *whereas the number of female homicide victims has remained broadly flat over the last five years (fewer than 200).*' (Emphasis added) The homicide rate for males (15 per million population) was 150% greater than that for females (6 per million population), that is, one and one half times greater than for females. As recently as the 1960s, the proportion of homicide victims was more or less the same for male and for female victims. Over the next 50 years, while the number of female victims has remained more or less constant, the number of male victims has doubled! Between 2011 and 2015, the number of female victims declined to under 200, while the number of male victims fell significantly to just over 300. In the last two years, however, the number of male victims has increased by over 30%. A 2009 policing report found that around two thirds of all murder victims are men.

Children under the age of one are the victims who suffer the highest rate of homicide (36 per million population). Fiona Brookman and Jane Nolan note that 'Infants aged younger than 12 months have the highest homicide victimization rate of any single age group in England and Wales.' (Brookman & Nolan) Most such deaths are cases of infanticide, where the perpetrator of the homicide is, despite the inroads of transgenderism, always a woman and the child's mother. (Infanticide Act, §1) In law, infanticide can attract a penalty of life imprisonment but, in practice, sentences are normally non-custodial. After young babies, the group next most likely to be killed are young males aged between sixteen and twenty-four. Of course, the statistics on homicide don't take into account the many thousands of very small human beings who every year are legally killed while still in the womb (just under 220,000 in the UK for the year 2018), the prime agents of whose deaths are usually their own mothers.

What can we conclude from this cascade of figures? Is it the case, as Ms Bindel thinks, that in the UK we are witnessing a war on women? I suggest that any unbiased examination of the statistics on homicide will tell us that if we were asked to decide whether they indicated a war on women or a war on men, there is only one honest answer, and it is not the one proposed by Ms Bindel. Once again, the patriarchy seems to have fallen down on the job. Putting it all together, it is hard to better the words of Steve Moxton when he writes that we are told

> that women are disadvantaged, and that they've got this way because of the oppression of men. We're never told how or why this could be. We're not told why—especially if men and women are supposedly the same—there would be any

point in one sex oppressing the other. We're not told how it can be—if indeed men are different to women and oppress them—that by most measures it is not women who are disadvantaged but men (or, at least, a large sub-group or even the majority of men). Nobody tells us why men are maligned as if they are at one with the very few at the top of the pile, whereas all women are championed irrespective of who they are, what they have done, or how they have lived their lives. Confused? You should be. (Moxon, 1)

The banal truth about the patriarchy

Let's return to where we started this chapter, with the idea of an all-powerful, omnipresent, misogynistic patriarchy. Is it all a matter of feminist conspiratorial nonsense or is there any element of truth in the idea of a patriarchy? Yes, the idea of a patriarchy contains an element of truth, but it is much more mundane and humdrum than the conspiratorial nonsense that is the usual burden of the feminists' tale. If patriarchy were anything like it is depicted by feminists—all-powerful, omnipresent and ineradicable—as a system constructed for the exclusive benefit of men at the expense of women, then feminism could never have existed and this discussion wouldn't ever have seen the light of day.

In prehistoric times, pregnancy and childbirth were likely to be constant conditions for most women of childbearing age, especially given the evolutionary loss of oestrus by human females. 'Man,' writes John M. Roberts, 'is the only animal in which the mechanism of the oestrus (the restriction of the female's sexual attractiveness and receptivity to the limited periods in which she is on heat) has entirely disappeared. It is easy to see the evolutionary connexion between this and the prolongation of infancy ... ' (Roberts 1993, 10) Roberts believes that this loss of oestrus has had radical social implications. 'The increasing attractiveness and receptivity of females to males make individual choice much more significant in mating,' he writes. 'The selection of a partner is less shaped by the rhythm of nature; we are at the start of a very long and obscure road that leads to the idea of sexual love. Together with prolonged infant dependency, the new possibilities of individual selection point ahead also to the stable and enduring family unit of father, mother and offspring, an institution unique to mankind.' (Roberts 1993, 10) The physically debilitating (and oftentimes dangerous) effects of pregnancy and childbirth, and the subsequent demands of childcare extending over a long time, produced a differentiation of social function along sexual lines. The sex-based division of labour meant, Azar Gat remarks, that 'women specialized in child bearing and rearing and in foraging close to the home base, whereas men specialized in long-distance hunting and in the struggle to acquire and defend women and children .... ' Despite the cooperation of both parents in child-rearing, it is significant that 'the father ... was more expendable than the mother' so that when the group came under attack, 'the men formed the group's main line of defence, while the women covered the children to the best of their abilities.' (Gat, 80, 81) C. Northcote Parkinson remarks that 'women and children must be kept out of danger if the family group is to survive. If men are killed in hunting, the survivors may still be enough for breeding purposes. The same is not true of women, upon whose number the natural increase must depend.' (Parkinson, 17)

Not everyone is convinced by this line of reasoning. Rosalind Miles considers the argument that 'Mother Nature having saddled women with an unequal share of the work of reproduction...[women] had to consent to male domination in order to obtain protection for themselves and for their children', but she counterargues that 'the historical record clearly shows that women in "primitive" societies have a better chance of equality than those in more "advanced" cultures.' She believes that it's a paradox of our age that 'women were freer in earlier times than in our own. Prehistoric women hunted and ran at will, roamed where they would and freely lay down with the partner of their choice. They created pottery and cave painting, they planted and wove, danced and sang.' Prehistory is *pre*history, and so we have no written records to rely on to prove or to disprove such assertions. While it isn't necessarily a reliable procedure to take the constitutions of traditional societies that have survived into modernity as a guide to the constitutions of those of the remote past, in the absence of hard data, a consideration of their customs and *mores* would suggest that there is more than an element of wishful thinking and anachronistic retrojection, perhaps—dare I say it?—even of feminist fantasy, in Miles's imaginative account of the 'primitive' woman. 'What egalitarian feminist ideology fails to realize,' writes Camille Paglia, 'is that tribal cultures suppress individuality. The group rules. Our distinct, combative, intro- spective, conflicted, and highly verbal and creative personalities are a product of Western culture. Feminism itself has been produced by Western culture.' (Paglia, 1992)

In hunter/gatherer societies, in respect of the three essential social roles of procreation, provision and protection, men played two roles that were danger- ous and arduous (provision [hunting] and protection) and one that was normally neither dangerous nor arduous (procreation); women played one role that was dangerous and arduous (procreation), one that was neither danger- ous nor arduous (protection) and one that was arduous but not dangerous (provision [gathering]).

	Men	*Women*
Procreation	Neither dangerous nor arduous	Dangerous and arduous
Provision	Both dangerous and arduous	Not dangerous but arduous
Protection	Both dangerous and arduous	Neither dangerous nor arduous

The burdens and responsibilities of social life were thus roughly equal for both sexes, men having slightly the worst of the bargain, with two dangerous roles to women's one. After the Agricultural Revolution and the relative decline in the importance of hunting as a primary means of provision, men's role in provision remained arduous but was no longer inherently dangerous, so that the number of dangerous and arduous roles of men and women effectively balanced. For almost all of human history and prehistory, females have chosen their mates in respect of their abilities to be successful and to provide food and protection for them and for their children; men have chosen women for their fertility, the outward indication of which is physical attractiveness. And so things remained (with minor local variations) until the occurrence of the Reproductive and Technological Revolutions of the second half of the twentieth century, the social and cultural consequences of which we are still working out with fear and trembling. (see Nathanson & Young 2001, 2006 and 2015, passim.) Reflecting on these issues, Meghan Daum writes,

> the questions we face now when it comes to men and women are questions that arose a split second ago. Modern humans have been around for about 200,000 years. Civilization as we know it has been churning away for perhaps 6,000 years. Until the birth control pill came along in 1960, we were all essentially prisoners of nature, with women's conditions being markedly worse, sometimes obscenely so. Until 1960, the idea that women could compete with men in the job market, that men should do housework, that women had any purpose in life higher than having babies and men had any purpose higher than financially supporting those babies or going to war to protect them, was something close to unthinkable. That we have come so far in so little time is a marvel. That we should expect all the kinks to have been worked out by now is insane. In the scheme of things, the 59 years that have elapsed between 1960 and today is a nanosecond, a flash of time so imperceptible that it has passed in increments of billions by the time you have read this sentence. (Daum 2019a)

The depth and extent of the changes wrought by these two Revolutions and their social implications cannot be overstated. In the space of forty years, abortion has gone from being either illegal or exceptional to being in effect a relatively routine backup form of contraception. Divorce no longer has any social stigma attached to it and is generally available in 'no-fault' form, that is, on demand by one or other of the parties. The concept of illegitimacy, even the use of that term, is *streng verboten*, and in its place we have the brave new world of single-motherhood, stigma-free and state supported. Homosexual conduct has moved from being vilified and illegal to being tolerated to being valorised, with the state offering its support to the new normative environment in its recognition of so-called gay marriage. All these changes, and others, stem from our increasing ability to separate sex and reproduction. Sex without reproduction has been commonplace for almost fifty years; reproduction without sex is already with us, and is set to become increasingly common. The biological constraints that informed human sexual morality from our very beginnings are no longer operative.

The social, economic and political consequences of these two 20th-century revolutions rank in significance with the Agricultural and Industrial Revolutions. The Technological Revolution freed men in large measure from the exhausting and debilitating physical toil that made so many of the men of my father's generation physical wrecks by the time they were in their forties. It also drastically expanded the job opportunities open to women while simultaneously steeply discounting the economic value of men's superior muscle power. The Reproductive Revolution gave women the power to control their fertility and thereby freed them, in some ways at least, from the biological imperatives that have cabin'd, cribb'd and confined them since sentence was first pronounced on Eve. Chemical contraception, together with the widespread acceptance of effectively unrestricted abortion, constitutes an experiment in radical social re-engineering whose personal, social, sexual, demographic and political implications are difficult to foresee.

The *Times*'s columnist, Caitlin Moran, remarks that 'It's not a coincidence that efforts towards female emancipation only got going under the twin exegeses of industrialisation and contraception—when machines made us the equal of men in the workplace, and The Pill made us the equal of men in expressing our desire.' (Moran, 138) 'The so-called "sexual revolution" of the 1960s,' writes Catherine Hakim, 'was made possible by the contraceptive revolution. For the first time in history, the pill and other modern forms of reliable contraception controlled by women gave women easier access to recreational sex without fear of pregnancy. The uncoupling of sexuality and fertility led to an increase in marital sexual activity in the West. It also made premarital sex more common, and eventually facilitated extra-marital sexuality as well. Possibly for the first time in history, recreational sex became far more important than reproductive sex—for people of all ages, and in all socio-economic groups. Marriage is no longer the precondition for an active sex life.' (Hakim 2015, 8) These revolutions also irrevocably altered the relationship between the sexes— in precisely what ways and whether for good or for ill only time will tell. (see Penman, 549-50) Writing in the early 90s, David Thomas remarked, 'We are, after all, only thirty years into the greatest shift in sexual patterns ever known to human kind: the freedom from pregnancy caused by the arrival of the Pill.' (Thomas, 180) Thirty years later and matters have become, if anything, even more confused. All that can be said with certainty is that since the 1960s, in the matter of sexual relationships, all is changed, changed utterly: a terrible bemusement is born. (see Moxon, 4-5)

John M. Roberts lists three factors he believes to have contributed to the social emancipation of women, two of which coincide with the factors I have already identified. These factors are: first, the creation of the advanced industrial economy which provided women with significant numbers of new jobs, none of which had existed even a century earlier; second, contraception, which gave rise to a 'revolution in outlook as more women absorbed the idea that they might control the demand of childbearing and rearing which hitherto had throughout history dominated and structured the lives of their sex'; and third, technological changes, such as piped water, gas, imported foods, detergents, gas cookers, vacuum cleaners, washing machines—'Historians who would recognise at once the importance of the introduction of the stirrup or lathe in earlier times, have strangely neglected the cumulative influence of such humble agencies.' (Roberts 1997, 475-476) It may, perhaps, be worth pointing out that all three factors indicated by Roberts—the advanced industrial economy, chemical contraception, and the technological inventions that have transformed our lives—were the product of male energy and ingenuity.

An obvious but not-often-adverted-to fact is that the infrastructural environment in which radical feminists operate has been designed, constructed and maintained almost entirely by men: the lecture halls in which radical feminist doctrines are espoused; the roads that radical feminists drive on to get to their universities; the iPads, iPhones and the computers on which they write papers about the all-encompassing and all-powerful patriarchy; the airplanes they fly in to attend radical feminist conferences—these are all the product of largely male ingenuity and labour. Writing of Suzanne Gordon, the founder of *Women*, one of the first feminist journals in the USA, Camille Paglia notes that while Gordon thinks of the patriarchy as tyrannically oppressive, she 'never pauses to note the benefits, gifts, and privileges she takes for granted in the male-created world around her—the hot showers, flush toilets, automatic washers and dryers, electric lights, telephones, automobiles, the grocery stores overflowing with fresh, safe food, the high-tech network of medicines and life-saving hospital equipment.' (Paglia 1992, 88.) In an earlier publication, Paglia had remarked, perhaps provocatively, that 'If civilization had been left in female hands, we would still be living in grass huts.' (Paglia 1991, 38; but see Miles 2001 for another perspective.) Using the pregnant words of Francis Urquhart in the original British version of *House of Cards*, I can only say that whereas Paglia might very well think that, I couldn't possibly comment. According to Caitlin Moran, 'even the most ardent feminist historian, male *or* female...can't conceal that women have basically done **** all for the last 100,000 years .... Our empires, armies, cities, artworks, philosophers, philanthropists, inventors, scientists, astronauts, explorers, politicians and icons could all fit, comfortably, into one of the private karaoke booths in SingStar. We have no Mozart; no Einstein; no Galileo; no Gandhi. No Beatles, no Churchill, no Hawking, no Columbus. It just didn't happen. Nearly everything so far has been the creation of men...' (Moran, 134, 135)

Steven E. Landsburg describes the typical laundry day for a housewife in the 1900s: 'First, she ports water to the stove, and heats it by burning wood or coal. Then she cleans the clothes by hand, rinses them, wrings them out... then hangs them to dry and moves on to the oppressive task of ironing, using heavy flatirons that are heated continuously on the stove. The whole process takes about eight-and-a-half hours and she walks over a mile in the process .... By 1945, our heroine probably had a washing machine. Now her laundry chores took just two-and-a-half hours instead of eight-and-a-half and instead of walking a mile, she walked just 665 feet.' (Landsburg, 29-30) George Catlin, writing of his experiences among the Sioux in the 1830s, says,

> It is proverbial in the civilized world that "the poor Indian woman has to do all the hard work." Don't believe this, for it is not exactly so. She does most of the drudgery about the village and wigwam and is seen transporting heavy loads, etc....*His* labours are not seen, and therefore are less thought of, when he mounts his horse with his weapons in hand, and working every nerve and every muscle, dashes amongst the herds in the chase, to provide food for his wife and his little children, and scours the country both night and day, at the constant risk of his life, to protect them from the assault of their enemies....The education of woman in those countries teaches her that the labours are thus to be divided between herself and her husband; and for the means of subsistence and protection, for

which she depends upon his labours, she voluntarily *assumes* the hard work about the encampment, considering their labours about equally divided. (Catlin, 60-61; emphasis in original; see also Purdy, 90-114)

Men, it is said, have all the power. If power is defined as *the possession of superior upper body strength*, then men as a whole are indeed in a position to dominate over women as a whole although, as with all such aggregates, any given woman may well be physically stronger than any given man. If, however, one thinks of power not just as raw physical strength but as *an aspect of the complex of sexual psycho-social relationships*, then, given the existence and persistence of the radical imbalance in the demand for sex by men and by women, women, as a whole, are in a position to dominate over men, as a whole and thus might be said to have, if not quite all the power, at least a preponderance of it. This point is made, humorously in the film, *Annie Hall*. Alvy (Woody Allen) and Annie (Diane Keaton) are each at their psychiatrist's. On a split screen, Alvy's psychiatrist asks him: 'How often do you sleep together?' Annie's psychiatrist asks her: 'Do you have sex often?' Alvy replies: 'Hardly ever. Maybe three times a week.' Annie replies: 'Constantly! I'd say three times a week.' 'The casting of the two genders into the roles of male oppressors and female oppressed ignores the possibility that the balance of power may be far more complex and flexible than that.' (Thomas, 8)

As Catherine Hakim notes, 'male demand for sexual entertainments and activity greatly outstrips female sexual interest even in liberal cultures. This gives women an edge, although many are still unaware of it.' (Hakim 2015, 9) Hakim provides conclusive evidence, if evidence of such an obvious fact were needed, of the persistent and significant difference in demand for sex by men and by women. (Hakim 2015, 12-20) This difference in demand, she believes, is 'not due to socialisation, the repression of female sexuality, or women's lesser sexual enjoyment, and may be due to the female sex drive being more plastic, malleable, responsive to social influences, whereas the male sex drive is less compliant.' (Hakim 2015, 19) If power is defined as *political dominance* then, while most of the politically powerful human beings may be men, it's perhaps worth noting that most men are *not* among the politically powerful! The ruler-ruled relationship is one of domination and subordination, and it is of little or no consolation for politically subordinated men to reflect that the orders they have to obey issue from a male rather than a female. Even if we limit our power focus to politics and economics, it's not true that men have all the power. Even if it were to be the case that the most powerful political and economic personages in the world were men, it is also the case that almost all men are not among this elite group.

It would seem that, at least from the ordinary man's perspective, the perspective of those men (almost *all* men) who do *not* have (and never have had) all the power, sexual or political, that the patriarchy isn't all it's cracked up to be. Men must be the only supposed oppressors in history that are *less well-served by the education system* they have permitted to be created than the allegedly oppressed other, are *greater victims of physical violence* (including the socially sanctioned violence of military conscription and military service which was, and still largely is, exclusively applied to disposable men) than the allegedly oppressed other, are *treated with greater severity by the justice system in respect of divorce and custody and in criminal sentencing* than the allegedly oppressed other, do, as they have done throughout history, a *staggeringly greater proportion of society's dirty jobs* than the allegedly oppressed other, *are treated less well by their health systems* than the allegedly oppressed other and live *statistically significantly shorter lives* than the allegedly oppressed other.

If patriarchy is all-powerful and all pervasive, as some feminists claim, it would seem to be correspondingly all-stupid and omni-ineffective in its manifest inability to construct and maintain a social order that transparently benefits all and only men, which, given that the patriarchy is supposed to be, according to Tuttle, 'the universal political structure which *privileges men at the expense of women*,' makes no sense.

Toxic Masculinity *or* Why Can't a Man be more like a Woman?

Man will swear and man will storm —
Man is not at all good form —
Man is of no kind of use —
Man's a donkey—Man's a goose—
Man is coarse and Man is plain—
Man is more or less insane—
Man's a ribald—Man's a rake,
Man is Nature's sole mistake!
—W. S. Gilbert

I'm as mad as hell, and I'm not going to take this anymore!
—Howard Beale (Paddy Chayefsky)

It would appear that the Preacher had it right when he told us that 'there is nothing new under the sun.' Today's radical feminists have their intellectual progenitrix in one Frances Swiney who was president of the Cheltenham Branch of the National Union of Women's Suffrage Societies. Back at the start of the twentieth century, she was of the opinion that if only women got the vote, it would lead to a brave new world of asexual reproduction and the birth of only female children. Men were to be abolished. Back then, feminists tended to think of women as morally superior to men. Today, feminists are torn between taking the high moral ground ('isn't it obvious—men are such brutes!') and, alternatively, since men seem to have all the fun, thinking that women should behave just like them, drinking irresponsibly, smoking, using foul language and, above all, having promiscuous sex which, as we have seen, can only lead to a paradisal situation in which women flourish in all aspects of their lives, and relations between the sexes are forever untroubled, exquisitely courteous, honest and harmonious.

Emotional repression and other male failings

Discussing what she calls, with just a *soupçon* of tendentiousness, toxic masculinity, Kirby Fenwick describes it as consisting of male dominance, emotional repression and self-reliance. These characteristics, it appears, manifest 'aggression and superiority in men at the expense of community and emotional expression.' (Fenwick) A brief word about male dominance and self-reliance before I turn my attention to emotional repression, the most important item on Fenwick's charge sheet. As I mentioned in the chapter on patriarchy, I don't know which world in is in which men are supposed to be dominant but it certainly isn't this one. I'm also puzzled by the imputation of 'self-reliance' to men as if it were somehow a deep defect of character. I should have thought in my naïvety that self-reliance was a virtue rather than a vice, whether manifested by men or women. But let's move on to the really important item on Fenwick's list: emotional repression.

That men are emotionally repressed is a truth universally acknowledged, at least, it is universally acknowledged in the narcissistic universe inhabited by radical feminists and their fellow travellers. Men, they believe, are emotionally stunted and do not feel emotions or, if they do feel them, they cannot bring themselves to express them. While the assertion that men are emotionally repressed may be a feminist dogma, it is, of course, palpable nonsense, and demonstrable palpable nonsense at that. Men, despite what feminists think, are human beings, and so both experience and express emotions. They laugh at jokes and absurdities, exult in victory, sing loudly and out of tune at football matches to show solidarity with their teams, sympathise with others in trouble, admire bravery, display contempt for cruelty and cowardice, regret irrational impulses, are indignant at injustice, feel pity for the unfortunate, take pride in their children's achievements and experience and express disgust, shame, trust or love. When the charge of emotional repression is made, those making it seem to have in mind a strangely limited set of emotions, usually fear and sorrow, so that, in effect, what is really meant by the peculiar assertion that men either don't have or don't express emotions is that men do not usually cry or weep in public, allow fear to prevent their undertaking their duties or—and this is where the shoe pinches—talk incessantly about their feelings to all and sundry. On the latter point, it should be obvious that you can *have* feelings and emotions without talking about them all the time. It might even be the case that there is an inverse relationship between having them and talking about them. As Mr Knightley says to the eponymous Emma, 'If I loved you less, I might be able to talk about it more.'

So, what *is* toxic masculinity? Short answer—pretty much anything that radical feminists don't like about men, which is pretty much everything. For radical feminists, *masculinity* is not a term referring to what is best about men but, prefaced by the word *toxic*, it signifies all that is bad and dangerous about them. Would it be acceptable to routinely characterise any other group in society in such an insulting and demeaning way? Men could, if they wished, and if they weren't gentlemen, turn the tables and charge women with, let's say, toxic femininity, which might be said to be characterised by emotional incontinence and verbal diarrhoea! I wonder how *that* charge would be received! The #MeToo campaign, takes its point of departure from a very specific context, the world of entertainment, a world hardly representative of the wider society. From this narrow base, it has been extended not just to one or other dodgy profession but to men as a whole. It is as if those of us who are critical of the manic machinations of radical feminists were to extend our criticisms of that tiny but noisy bunch of cranks to all women. Masculinity, writes George Gilder 'is treated like sex in Victorian England: a fact of life that the society largely condemns and tries to suppress and that its intellectuals deny.' (Gilder, xi)

The notion of toxic masculinity is so wide, so free-floating, so expressive of a distaste for a whole range of masculine characteristics, that it has little or no explanatory value. As Fraser Myers puts it, 'Toxic masculinity is merely a meaningless buzz-phrase used to express disapproval of certain forms of behaviour. It can encompass anything from the mass murders committed by violent misogynists like in Toronto to minor, everyday behaviour and beliefs— including some which would once have been seen as positive.' (Myers) This last point, about the once-positive-now-negative male characteristics, is signif- icant. For while few would not join with (some) feminists and sane people in condemning terrorism, toxic masculinity is used to call into question not only extreme violence, but also certain characteristics that have traditionally been seen as masculine virtues, though not, of course, exclusively so. Many men believe that they are called upon to be responsible for maintaining order in crisis situations, to accomplish which, they have learned to keep certain—not all—of their emotions (such as fear and anguish) in check. Keeping their fears under control and not crying or weeping in public, apart from truly exceptional circumstances, has been a way that men, traditionally, have respected the privacy of others and tried to manage difficult situations *for the sake of others*. We can't all cry at the same time; someone has to deal with crises, and not everyone gets to have the luxury of emotional catharsis when things need to be done. Of course, it's not only men who can take on this role, but such has been seen as something one did as a man, indeed, something one was obliged to do as a man. Now, some see such virtues as old-fashioned and sexist, and damaging to men and to others around them.

Most normal men don't talk about their feelings, at least not directly. Four words guaranteed to strike terror into any normal man's heart are hearing his significant other say, 'we need to talk.' Men's posture in relation to other men is side-by-side, not face to face, and while women may find talking about their feelings cathartic and a source of social bonding and solidarity, most men understand what another man is feeling and can support that other man without necessarily talking about it, certainly without talking about it incessantly. It is, perhaps, ironic that some men who have manifested an unquestionable antisocial toxicity have displayed a conspicuous lack of reticence when it came to talking about their feelings, being willing to talk about them to all and sundry *ad nauseam*. Myers once again: '[Elliot] Rodger [a so-called incel killer] spent 14 of his 22 years on the planet visiting multiple therapists, even writing a 141-page manifesto about his feelings of hatred for the world and himself. The incel subculture appears to reflect today's therapeutic sensibilities much more than any long-gone notion of traditional masculinity.' (Myers)

Here's a take on male emotional sensitivity from the film *Bedazzled* that pretty much tells it like it is. It's funny 'cause it's true! The scene is sunset at the beach. Elliot comes running back to his new love, Allison. She asks where he's been and he replies, in a nauseatingly saccharine voice, 'I went to make a garland of beach plums to place atop your glorious head, but then I caught sight of that sunset ... I don't know, something stirred inside me and I had to stop and weep.' Allison agrees, 'Mmm ... it's beautiful.' Elliot, overcome with emotion says, 'It is' and snivelling loudly, adds, 'Here I go again' Allison offers him a tissue. Elliot tenderly rejects her offer. 'No,' he says, 'I never wipe my tears away, I'm not ashamed of them, I'll wear them proudly like small, wet, salty badges of emotional truth.'

Allison clearly has something on her mind. 'Elliot, um, there's something that I think we should talk about, um, we've been together for what, about three weeks now ...' Elliot interrupts, sensitively, 'Three magical weeks.' She continues, ' ... three *magical* weeks ... and I don't think that I've ever met a man who's been more in touch with his feelings ....' Elliot, interrupting her again, but sensitively of course, says 'I love you so very much', to which she responds, automatically, with 'I love you too', and they move towards a kiss. They are interrupted by an appearance of the Devil (Liz Hurley in a bikini!) who, barely restraining two snarling large black attack dogs, bursts in on them, preventing the kiss from taking place.

When the Devil has left, Elliott says to Allison, earnestly, 'I'm sorry, are you ok? Do you need comforting on any level?' Allison says she's fine, but Elliot persists with the emotional inquisition: 'Have I done or said anything to make you feel less good about you?' She repeats that she's fine. Elliot, changing the subject abruptly, asks her, 'Would you like something to eat? I made a salad nicoise with dolphin-safe tuna.' He starts to blubber again and Allison asks him (impatiently), 'What is it?' 'It's the sunset again,' he says, 'and I worry about the dolphins. I wrote a song about them. Would you like to hear it?' Allison is incredulous. 'Now? I ... ' Elliot picks up a guitar and starts to sing (very badly): 'Swimming by the sandy shore, dancing up among the waves, dolphin, dolphin I adore, everything you are. You're so much more than a fish to me, my playful friend beneath the sea, eek, eek, eek, eek ....' At this point, Allison turns away in embarrassment. Elliot stops: 'I have to stop.' Allison, relieved, says 'Good ... I mean, why?' 'Because I'm looking at you and I'm seeing all the beauty of the world shining at me through your eyes—would you mind if I sketched you?' Allison is surprised. 'I didn't know you could draw?' she says. Elliot, modestly, 'I'm not an artist *per se.*' Allison once more tries to tell him what's on her mind. 'OK Elliott, there's something that I think I really have to say ... ' Elliot shows her a remarkably skilful and finished portrait which he has completed in about 1.8 seconds flat! She's astonished: 'Elliott! That's amazing!' 'Compared to you,' he says, 'it's nothing, compared to your smile and the blush of your cheek and the sound of your voice as it floats on the evening breeze ... compared to you, that sunset's just (he snivels again) ... when is that darn thing going to set?'

Allison suggests that they might leave the beach but Elliot says, 'No, wait, um, there's so much that I want to say to you but I just ... I can't find the words. I have an idea! I would like to improvise a sonnet about your hair. "How wonderful my fair one's hair " .... ' He's rudely interrupted by a shower of sand hitting him on the side of his head. Two tough-looking roughnecks (whom I shall call Zig and Zag) are standing there. 'Excuse me, fellas,' says Elliot, 'might I ask you to take the horseplay down to another part of the beach?' Zig, pretends to consider the request, then says 'Nooo', and kicks some more sand in Elliot's face. Elliott, spitting sand out of his mouth, says, 'You know, rather than get confrontational, why don't we all just sit down together and have some salad with dolphin-safe tuna and see if we can't start a dialogue ... ' More sand approaches Elliot's face but he blocks it with his sketch pad. 'You know,' he says, 'I had a feeling you were ...', just as the next shower of sand arrives in his face. He gets to his feet. 'OK guys, I'm afraid I'm going to have to ask you to respect the moment that my woman friend and I are sharing because it's a special celebration of love and caring and unique spiritual and emotional understanding.'

Zig is bemused. Then he says to Allison, 'You wanna get a beer?' 'Sure!' she replies. Elliott is taken aback. 'Allison! I'm ... Excuse me, but I thought that this was our time together?' 'It's just a beer!,' she replies, 'I'll be back in two secs....' Zig interrupts, 'Actually, my place is like 40 minutes from here.' Allison, with heartfelt relief, 'That's fine! Which way's your car?' Zig: 'Van.' Allison: 'Great!' Elliott speaks. The roughnecks, now three in number, stand around looking embarrassed for him. 'Allison, I respect your uniqueness and your individuality and you're your own person ... if you want to go with our new friends here to get a drink, I won't stand in your way.' Allison, pleased, says, 'Hey, thanks El, I knew you'd understand.' Elliott, abandoning all pretence of acceptance, goes down on his knees to beg, 'No, wait, don't go, don't go! Why can't we have this time together? Why don't you want to stay here with me?' Allison looks him straight in the face. 'You want to know why, Elliott? It's because you're just ... too ... sensitive. I'm about to go out of my mind here. It's been wonderful and God's knows, I love you, but enough is enough. I just want to be with a man who'll ignore me and take me for granted and who's only pretending to be interested in who I am and what I think so he can get into my pants.' Zig, deprecatingly, 'That would be me!' Allison: 'Thank you! Let's get out of here.' Elliott pleads, 'Allison, wait! I'll get into your pants.' Allison leaves with the roughnecks. Elliott, left alone, looks at the sunset and, yes, you've guessed it, breaks into a bout of weeping.

'Some of my best friends are men'

Rhiannon Lucy Cosslett is eager to assure us that she and her feminist sisters are not the man-hating crazed maenads of lore. Unlike Lilli Vanessi in *Kiss Me, Kate*, she and her sisters do not sing 'I Hate Men!' at the drop of a hat. From the way she puts it, indeed, it sounds almost as if she's saying that some of her and her sisters' best friends are men! And who are these men whom Ms Cosslett and her fellow feminists live with, work with and socialise with? In her words, 'We have male friends and loved ones who have suffered anxiety, anorexia and gym addiction, have sat with our male friends as they describe their depression, loneliness, problems with alcohol abuse, feelings of worthlessness, or express frustration with their fathers and the model of being a man that were offered to them.' (Cosslett) Crikey. What a bizarre set of male acquaintances you have, Ms Cosslett! One wonders how you manage to be acquainted with so many losers! Don't you know any men who *don't* suffer from anxiety, anorexia, gym addiction (what the hell is *that*?), depression, loneliness, problems with alcohol, feelings of worthlessness, and father-problems? And what lies at the root of the multitudinous problems her male acquaintances suffer from? Why, you've guessed it: repressed emotion, of course! Cosslett seems to adhere to a fluid dynamics theory of emotions. Emotions are like water, which if it doesn't go to one place has to go to another. So all the emotions repressed by her male friends during their lives burst out in aggression and violence, depression or suicide.

Former bad boy Chris Hemmings, now repentant, has written a book entitled *Be a Man*, which is all about toxic masculinity. It sets out to deconstruct the strict gender roles that men have been required to play, roles which, it seems, make them radically unhappy. He doesn't tell Ms Cosslett anything she doesn't already know but since she thinks men are 'socialised to value the words of other men more highly than those of women', his book might ensure that what he has to say about toxic masculinity will get a hearing that it wouldn't get if it came from the pen of a woman. Yes, indeed. I can remember my father taking me aside and saying, 'Son, whenever you read something that seems to make sense, check first to see if it's written by a man or a woman. If by a woman, just disregard.' Standard father-son patriarchal stuff. Ms Cosslett believes that we need to have an urgent conversation about masculinity and men and that those who should lead that conversation are not the sexually frustrated internet hate-preachers but what she calls 'kind, rational men'—by which she seems to have in mind men who suffer from anxiety, anorexia, gym addiction, depression, loneliness, alcohol abuse and feelings of worthlessness. Doesn't she know any *normal* men—men who are neither emotional wrecks nor internet trolls, men with sisters and mothers whom they cherish, wives and daughters whom they love, and female friends and colleagues whom they like and respect?

In what, even by *Guardian* standards, is an exceptionally nauseating piece of cant, Tom Pessah treats us all to a Moscow-show-trial-type confession of his past sins of sexual transgression. (Pessah). He begins by telling us he has never raped anyone. Well, that's good to know, Mr Pessah. Congratulations! I have never raped anyone either, but I haven't felt the need to take to the opinion pages of a national newspaper to broadcast this astounding fact to the world. However, Tom is not perfect. When he was a teenager, he touched some women inappropriately 'by accident' (his inverted commas). What depravity! I tried to paraphrase what some of his grievous sins were but his *ipsissima verba* are priceless and deserve to be read for their spectacular cringe-worthiness. Here's how he tells it. 'Once, when I was about 18, I had a good friend whom I was attracted to. One day she came round and was tired so she went to sleep on a mattress, and asked me to wake her up after half an hour. So I did. She slept on her back. I could have touched her gently on her left-hand shoulder (closer to me) but I deliberately bent over and touched her on her right hand shoulder so that my elbow touched her chest. Of course this could have just been an "accident", but it wasn't.' My God, I can hardly bear to read this effusion, not because what it describes was so awful, but because his telling of it is so unintentionally funny. He goes on to reveal that he dared to tell a classmate that he had been looking at her chest and she later told him how uncomfortable he had made her feel. It's not clear from the telling of this ludicrous story whether it was the looking or the telling that made her feel uncomfortable but, if I had to put money on it, I'd plump for the telling. Weird, man, just weird! Why would you do that, Mr Pessah? But there's more. Tom (I think I may call by his first name someone who has been so revealing of his inner life) consumed (to use his own word) pornography for years, but—and this is the awful part—not just pornography but *sexist* pornography. Too much information, Tom! I'm no expert in this area but could any form of pornography conceivably be *non*-sexist? I'm just asking. So, what has our Tom done by way of atonement for his terrible sins? Well, unfortunately, he tells us this too. Once again, his *ipsissima verba*: 'I try to take up less space. I wait until a woman in the room has spoken before I chime in. I walk in the street in a non-intimidating way—if it's late at night and there's a woman in front of me, I keep my distance or cross to the other side.' When I had stopped laughing at this creepy piece of self-hating exhibitionist flagellation, I began to wish that our Tom had adopted a policy of verbal reticence and had taken up less space, not only around women, but also in the pages of what used to be a respectable national newspaper.

In the film, *Butch Cassidy and The Sundance Kid*, our anti-heroes are chased relentlessly by Pinkerton men. Exhausted and frustrated, they look at their dogged pursuers and ask, 'Who *are* those guys?' That's a question I felt rising to the top of my mind repeatedly when reading about the members of The Huddle, a Toronto-based male bonding group that meets on Tuesday nights at The Local. Once a month, Marvin, Alex, Chris and Cameron get together to talk about their feelings. What kind of things do they say to each other? Marvin opines that male conversations are usually 'very superficial'. 'It's always about sex and money,' he says. One of his fellow bonders agrees, 'Like, "Oh, I got laid last night." It gets boring.' I've never talked about getting laid with anyone, man or woman and I rarely talk about money if by that you mean salary—it's considered impolite where I come from! One commentator online made more or less the same point, remarking, 'If I spoke with any of my male friends about sex or money they'd laugh me out of the building, unless I had a problem with either. Maybe this guy grew up in a bad film.' Another commentator said, 'Where do you work? I've never worked anywhere where men have talked like that at work.'

Chris tells us that 'emotions are energy and they have to move, they have to be released.' Many men never learn 'to release that energy without using force.' Another fluid dynamics theory of the emotions! A moment's reflection and a little knowledge of social history will show that most men release their energy through work or hobbies or sport, not by talking about their feelings. As I mentioned already, most men really dislike talking about their feelings, which doesn't, of course, mean that they don't have them, just that they don't find it helpful to talk about them directly. Switching images from fluid dynamics to structural engineering, Alex is of the opinion that anger is like an iceberg, 'Anger is what you see,' he says, 'but it comes from everything else below the surface—shame, fear, guilt. For most men, it feels safer to get angry than express sadness or vulnerability.' In confessional mode, he reveals that when he feels vulnerable, he cries. 'It looks like sadness on the outside, but it feels powerful.' I'm sure it does, Alex, I'm sure it does—to you! Other topics for discussion in The Huddle: mental health, substance abuse and mistreatment of women. The group, so we are told, consists mainly of straight, unmarried men in their thirties with a common interest in fashion, athletics and wellness trends—the tattoo quotient is high. Straight? Fashion? Tattoos? Unmarried—no surprise there! Who *are* those guys?

Publishers are falling over themselves to publish books that tell us how terrible toxic masculinity is and how men can redeem themselves. A Google search will turn up dozens. In April 2018, the author, Tim Winton gave a speech about his new book, *The Shepherd's Hut*, an excerpt from which was published in the *Guardian*. 'Boys and young men,' he tells us, 'are so routinely expected to betray their better natures, to smother their consciences, to renounce the best of themselves and submit to something low and mean.' (Winton) Crikey! Is that so, Mr Winton? Tell us more. 'As if there's only one way of being a bloke, one valid interpretation of the part, the role, if you like. There's a constant pressure to enlist, to pull on the uniform of misogyny and join the Shithead Army that enforces and polices sexism.' I see. That wasn't my experience as a young man, but let that go.

Mr Winton does make one important point—one out of fifteen or twenty isn't bad I suppose—which is that 'modernity has failed to replace traditional codes with anything explicit, or coherent or benign. We're left with values that are residual, fuzzy, accidental or sniggeringly conspiratorial.' I would rather say that the erosion of traditional codes, an erosion promoted by feminists and their fellow travellers such as Mr Winton, has pretty much left sexual relations in a state of chaos, but let that go too. Winton is unrepentant about the elimination of our traditions. 'There are,' he says, 'lots of reasons for having clear-felled and burnt our own traditions since the 1960s, and some of them are very good reasons. But I'm not sure what we've replaced them with.' Just so, Mr Winton, just so. It's one thing to burn down the house, quite another to find adequate shelter in the ruins.

He tells us that 'toxic masculinity is a burden to men', being very careful to make it clear that it's much less of a burden to them than it is to women. But, trivial as the effects of misogyny may be on men compared to the hideous burdens it places on women, misogyny affects men too, it 'narrows their lives. Distorts them .... Misogyny, like racism, is one of the great engines of intergenerational trauma.' Men, it seems, are bred for mastery, and when the world cannot be mastered, what do men do? 'Too many men are blunt instruments. Otherwise known, I guess, as tools. Because of poor training, they're simply not fit for purpose.' Children are reservoirs of tenderness and empathy but, alas, some of them turn into savages and, wouldn't you know it, 'most of those are boys. They're trained into it.' Charming stuff, Mr Winton, if somewhat sweeping and condescending. How lucky you were to be able to escape this toxicity. However did you manage to do it?

What can we do, Tim? Tell us, please. 'Boys need help.' Yes, Tim, we've got that. 'And, yes, men need fixing—I'm mindful of that.' We've got that too, Tim. Tell us what we can do. Set up extermination camps for these savages? Breed them out of the population? Emasculate them? What? While we're waiting for an answer, let's check out some more of Tim's deathless prose. 'Males,' he tells us, 'arrive in our community on the coattails of an almost endless chain of unexamined privilege. I don't deny that for a second.' You might not deny it Tim, but the rest of us might have some difficulty identifying the links in this chain. Some examples would help. Evidence would be nice. I, and most other men, must have been on vacation the day they were distributing that endless chain of unexamined privilege. 'Patriarchy'—ah yes, here it comes, that great, invisible, all-powerful and quasi-demonic force—'is bondage for boys, too. It disfigures them. Even if they're the last to notice. Even if they profit from it. And their disfigurement diminishes the ultimate prospects of all of us, wherever we are on the gender spectrum. I think we need to admit this.' You go ahead and admit it, Tim. The rest of us men who know precisely where we are on the gender spectrum—not on it at all—will get on with our usual tasks of making a living, providing for our families, and doing our bit too keep society functioning.

How to treat men and boys

In addition to the confessional 'toxic masculinity' genre, there is yet another genre which, as well as tearfully convicting men of toxic masculinity, recommends ways in which these macho monsters might be reconstructed in the image and likeness of the goddess of gentleness and general niceness. One volume in this mini-avalanche of volumes is J. J. Bola's *Mask Off*, in which he tells us that we need to junk the whole idea of maleness as we've known and loved it to date, and replace it with 'a masculinity that sees the necessity of the equality of genders for it to not only survive, but to thrive.' In the course of what the *Guardian* reviewer describes as 'an antidote to Jordan Peterson', Mr Bola introduces his intended audience to such entrancing ideas as 'slut-shaming, male privilege, emotional labour, victim-blaming and intersectionality.' (Barekat) In a variant of what Disraeli is reputed to have written to the senders of unsolicited manuscripts, I recommend that we should lose no time in reading *Mask Off*, and that we should adopt a similar time-saving approach to the many published effusions of the same type.

But it's not only popular non-fiction publishing that engages in the subtle art of man bashing. Now the American Psychological Association has got in on the act. In August 2018, the APA released a document containing clinical guidance for treating men and boys. (see APA) The document links traditional masculinity—comprising anti-femininity, achievement, eschewal of the appearance of weakness, and adventure and risk—to sexism, homophobia, suicide and violence. According to the APA, traditional masculine norms tend to harm the health of men and boys. Conspicuous among these norms is the pressure (as the APA sees it) to suppress their emotions. Boys, it seems, are not meant to cry, and this norm leads to increased negative risk-taking and inappropriate aggression. The APA document is fully on board with the current feminist and social justice dogmas regarding male privilege, power and sexism. (APA, 9 ff.) Gender (of course 'gender'—298 mentions) is socially constructed and, of course, is non-binary. Sex is—you know what's coming—assigned at birth, not, as you might naïvely have thought, identified by taking a look. ('Is it a boy or a girl?' 'Whichever one you'd like, dear.') The dominant idea of masculinity was, according to the APA, historically predicated on the exclusion of men who were 'not White, heterosexual, cisgender, able-bodied, and privileged.' (APA, 6)

It seems that the only acceptable form of masculinity for the APA is femininity. To invert the sentiment of Professor Higgins's song in *My Fair Lady*, the APA appears to be asking us 'Why can't a man, be more like a woman?' Toby Young tells us why:

The 'unhealthy' male characteristics the APA believes are created by 'gender stereotypes', such as a reluctance to spend hours talking about your feelings, are not foisted on men by white, heteronormative society. Rather, they're rooted in our biological nature. Contrary to the postmodernist dogma that the differences between men and women are 'socially constructed', men exhibit the same basic qualities regardless of what sort of society they're brought up in. The psychological drives experts attribute to 'Western culture', such as territorial aggression, date back to the emergence of homo sapiens from the primeval forest. Indeed, many masculine traits are cross-species, too. When baby monkeys are given the option of playing with toys, the males choose trucks and the females pick dolls. The traditional male characteristics these pseudoscientists are objecting to are part of our ineradicable essence. What does appear to be genuinely psychologically harmful is this unending war on masculinity. The effect of telling men that their desire to protect and provide is 'sexist', as well as persuading women they're better off without us, has been to unleash an epidemic of family breakdown. A whopping 25 per cent of American children are being raised by single mothers. No doubt the APA thinks boys who grow up without fathers are better off. After all, they've been spared exposure to noxious male role models. But the grim reality is they're more likely to drop out of school, become alcohol and drug addicts and end up in the criminal justice system. (Young)

The APA document sees itself as highlighting only the destructive aspects of what it is to be male; critics on the other hand, have tended to view it as smugly patronising and as pathologising maleness itself. The Guidelines will expire as APA policy after ten years. Some unkind people might think that it was a pity that they weren't stillborn and would be happy to see them die an unnatural death a long way short of ten years.

It's bad enough to have to endure the smug condescension of the APA, but when a commercial firm whose clients are almost exclusively male gets in on the 'toxic masculinity' act, things have come to a pretty pass. An advertisement from Gillette (owned by Proctor & Gamble) could have taken the pronouncements of the APA as its guideline. Riffing on their well-known promotional line 'The Best a Man Can Get', Gillette asks, 'Is this the best a man can get?' The advertisement, a masterpiece of caricature and misandric prejudice, has to be seen to be believed—a montage of news reports on the #MeToo movement, sexual harassment, images of boys fighting, and so on. (see Gillette). Gillette are in the business of selling shaving products, or at least they were. I'm not sure what they're selling now, but whatever it is, I'm not buying it.

Noah Berlatsky is one commentator who is taken aback that not everyone is pleased that the APA and Gillette are 'trying to understand and address the difficulties which men in particular face, and that corporations like P&G, which owns Gillette, are doing the same.' (see Berlatsky) Those who are not pleased, Mr Berlatsky, are not pleased because they see clearly that it is a deeply patronising, radical-feminist-inspired, misandrist attack on men. Berlatsky thinks the critics of the Gillette advertisement 'all talk about the glory of all men embracing manliness, and being strong, stoic, fearless, and competitive. They suggest that this is biological, that men just are this way.' And then he gives us what he obviously regards as a zinger. 'But what if you're not that way? What if you're a boy who would rather play with dolls than guns? What if you're queer or trans?

What if, as a man, you're sometimes depressed, or scared, as all human beings are? Superman and James Bond are fictions. Real human men are more vulnerable and more various. Conservatives want to put all men in a single, small box. The APA guidelines suggest we let them out—for the good of men, of women, and of people of every gender.' (Berlatsky)

To find the Gillette advertisement deeply offensive is not to defend sexual harassment and violence. It is to reject the simple-minded (and offensive) contention that such things are an intrinsic part of what it is to be a man. Those who are on board the toxic masculinity train might agree, saying that what they are attacking isn't masculinity *per se* but masculinity merely in its toxic variety, but the scope of the attack on toxic masculinity is so wide that it catches pretty much *any* form of masculinity in its nets. (see Sigillito) Of course, the denigration of men as emotional incompetents is just one way in which feminists persist in crude forms of stereotyping. Not only are men emotionally retarded, but men, white men at least, are also typically racist. Toxic masculinity is supposedly manifested in men's barely repressed propensity to use violence at the drop of a hat, especially towards women and vulnerable groups. If you don't accept the toxic idea of toxic masculinity then, if you're a man, you'll be charged with being in denial or, if you're a woman, with internalising misogyny. Men must accept the toxicity of their sex and pre-emptively regulate themselves, or face denigration.

Any disinterested account of social toxicity, however, will show that it is not a phenomenon confined exclusively to men. One woman writes, 'the most toxic people I've met in my life socially and professionally (education and public services) have been predominantly women, feminazis and just plain bitches. Yes, there's been a few men too, but greatly outnumbered by women. Men's toxicity tends to be a kind of cluelessness mostly. The women's is calculated and targeted.' Another woman, agreeing with her, writes, 'what you say reflects my experience too—with perhaps one exception, the really deranged, emotionally damaging and out of control individuals that I have had to deal with professionally have been women. In fact, if given a blind choice today between a male and female manager, I'd take my chances with the male ... that's what it boils down to.' Yet another woman writes, 'I couldn't agree more. All the women bosses I've had have had "issues" or been very tricky and manipulative. The men have been refreshingly straightforward. Furthermore, I actually like men as they are. I don't want them to be feminised. I think society will really suffer if we lose vital male qualities.'

Not all women think this way, of course. Some women, like Howard Beale in the film *Network*, are as mad as hell, and they're not going to take it anymore.

One such non-taker is Charlotte Riley, a lecturer in British History at the University of Southampton, who published an intriguing article entitled, 'How to play Patriarchy Chicken: why I refuse to move out of the way for men' in *NewStatesmanAmerica*. (Riley 2019) Patriarchy Chicken is a simple game: all you have to do is be a woman and refuse to move out of the way for men. In the course of her bizarre piece, Dr Riley writes, apparently with a straight face, 'The point is that men have been socialised, for their entire lives, to take up space. Men who would never express these thoughts out loud have nevertheless been brought up to believe that their right to occupy space takes precedence over anyone else's right to be there. They spread their legs on tubes and trains, they bellow across coffee shops and guffaw in pubs, and they never, ever give way.'

On the contrary, Dr Riley, if I might be so bold as to contradict you, respectfully, of course, men have a deep-rooted socially reinforced inhibition against causing harm to women, and are socialised to be as unthreatening as possible to them—not to walk directly behind them at night, or even during the day if that could be perceived as a kind of stalking; in a lift, to push their floor buttons first, not out of some sense of superior entitlement or masculine assertiveness, but just in case she's getting off on the same floor and you don't want to give the impression you're stalking her; to step to the outside of the pavement to allow women to walk on the inside, to walk up a narrow stairs after a woman, but before her on the way down; apart from a formalised 'good morning' or when, *in extremis*, lost and looking for directions, not to start a conversation with a strange woman; and—wait for it—if there's a head-on collision coming on the street or a Tube platform *to give way*. This often leads to a pedestrian *paso doble* as both parties shift to one side and then to the other side until the seeming impasse is finally resolved, usually not with fisticuffs, but with a smile. In contrast to those brutish men who have been socialised to take up space, Dr Riley tells us that 'Women have not been socialised to take up space. Women have been socialised to give way, to alleviate, to conciliate, and to step to the side.' I see. Try getting past a woman in a supermarket aisle when her shopping trolley completely blocks your passage.

Leg spreading? Well, perhaps, if nobody's occupying the space next to you— what's the problem there? As a matter of fact, Dr Riley, most men are social-ised to give up their seats to women on public transport. This particular bit of training can produce some painful frisson for men in the early 21st century. Do you offer your seat, and risk being attacked as patriarchically patronising; or do you stay seated, while around you women stand and you risk being taken for a jerk instead of the truly woke dude that you really are? It's lose-lose. This has happened to me on more than one occasion. What's next from the feminist hyperbole-space? Could it possibly be something like: 'Men giving way to women is just another manifestation of patriarchy! Men have been socialised to assume that the public space is their possession and at their disposal, and this attitude is expressed when they step aside to let a woman pass. This so-called gentlemanly act in reality serves to marginalise women by implicitly placing them as "the other", playing the role of propertyless trespassers on male territory, able to go about their business only by the tacit permission of men.' Ah yes, the old, old game of heads you win, tails I lose.

Bellowing across coffee shops? What? If that happens, it's presumably because of the deafening racket that's been caused by the 95% female occupation of such shops, so perhaps it's the only way to make yourself heard if you're a man. Just joking! Guffawing in pubs? Crikey! Now there's a cardinal sin if ever there was one! Women, of course, never shriek or scream in public. By the way, why does Dr Riley think that *anyone* has the obligation to give way to *her*? Over a hundred years ago, E. Temple Thurston wrote, 'The man who runs into you on the pavement is going in his direction as well as you in yours, and it is a nice point to decide whether you ran into him or he into you.' (Thurston, 31)

Women, it seems, are emotionally strong and independent and, if you watch some recent movies, they're also physically fierce. So fierce, in fact, that they can kick men's arses, quite a few of them it seems, in rapid succession. No woman needs to be rescued by a man; instead, if there's any rescuing to be done, our formerly fragile females will do some rescuing themselves! By all means be fierce, if that's your natural bent. But fierceness isn't a moral virtue that one can acquire through repeated actions. It's an innate psychological characteristic, one that is associated more with men in the aggregate than with women in the aggregate. Our feminist social engineers push women to manifest the overwhelmingly masculine characteristic of fierceness while, at the same time, deprecating men's acting in accordance with that precise characteristic which, for our friendly feminists, is an aspect of masculinity at its most toxic.

Given that women are now strong and independent, it may seem odd that in some universities (you know who I mean, University of Melbourne!) men are being urged to speak more like women so that women won't be interrupted when they speak, and will feel confident about raising their voices in classroom discussions. 'More like women'? There's a special way that women speak? Here's a crazy idea—why don't women speak more like men! Here's an even crazier idea. Why don't we let both men and women speak as they wish, and trust women—our strong, independent, fierce women—to look after themselves.

But not every feminist is willing, like Rhiannon Lucy Cosslett, to admit that some of her best friends are men. Some, refreshingly, tell it like it is. Suzanna Danuta Walter, professor of sociology and, surprise, surprise, director of the Women's, Gender, and Sexuality Studies Program at Northeastern University, thinks that it is logical to hate men. (Walter; see also Friedersdorf) She thinks that women experience sexual violence pretty much everywhere in the world— this violence includes terrorism and mass gun violence. Moreover—wait for it, here it comes—women are underrepresented (there's that word again!) in high paying jobs, in local and federal government, in business and in educational leadership, and so on and so on, and on and on. In the USA, which she describes as the 'land of legislatively legitimated toxic masculinity', what could possibly be wrong with hating men? Nothing, according to Professor Walter. To atone for their multiple systemic abuses of women and to avoid being hated by such as Walter, men must vote for feminist women, decline to stand for election to public office, and step away from power. Somehow, despite the omnipresence of male domination and the machinations of the repressive patriarchy, Professor Walter managed to get her anti-men rant published not in the *West Virginia Pig Breeder's Gazette* but in the *Washington Post*! I suppose the all-powerful patriarchy must have taken their collective eyes off the ball for a moment and allowed this piece of perverse invective to slip under their repressive radar. Her piece is not much above the level of the song 'I Hate Men' from *Kiss Me, Kate*, which has the immortal lines, 'I hate men! I can't abide them, even now and then! ... They should be kept like piggies in a pen!' But that song was meant to be humorous. Professor Walters' piece is humorous too, but unintentionally so.

When I read the effusions of such as Professor Walter, I am overcome with guilt. I'm such a terrible person. I'm white (that's bad), I'm old (that's almost as bad), I'm conservative (that's almost criminal), I'm Catholic (that's just ridiculous), I'm heterosexual (that means I'm a possible rapist), and I'm a libertarian (which means that I am a staunch believer in, among other things, free speech which, as we all know, is simply a mask for oppression and a convoluted legitimation of 'punching down' on those less able to defend themselves). But, worst of all, I'm a man. There! I've said it! I've got it off my chest. Confession, they say, is good for the soul. How can I live with myself after reading the charge sheet that Professor Walter has so convincingly assembled?

A sign of the *Times*

Professor Walter is not alone in having the views she has. Sarah Jeong of the *New York Times* seems to have taken Professor Walter's correspondence course. If someone wrote: 'white men are [bullsh**]', '#cancelwhitepeople', 'oh man it's kind of sick how much joy i (*sic*) get out of being cruel to old white men'; 'f__ white women lol'; 'National/ Pretty goddam white/ Radio,'" and 'are white people genetically predisposed to burn faster in the sun, thus logically being only fit to live underground like groveling (*sic*) goblins', would you consider that person a racist? If you are a normal human being I suspect you would, but if you were the *New York Times*, who hired Sarah Jeong, the author of the pieces of anti-white short-form literature I just cited, you wouldn't. In a statement in 2018, they wrote, 'We hired Sarah Jeong because of the exceptional work she has done covering the internet and technology at a range of respected publications. Being a young Asian woman journalist has made her a subject of frequent online harassment. For a period of time she responded to that harassment by imitating the rhetoric of her harassers. She sees now that this approach only served to feed the vitriol that we too often see on social media. She regrets it, and *The Times* does not condone it.' They continued: 'We had candid conversations with Sarah as part of our thorough vetting process, which included a review of her social media history. She understands that this type of rhetoric is not acceptable at *The Times* and we are confident that she will be an important voice for the editorial board moving forward.' (New York Times) And Jeong herself wrote, 'I engaged in what I thought of at the time of counter-trolling. While it was intended as satire, I deeply regret that I mimicked the language of my harassers. These comments were not aimed at a general audience, because general audiences do not engage in harassment campaigns. I can understand how hurtful these posts are out of context, and would not do it again.' Ms Jeong, now apparently regretting the language she used in those tweets, claims that they were intended to be satirical or, as one of her supporters put it, a way of using humour 'to get through the white supremacist bullshit this society shovels on WOC [women of color].' Maybe so, Ms Jeong, maybe so, but I wonder just how much credence the 'I was being satirical' defence would get if the shoe were on the other foot.

Appearances to the contrary notwithstanding, then, what Ms Jeong got up to in her tweets was only satire and counter-trolling, merely corroborative detail, as it were, intended to lend artistic verisimilitude to an otherwise bald and unconvincing narrative. And it was those bad white people who are really to blame for it all since it was *their* rhetoric that she was imitating. Bad, bad, white people, forcing that poor, defenceless Asian female to behave in this way! I think Phyllis Chesler has captured this self-deceptive disingenuousness well when she wrote (in another context), 'most women ... have learned how to pretend, even to themselves, that they have not been aggressive, especially when they have been; or that they didn't really mean it and, therefore, it doesn't count, or that no serious harm resulted from what they didn't "really" do.' (Chesler, 126; see also MacDonald)

The substance, if not the precise forms of expression, of what Ms Jeong wrote is more or less standard issue at the elite academic establishments she has attended: the University of California at Berkeley and Harvard Law School. The key tenets of progressive thinking she will have been exposed to on her academic travels would include: white people are *the* problem, especially if they are also men and old; due process is merely a poor substitute for justice, not a procedural bulwark against the conviction of the innocent; racism and bias are everywhere; truth is merely a cloak for the exercise of power by the dominant group in society; rape culture is endemic in the USA, especially on US campuses. (but see Gittos) On this last point, witness Jeong's defence of the *Rolling Stone* story of fraternity rape on the University Campus in a (now deleted) blog post that was posted *after* the story had been retracted by *Rolling Stone*! The fact-checking that eventually resulted in the discrediting of the *Rolling Stone* story is, it seems, simply more evidence of the patriarchy's attempt to deny the existence of rape culture. Discrepancies in dates and times don't matter when we all know that rape is all around us. The deleted blog has been recovered and can be viewed online. Here is an excerpt from that piece:

> I believe Jackie. It's a different kind of believe from believing that her story is a historical, factual account. But she's not lying. Her story is one she's pieced together through a haze of agony, even as every neuron in her brain worked to forget what had happened .... Rape is not some rarefied, exotic crime. It's all around us. Our rapists are acquaintances, family members, boyfriends, girlfriends, partners, spouses, trusted friends .... Of course no one should even be looking at the details. No one should be assessing Jackie's truthfulness .... In law school, after all, we learned that due process is what we get in lieu of justice. What's due process besides a series of rules that are meant to keep things as predictable as fucking possible? .... Something terrible happened to Jackie. I don't know what it was. Her suitemate doesn't know what it was. I don't even know if it's clear to Jackie. But something happened. (see Sailer)

Is comment on this bizarre free-association rhapsodic effusion really necessary? To see why Ms Jeong thinks (to use that term loosely) in this way, here are some examples of the kind of material you can find in ostensibly respectable academic journals, material that students like Ms Jeong are routinely exposed to on liberal university campuses, which is to say, *most* university campuses.

Published in *Cultural Studies of Science Education*, the abstract for the paper 'Towards a truer multicultural science education: how whiteness impacts science education' reads, 'The hope for multicultural, culturally competent, and diverse perspectives in science education falls short if theoretical considerations of whiteness are not entertained. Since whiteness is characterized as a hegemonic racial dominance that has become so natural it is almost invisible, this paper identifies how whiteness operates in science education such that it falls short of its goal for cultural diversity.' (Le & Matias) Good stuff, I think you will agree, but there's more. An article written by Carrie Mott and Daniel Cockayne entitled, 'Citation matters: mobilizing the politics of citation toward a practice of "conscientious engagement", published in a journal called *Gender, Place & Culture* (A Journal of Feminist Geography) holds that 'An increasing amount of scholarship in critical, feminist, and anti-racist geographies has recently focused self-reflexively on the topics of exclusion and discrimination within the discipline itself. In this article we contribute to this literature by considering citation as a problematic technology that contributes to the reproduction of the white heteromasculinity of geographical thought and scholarship, despite advances toward more inclusivity in the discipline in recent decades.' Hetero-masculinity, eh! That sounds pretty bad! Heteromasculinity apparently ignores the contributions of people of colour and women and the poor, so as to benefit those who are—here comes the customary litany—'white, male, able-bodied, economically privileged, heterosexual and cisgendered.' So there! We've got to stop citing those heteronormative males—it only encourages them! Ignore, of course, whether they have produced anything worth citing—that's not the issue.

You can see, then, from all this that there is nothing singular about Jeong's producing tweets that, on the face of it, appear to be racist and sexist and ageist, and blogs that are straight out of the twilight zone. She is the end product of an educational and social establishment that justifies and perpetuates acceptable forms of racism, sexism and ageism; racism, as long as it is racism against whites, sexism, as long as it is sexism against males, and ageism, as long is it is ageism directed against old white males. Truly, Jeong is a sign of the *Times*.

No toxic masculinity, please, we're opera singers

Carmen must be one of the most instantly recognisable of all operas. In a new makeover at Florence's Opera House in January 2018, it became somewhat less recognisable. Violence against women is a big no-no in our contemporary world, so much so that even its portrayal on stage has become problematic. No longer will we see José stab the errant Carmen—instead, Carmen, in a turn-about-is-fair-play move, gets to shoot José with his own pistol! Old fuddy-duddy opera-lovers might object that this isn't just a creative interpretation of the old *Carmen* that we all know and love but a hermeneutical and directorial step too far. But who cares what such reactionaries think? Paolo Klun, speaking for the

Opera House, said that they thought it important that 'the theatre should not be a conservative place of musical culture, it should not be a museum. It's a place where debate can be initiated. *Carmen* was written 150 years ago in a very different cultural context. Times change.' (see Squires) Because of what they see as the increasing number of horrific instances of domestic violence, the directors of the new, improved and sanitised *Carmen* said that they weren't comfortable with audiences applauding the final scene in which Carmen, in the traditional version of the opera, meets her doom.

May I make three small points? First, if you, the directors, felt that strongly about these matters, *why did you put Carmen on in the first place*? Second, don't you realise that a dramatic depiction of any given event—murder, rape, strangulation, adultery—doesn't imply the approval of such things in the real world, either by the writer of the libretto, or the composer of the music, or by the audiences that go to see the resultant operas. And third—and I feel a bit silly having to say this—when the audience applauds at the end of a performance of *Carmen*, they're not endorsing femicide but showing their appreciation of the composer, the singers and the orchestra.

The move to emasculate *Carmen* seems to have had its origin in the comments of Cristiano Chiarot, the head of the Teatro del Maggio Musical Fiorentino. At a time when our society is having to confront the murder of women,' he said, 'how can we dare to applaud the killing of a woman?' (Squires) Once again, we are not applauding the killing of a woman. No women were ever harmed in the presentation of *Carmen* except by having to get up close and personal with bad tenors. What we applaud when we do applaud is a dramatic representation set to music of a love affair gone wrong. It is unlikely that there are many murder sympathisers in your audience. One might think that you've been in the theatrical business so long that, like a boxer who has taken one blow too many to the head, you can't tell the difference between acting and reality. If the director and producer really thought that what the audience is applauding in the traditional version of the opera was the killing of a woman by a man, did they, in the new politically-sensitive version with the victims reversed, think the audience would be applauding the killing of a man by a woman? If not, why not?

The director of this version of *Carmen*, Leo Muscato, was initially opposed to the idea of mangling the ending for the very good reason that, as he put it himself, 'The death of Carmen is the engine that drives the opera.' Well said, Signor Muscato, I couldn't have put it better myself. But then, he saw the light. 'The theme of death in the opera has a strong masculine element—the woman must sacrifice herself in order to save her freedom. It is a point of view that today makes no sense.' Do we only stage operas or plays that 'make sense' today? Is it not possible for an audience to understand the historical situatedness of an opera set in earlier times? Ah Leo, you had it right the first time. Here's an idea, Mssrs Klun, Chiarot and Muscato. Commission a libretto that is ultra-modern, up-to-date, something solidly in tune with the new, normative environment. Get someone to write a new opera based on this libretto, all about violence against women and how wrong it is and how terrible men are and see how many people turn up to listen to it. No one is forcing you to stage *Carmen*. If *Carmen* contains an essential but problematic depiction of heteromasculinity, why put it on? Why not put on another opera? The answer to that question is that *Carmen* brings in audiences and revenue, whereas a right-on politically correct contemporary opera is unlikely to have many takers.

In a similar vein to the bowdlerisers of *Carmen*, Michael Fabiano, who starred as the Duke of Mantua in the Royal Opera House's 2018 production of *Rigoletto*, recounted how he had, as he put it, resisted demands to perform sexually violent scenes on stage because he believed that the treatment of women in operatic productions should better reflect the modern world. Precisely! Politically correct realistic treatment of women is what we desperately need in that most irrational of entertainments in which, when a man gets stabbed in the back, he sings and sings and sings instead of bleeding to death quietly like a normal human being. Reasonableness, that's what opera is all about! Let's not have any representation of murder on stage or screen. After all, we don't want to appear to condone murder or suggest that it's acceptable in today's enlightened and sensitive society. No violent sex either, or theft or, indeed, anything of that kind. Down with this sort of thing! Instead, let's have just generalised niceness. Not much drama in that, of course, but why should that be a problem? Mr Fabiano said that he had been asked to 'do things with women on stage that were... strong' (strong?) but that he had asked to develop his character instead.' (Furness) What kind of things: real violence or merely simulated violence, such as, you know, acting? Of course if his principles were all that sacred to him, he could just have declined the role but that's too obvious a solution to his ethical dilemma. Once again, I feel I need to point out the bleedin' obvious. Acting (or singing in an opera) is all about make-believe. It's not real. Robert Mitchum remarked that acting 'is not a tough job. You read a script. If you like the part and the money is OK, you do it. Then you remember your lines. You show up on time. You do what the director tells you to do. When you finish, you rest and then go on to the next part. That's it.'

So, what can we expect in the future? A production of *Otello* in which Otello and Desdemona go to a marriage counsellor, Otello resolves his jealously and anger-management issues and they go off on a Mediterranean cruise for a second honeymoon, or perhaps even better, an *Otello* in which Desdemona smothers Otello and not, as is customary, *vice versa*? What about a *Tosca* in which she rescues Mario from the firing squad and Scarpia ends up jumping out the window of the castle? Or a *Madama Butterfly* in which Butterfly goes off on an extended junket with the girls, leaving Pinkerton holding the baby? The only limitations on artistic politically correct bowdlerisation are the paucity of our imaginations and the inexhaustibility of our stupidity.

But back to Michael Fabiano who seems to be a sensitive and caring chap. He wanted to make the Duke of Mantua dark but questioning, as it were, a man with doubts. There is, according to him, 'a huge hole inside him' but 'he's not really an evil guy.' (Furness) Yeah, the poor bastard. The Duke only does the awful things he does because he had a tough upbringing. Fabiano wondered if the Duke really wanted to be this person at the top of the feudal system, watching men assaulting women all the time. If things had only been a little different, I suppose he could have been a birdwatcher of a different kind, providing free corsets for the under-fives (*Blackadder*) and turkeys for all at Christmas (*A Christmas Carol*).

A spokesman for the Royal Opera House said, presumably with a straight face, that the depiction of sexual violence against women didn't imply its endorsement. My goodness, how lucky were we that he said that, otherwise we might have had a rash of copycat sexual assaults against women all over London, perpetrated by deranged opera-goers, and when the assailants were charged their defence would be, 'Well guv, so 'elp me, I seen it done on styge in Covent Gaaaden so I fought i's gottabe orl korrect!' It is interesting that the ROH spokesman didn't feel obliged to say that the depiction of violence against men didn't imply *its* endorsement because, presumably, they're only men and so don't count or—and I know this is a really wild surmise—because people aren't stupid and can tell the difference between fiction and fact, without the need to be enlightened and lectured by po-faced opera singers, directors and theatrical spokesmen.

#MeToo

'Keep your hands to yourself'
might almost be put at the head of the
first chapter of every book on etiquette
—Emily Post

I have never had any great esteem for the generality of the fair sex,
and my only consolation for being of that gender
has been the assurance it gave me of
never being married to anyone amongst them
—Lady Mary Worley Montague

You would have to have been marooned on a desert island since before 2017 not to be aware of the Harvey Weinstein imbroglio. In October of that year, the *New York Times* published a story alleging decades of sexual harassment by the Hollywood producer Harvey Weinstein. Weinstein denied that he had sexually harassed anyone, and threats were made to sue the *New York Times*. The Weinstein Company says it took the allegations seriously and it would seem that they did, since they eventually sacked Mr Weinstein. More allegations of sexual misconduct on Mr Weinstein's part emerged in the months following, including allegations of rape by Rose McGowan, Lysette Anthony, Mimi Haleyi, Dominique Huett, Natassia Malthe, Annabella Sciorra and Paz del la Huerta. The Producers Guild of America banned Weinstein for life. Eventually, Weinstein was charged with rape and indicted in May 2018. The story continues to unfold. (see BBC 2019a for a Weinstein timeline.) As some of these matters are *sub judice* at the time of writing, nothing I say here is to be taken as characterising Mr Weinstein's actions as criminal.

One of the odd things about the Weinstein revelations is just how many people quickly jumped on the bandwagon. One wonders where these people were before 2017. Taki captures the point nicely, 'It's funny,' he says, 'how feelings of anxiety and degradation suddenly appear when these kinds of revelations hit the papers. What I'd like to know is why it's taken some 20 years, and others ten years, to come out with it.' (Taki) Now that it's fashionable to diss Harvey Weinstein, it's conveniently forgotten that, as well as being a stern liberal critic of various non-liberal 'isms', Weinstein was a big supporter of liberal politicians, among them Barack Obama and Hillary Clinton, and a spectacular fundraiser for progressive (so-called) causes, including Mothers Opposing Bush.

Harvey Tell-Tales

A thought that must have must have occurred to those reading the stories of Weinstein and his sexual propositions is why the objects of these propositions didn't just tell him to 'F@£$ off'! So, for example, the actress Ashley Judd relates that Weinstein invited her to a hotel for a business meeting. As she tells the story, he had her sent up to his room where, dressed in his bathrobe, he asked if he could give her a massage or, alternatively, if she could watch him shower. (Hayden) Now, there are a number of peculiar aspects to this story. First, why would a business meeting take place in a hotel bedroom? Don't these people have offices for business? Second, saying that Weinstein had her sent up to his room makes it appear as if Judd were some offering from room service, instead of a human being with a will which she could exercise to say something like, 'Thank Mr Weinstein for his invitation, but I'll wait here in the lobby until he's ready to come down.' Her thought on receiving the admittedly bizarre massage-or-shower invitations from Mr Weinstein was, 'How do I get out of the room as fast as possible without alienating Harvey Weinstein?' Why should she care about alienating him? Would she care about alienating a potential murderer? If it had been a regular Joe Soap who'd propositioned Ms Judd, I very much doubt if she would have worried about alienating him. The difference between Joe Soap and Harvey Weinstein, of course, is that Harvey Weinstein had jobs to offer and favours to grant. In 2019, a US District Court in Los Angeles dismissed Judd's sexual harassment suit against Weinstein. (Barnes 2019) Other women too claim that they were similarly propositioned by Mr Weinstein. One was told that if she went along with Weinstein's sexual advances, he would give her career a boost. What prevented these independent and empowered women saying 'Fx£& off, Harvey' or 'Get a grip, Harvey' or, if they were very polite, 'Thanks, Mr Weinstein, but no thanks. Perhaps we can continue our discussion at your office at some mutually convenient time.'

It seems that Harvey's hotel-room proposals were well known in Hollywood circles. The casting couch, of which Harvey's alleged propositions would appear to be latter-day variations, is a cliché of Hollywood. Why, then, if invited to a meeting, at his hotel, couldn't the apparently helpless young ladies bring their agents with them? This wasn't the 1940s or even the 1960s. By the 1980s and 1990s, sexual harassment claims had already become common. Such claims put huge power into women's hands. Weinstein could have been brought down at any time by the making of such allegations. Why did it take until 2017 for this to happen? Oh, but the propositionees were worried about their careers! *They had no choice*! So, they accepted his behaviour in return for favours? Did they get those favours? Yes? Well, they made a deal, in which case they're not victims, just people with very strange and embarrassing stories to tell their grand-children, if they can bring themselves to do so. Terry Gilliam attracted the ire of the #MeTooers after he remarked that #MeToo was creating a world of victims, suggesting that many of the women who met up with Harvey Weinstein knew exactly what they were doing.

Léa Seydoux does a little Weining of her own. (Seydoux 2017). She tells us that when she met Weinstein he was charming, funny and smart—but very domineering. 'He wanted to meet me for drinks,' she writes, 'and insisted we had to make an appointment that very night. This was never going to be about work. He had other intentions—I could see that very clearly.' What great percep-tion you have, Ms Seydoux! What intuition! Having seen so clearly through Weinstein's evil intentions that, one supposes, was the end of that. Goodbye Harvey! But no! Despite knowing in advance that any appointment she made with Weinstein was not going to be about work, she still agreed to meet him! One wonders why? The plot thickens. 'We met in the lobby of his hotel,' she tells us. 'His assistant, a young woman, was there. All throughout the evening, he flirted and stared at me as if I was a piece of meat.' This is very interesting! I've never flirted with or stared at a piece of meat, so I'd like more information on how (and, not least, *why*) this is done but, alas, on this issue Ms Seydoux is modestly reticent and such information is not forthcoming.

But back to our story. 'He acted as if he were considering me for a role. But I knew that was bullshit. I knew it, because I could see it in his eyes. He had a lecherous look. He was using his power to get sex.' Yet another amazing demonstration of intuition on Ms Seydoux's part—she could see it in his eyes. Truly wonderful! So, at *that* stage, she must have parted company with Weinstein forever. But again, no! 'He invited me to come to his hotel room for a drink,' she tells us. 'We went up together. It was hard to say no because he's so powerful.' Powerful? What, did Weinstein pick her up bodily and carry her, Tarzan-style, back to his hotel bedroom lair, or did she, as I suspect, manage to get there under her own steam, using her own legs? The saga continues. 'Soon, his assistant left and it was just the two of us.' So *now*, Ms Seydoux must surely have acted on her amazing intuitions and left the room with the assistant. But again, no! She stayed. 'We were talking on the sofa when he suddenly jumped on me and tried to kiss me,' she says. 'I had to defend myself. He's big and fat, so I had to be forceful to resist him. I left his room, thoroughly disgusted. I wasn't afraid of him, though. Because I knew what kind of man he was all along.' At this stage, one begins to wonder what the point is of having the amazing powers of intuition that Ms Seydoux appears to have if one never acts in accordance with the warnings they deliver. She knew that a meeting with Mr Weinstein would not be about work, but she agreed to meet with him anyway. *Why?* She went back to his hotel bedroom with him. *Why?* She stayed on with him alone when his assistant left. *Why?*

After the trauma Ms Seydoux would have us believe she went through at the hands of Mr Weinstein, that, surely, must have been the end of any possible relationship between them. Incredible as it may seem, that appears not to be the case! Since that night, she tells us, she's seen him on many occasions, including one where she went with him to a restaurant! Why did she go with him to a restaurant? Did she do so willingly or was her attendance compelled at the point of a gun, or was Mr Weinstein once again 'so powerful' that she was unable to resist? Was this a case of Weining and dining? At the restaurant—I know this kind of behaviour is hard to credit from a Hollywood mogul—Ms Seydoux tells us that 'when he couldn't get a table he got angry and said: "Do you know who I am? I am Harvey Weinstein." That's the kind of man he is.' Has Ms Seydoux had any other bad experiences with our friend Harvey? Well, yes. He has said misogynistic things to her over the years that shocked her, such as that she'd be better if she lost weight. Can you imagine that? A Hollywood producer suggesting that an actress—excuse me—an ac*tor* lose weight. Outrageous!

Acting it would seem on the old street-fighting principle, 'Never kick a man unless he's down,' Kate Winslet informed readers of the *Los Angeles Times* that her failure to thank Harvey Weinstein when she won her best actress Oscar in 2009 was 'absolutely deliberate', even though it was Weinstein's company that financed and distributed the film. (see Whipp 2017) She said that whenever she would bump into Weinstein, 'he'd grab my arm and say, "Don't forget who gave you your first movie". Like I owe him everything.' When it came to the movie *The Reader*, he would say to her, 'I'm gonna get you that Oscar nomination, I'm gonna get you a win, I'm gonna win for you.' I think we'd have to concede that Harvey may have been somewhat boorish in constantly reminding the winsome Winslet that he had kick-started her career. Crass behaviour indeed, but hardly criminal. He promised to get her an Oscar nomination, which, it seems, he did! And that's bad? Winslet remarks that Weinstein was 'bullying and nasty. Going on a business level, he was always very, very hard to deal with—he was rude.'

Goodness gracious me! He was rude and hard to deal with. Is that it, Kate? Is that the full rap sheet?

Despite the oddly passive behaviour of these strong and independent women, perhaps the #MeToo movement is not without some point. Jenny McCartney writes, 'Over the past 20 years, we've seen the emergence of a nasty, reductive sexism in the mid-1990s in lads' mags, under the flimsy guise of irony; the rise of sex trafficking and tourism; the advent of 'porn chic'; the popularisation of plastic surgery; the prime-time Channel 4 "rape jokes" of Jimmy Carr and others; the regular exposure of boys and young men to hardcore internet pornography, with powerful, crass effects on their expectations of how women should behave in bed; and the rapid rise of the selfie and the dating app.' (McCartney)

Whoa, Ms McCartney! Hang on just a second. Sex trafficking is illegal, as it should be, involving, as it does, kidnapping and false imprisonment which, the last time I checked, were criminal activities. I'm not a fan of the selfie, and dating apps are above my pay grade, but it's difficult to see what is intrinsically wrong with either. I cannot recall reading reports of women being herded into plastic surgery clinics at the point of a gun, but perhaps I didn't buy the *Guardian* that day. You say that today's twenty-something women feel panicked and disrespected by the social climate in which they grew up, so much so that they 'find it virtually impossible to refuse a man in the moment.' In discussing a short story and the infamous experiences of Grace with Aziz Ansari, [more on this below] you say that they described young women going along sexually with things they didn't want. 'That semi-detached acquiescence,' you say, 'can send confusing signals to men, even those who regard themselves as enlightened.' Yes, Ms McCartney, you've got it in one. We men are simple creatures. If someone 'goes along' with what we're doing, we assume they're OK with it. Despite being all-powerful patriarchs, we're not mind readers.

You wonder, as I have just done and as others have done before me, why women who aren't enjoying an activity and are not under coercion wouldn't just walk or run away, but, you say, somewhat obscurely, 'today's twenty-somethings grew up trapped in a different script, one they're struggling to rewrite. It needs rewriting .... ' No, Ms McCartney, I'm not buying this nonsense about a script, whatever it means. Young women of today, just as young women of yesterday, have voices with which they can speak, and legs which they can use to run away on. What is so difficult about saying *no* politely and, if that doesn't work, saying *f@£$ off* very loudly and impolitely? So much for empowerment and the strong and independent woman created by fifty years of feminism. Either women are strong and empowered or else they are weak and fragile. Which is it to be? You can't have it both ways. And it's a little hard to take the 'strong and empowered' characterisation seriously if a woman who finds a man's hand on her knee or overhears a sexual remark has a nervous breakdown as a result. In the context of the Hollywood kerfuffle, Germaine Greer, doyenne of the feminist movement, has said: 'If you spread your legs because he said, "Be nice to me and I'll give you a job in a movie", then I'm afraid that's tantamount to consent and it's too late now to start whingeing about that.' Reviewing Kantor & Twohey's *She Said*, Helen Lewis writes, 'by definition, everyone with power in modern Hollywood has succeeded within the current toxic, compromising system. No wonder so few wanted to speak out. Some of them must have taken Weinstein's bathrobe bargain. Others said no and kept quiet about it. Others passed on a warning—don't be alone with him—and considered their job done.' (Lewis 2019)

Today's feminists appear to be obsessed with the topic of sexual harassment. But sexual harassment is not something new. In 1993, David Thomas wrote, 'Sexual harassment in the workplace is rapidly becoming one of the great *cause célèbres* of the women's movement all over the Western world.' (Thomas, 148) Sexual harassment is a phenomenon that feminists see afflicting women always and everywhere, and they want something done about it, now, preferably by legally coercive means. The Weinstein effect, and the #MeToo movement that it spawned, have finally persuaded some governments to accede to feminists' demands and so we are starting to see the introduction of anti-liberal laws. The French government proposes to introduce laws that would impose fines for catcalling, and in Amsterdam, street harassment has attracted a €190 fine since January 2018. The police in Nottinghamshire, not content with preventing harassment, now record it as a hate crime!

Sexual harassment is usually characterised as any form of unwanted verbal, non-verbal or physical conduct of a sexual nature. It can include, but is not necessarily limited to, making sexually degrading comments or gestures, staring at or leering at a person's body, subjecting someone to sexual jokes or propositions, sending emails or text messages with sexual content, unwelcome physical behaviour such as sexual advances and touching, displaying sexually explicit pictures in your space or shared space at work, and offering rewards in return for sexual favours. The radical feminist discerns a criminal chain extending along a continuum from rape (the most serious form of sexual harassment) all the way down to what most people would consider to be trivial incidents of sexual bad taste. If radical feminists are to be believed, sexual harassment, like charity, covers a multitude of sins, from knee touching to rape. The continuum thesis is meant to raise the trivial to the level of the serious; in fact, however, the danger is that the truly criminal and serious risks being trivialised. Men are accused of 'not getting' the continuum thesis; in fact, men get it all too clearly, they just don't accept it, and neither do most women.

The really worrying thing about sexual harassment law is its radical subjectivity. Harassment is whatever is perceived by the putative victim to be harassment, not what a normal person with a skin somewhat thickened by regular contact with the real world would consider to be harassment. Moreover, in work environments, employers are obliged to protect their employees from such harassment, and they bear the burden of proof to show that they have done so. 'Once again, codified in law is a subjective flexibility for a woman rather than an objective rule by which people can know where they stand. The absurdity is complete with the general adoption into codes of practice by organisations and firms of the notion of harassment as anything considered as such by either the recipient or any witness.' (Moxon, 150)

Are women in constant danger of being sexually harassed or not? In her *Spiked* interview, Christine Hoff Sommers was asked if women are in constant danger of being harassed in the workplace. She replied, 'There's no evidence of that. Cases like Harvey Weinstein or Charlie Rose involve these very high-profile men in unusual environments where there was no accountability. So they're atypical.' But if that is so, why is it now widely believed that sexual harassment has reached epidemic levels? Because, Sommers replies, 'People get carried away with stories.' If statistics are brought into play to put things in perspective, the response is that statistics 'are shaped by masculine ways of thinking' so instead, we should just 'listen to women's stories'. So they're listening to women's stories and crediting them, because 'it's also a principle that you should believe women and not be sceptical. But you have to know if these stories are true, and whether or not they represent the experience of most women. The best research we have suggests that they do not.' (Sommers 2017)

Monica redux

It's an ill wind that blows nobody any good. Monica Lewinsky is on the way to being rehabilitated by the tail wind of the #MeToo movement. Twenty years ago she didn't receive much sympathy or support from her feminist sisters as they rallied around Brother Bill to defend him from the machinations of the evil Republicans. Now, in the heady atmosphere of #MeToo, Monica is back! Writing in *Vanity Fair* in February 2018, she now seems to believe that her liaison with Bill Clinton was a gross abuse of power on his part. (Lewinsky) Well, by all accounts, it was gross. Was it an abuse of power? Let's see. The answer to that question would seem to hinge on whether the sexual relationship/activity between them was consensual. Twenty years on, Lewinsky wonders if she really consented to what went on. She ruminates, 'Now, at 44, I'm beginning ... to consider the implications of the power differentials that were so vast between a president and a White House intern. I'm beginning to entertain the notion that in such a circumstance the idea of consent might well be rendered moot ... power imbalances—and the ability to abuse them—do exist even when the sex has been consensual.' But didn't she in fact consent? Apparently she did. Or at least, that's what she thought in her last *Vanity Fair* outing just a few years ago when she said, 'It was a consensual relationship... I will always remain firm on this point.'

'We're not against sex,' wrote one of her unsympathetic sisters, Gloria Steinem during the revelations in 1998. Phew! I'm sure that was a relief to men all around the world! But, Steinem went on, 'we're against the use of sex to cajole, humiliate, coerce.' Fair enough, Ms Steinem, it's hard to argue with that. Since Lewinsky was quite clear at the time that she *wasn't* coerced, she wasn't in line for any tea or sympathy from the sisterhood. After all, as Steinem went on to say, 'If we say a 21-to-24-year-old has no sexual will, we're going against the whole struggle for self-determination and taking responsibility for our own lives.' Just so, Ms Steinem, I couldn't agree more. But, stop the press; Ms Steinem seems to have changed her line on all this. That was then, this is now. Now she's in favour of what have been called 'affirmative consent' laws, laws that require partners in sexual encounters to request and receive explicit consent for every aspect of that encounter. We are supposed to ignore the patent unworkability of such laws, particularly when it comes to individuating the events that require consent. What counts as a discrete event? Is it body parts; a particular part of a body part; touch; length of touch, and so on? We are also supposed to ignore the peculiarly bloodless view this takes of sexual congress. Furthermore, you'd have to be a visitor from the planet Zog not to realise that these laws, while they purport to be equally applicable to both men and women, are predicated on a view of men as essentially sexual aggressors, and women as essentially sexual victims, so that their effective coercive force falls almost exclusively on men. I wait with interest to see the first case of the prosecution of a woman for violating these affirmative consent laws. I expect to be waiting for quite some time.

Now, however, Ms Lewinsky considers the whole notion of consent to be 'very, very complicated.' She muses, 'The dictionary definition of "consent"? "To give permission for something to happen." And yet what did the "something" mean in this instance, given the power dynamics, his position, and my age? Was the "something" just about crossing a line of sexual (and later emotional) intimacy?' One can't help wondering if, in speculating on what 'something' means, Lewinsky is mimicking (consciously or unconsciously) Bill Clinton's notorious 'It depends on what the meaning of the word "is" is!'

But back to the main point. Is Lewinsky now saying she *didn't* consent? Surely she doesn't believe that a strong and independent 22-year old woman is incapable of giving consent and yet, what are we to make of the following statement? 'He was my boss ... the most powerful man on the planet. He was 27 years my senior, with enough life experience to know better. He was, at the time, at the pinnacle of his career, while I was in my first job out of college.' So, she *didn't* consent? If Clinton has asked her to jump off the top of the Washington Monument, would the fact of his being the most powerful man in the world have removed her ability to tell him to f@£$ off? But then, with a refreshing burst of linguistic and moral transparency, Lewinsky admits that 'none of the above excuses me for my responsibility for what happened.' So, she *does* accept responsibility for what happened and she *did* consent? I'm confused! I suspect Ms Lewinsky is probably confused too.

The dis-Grace-ful outing of Aziz Ansari

Some women seem to think that men should be mind readers who can tell what a woman wants without her having to tell him. It's strange to think that strong and independent twenty-first century women seem to have lost their ability to speak in certain circumstances, a loss that is not much in evidence most of the time. Here's the problem for your normal heterosexual man. If he makes an advance to a woman that she deems to be unwanted (and how is he supposed to know before making an advance whether his advances are wanted or not?), his life and career could be ruined. On the other hand, women, it would seem, *do* want to have wanted advances made to them, at least, sometimes, and by some men. But again, how is a man supposed to tell before making it? And why in our enlightened and feminarchical age don't women initiate the advances? Who can tell?

The old norms of appropriate relationships between the sexes are apparently dead and gone, except, of course, when women want them to hold, but who can tell when or if that is so? The soft romantic light of candles has been replaced by the harsh searchlights of interrogation. And with the prioritising of consent, a consent that seems to be in principle revisable, before, during and after, we create opportunities for the spurned, the disappointed and the grasping to advance their causes pretty much without any risk to themselves. If the older definitions of rape were still in place, the ones that contained the use of force or violence, or the threat or force or violence (see chapter 6), things might perhaps be a little less confused and confusing. The let-it-all-hang-out post 1960s sexually permissive culture has thrown up some tangled conundrums. Is sex with everybody and anybody, anytime still OK, or do we live in a very different, post-post-1960s world?

The headline in *Babe* (yes, that's what this particular august publication is called) read: 'I went on a date with Aziz Ansari. It turned into the worst night of my life.' (see Way; also Davis) The 'I' in question is someone called Grace who went on a date with Aziz Ansari, a minor television celebrity. She didn't like what happened on the date. By the way, 'Grace' is not her real name whereas Aziz Ansari *is* his real name and, despite her being a shrinking violet with respect to her own identity, she displays no reticence at all in sharing his name with the public. I can understand such modesty. He's moderately well known but who, after all, is she?

Twenty-two year old Grace met Mr Ansari at a party when she approached him (not the other way around note) and they exchanged numbers. On their subsequent date, after dinner (which he paid for—why didn't she go Dutch?), they returned to his apartment. Why did she go back to his apartment? Was she eager to see his etchings? Grace complains that Ansari was a little too eager to get back to his apartment after the dinner ('Like, he got the check and then it was bada-boom, bada-bing, we're out of there') but doesn't explain why if that really bothered her she didn't say 'Thanks for the memory' and take a cab home? Meanwhile, back at the apartment, after some casual chat about counter tops (not etchings), Ansari invited Grace to sit on them. They started kissing. Did she protest or object at this point. Apparently not. He then undressed her. What was she doing while this undressing was going on? Did she object to this? Did she wonder why her clothes were being removed or did she just not notice? Then he undressed himself. Did she not notice this either? *Leave, Grace; leave right now.*

As *Babe* relates the story, 'When Ansari told her he was going to grab a condom within minutes of their first kiss, Grace voiced her hesitation explicitly. "I said something like, 'Whoa, let's relax for a sec, let's chill.'"' Well, you have to admit, that's something less than a definitive rejection! 'She says he then resumed kissing her, briefly performed oral sex on her, and asked her to do the same thing to him. She did, but not for long. "It was really quick. Everything was pretty much touched (*sic*) and done within ten minutes of hooking up, except for actual sex."' I'm not sure why the duration of sexual contact is supposed to be significant but it seems that Grace considers it to be so. *Leave Grace; leave right now.*

She says she tried to voice her hesitation but Ansari ignored her signals. Signals? Wait a second! They're both naked and they've been kissing. What kind of signals was she sending that he didn't get? Did she send them by means of Morse code or semaphore? Did it not occur to her to make use of the word *NO* or one of its many variants! Was she prevented from so doing by having a handkerchief stuffed in her mouth or was she temporarily afflicted with dumbness? Who can say? In any event, it would appear that she gave him oral sex twice. (Twice?) Then followed an episode in which, according to Grace, Ansari repeatedly took two of his fingers and kept putting them in her mouth, in her throat. She moved away from him (as would any normal person), but he followed her. 'It was 30 minutes of me getting up and moving and him following and sticking his fingers down my throat again. It was really repetitive. It felt like a fucking game.' Oddly, she still didn't seem to think that after 30 minutes of this bizarre digital steeplechase, it might now be a good time to leave. *Leave Grace; leave right now.*

Grace says she used verbal and non-verbal cues to let Ansari know how uncomfortable and distressed she was. In her own words, 'Most of my discomfort was expressed in me pulling away and mumbling.' She doesn't know whether Ansari simply didn't notice her reticence or just ignored it. She says, 'I know I was physically giving off cues that I wasn't interested. I don't think that was noticed at all, or if it was, it was ignored.' I don't know what and just how unambiguous Grace's non-verbal cues were, but the verbal cues, on her own admission, consisted of mumbling! *Leave Grace; leave right now.*

In the half-hour or so that followed, Ansari said he wanted to have penetrative sex with Grace. Oh my goodness, what a surprise! A man and a woman hanging out together naked and the possibility of sex arose. How crazy is that? She, apparently, was uncomfortable with Ansari's efforts at sexual congress. If so, one might wonder why she didn't put her clothes back on and leave? She says that she remembers him asking repeatedly "Where do you want me to fuck you?" while she was still seated on the countertop. She says she found the question tough to answer because, she says, she didn't want to fuck him at all.' Eh? *That's* a tough question? Now would have been a good time to stop mumbling, Grace, and to say something like, 'nowhere; not here, not now, not ever.' *Leave Grace, leave right now.*

Eventually, the possibility of expressing her reservations verbally and unambiguously did occur to Grace, and she said 'No' when Ansari suggested having sex in front of a mirror, at which point (how can I say this, it's so horrible), he suggested that they just chill out *with their clothes on*! So, after dressing, they sat on a couch and, wait for it, they watched *Seinfeld*. I can begin to see now why Grace thinks of this as the worst night of her life—discussing counter tops, watching *Seinfeld*—any woman would be psychologically scarred. What kind of fiend would make a woman watch an episode of *Seinfeld* with her clothes on? No wonder Grace finally complained to Ansari, saying 'You guys are all the fucking same.' If this has happened to her many times before, as that remark seems to suggest, why did she think that her rendezvous with Ansari on this occasion would be any different from her previous experiences? At this point, Ansari called an Uber to take Grace home. *Grace finally left.*

The next day, Ansari, instead of neglecting to get in touch with her as one of those guys-who-are-all-the-f@£$ing-same tend to do, texted her to say, 'It was fun meeting you last night' (which was probably not true, but polite), to which message Grace, with a conspicuous lack of the virtue signified by her pseudonym, replied, 'Last night might've been fun for you, but it wasn't for me. You ignored clear nonverbal cues; you kept going with advances. You had to have noticed I was uncomfortable.' Most men would have ignored this uncivil response to a routine courtesy or just told her to ... well, to cease and desist, but instead, just like one of those guys-who-are-all-the-f@£$ing-same, Ansari responded to this ungracious complaint with an apology: 'Clearly, I misread things in the moment and I'm truly sorry.'

As I may have mentioned already once or twice, one might wonder why Grace didn't leave at any of the many awkward moments that occurred during this sordid encounter. The reason was, she tells us, because of the gap between Ansari's comedy *persona* and his behaviour in the apartment. 'I didn't leave because I think I was stunned and shocked,' she said. 'This was not what I expected. I'd seen some of his shows and read excerpts from his book and I was not expecting a bad night at all, much less a violating night and a painful one.' I leave it to readers to make up their minds as to the plausibility of this explanation for Grace's not leaving.

What radical malfunction of the human will afflicted Grace during her strange encounter of the Ansari kind? Did some metaphysical singularity descend upon Ansari's apartment so that she ceased to be a human being capable of human agency? What stopped her at any stage from—and I know this is a really radical suggestion—getting up, putting on her clothes (better still, not allowing them to be taken off in the first place), and going home. What a paragon of female helplessness she seems to be which, however, we know cannot be true because all women are strong and independent. In a related context, Margaret Atwood, who is about as close as any woman can get to being a living feminist saint, wrote, 'My fundamental position is that women are human beings. Nor do I believe that women are children, incapable of agency or of making moral decisions. If they were, we're back to the 19th century, and women should not own property, have credit cards, have access to higher education, control their own reproduction or vote. There are powerful groups in North America pushing this agenda, but they are not usually considered feminists.' (Atwood) Exactly so, Ms Atwood.

In the end, what was Mr Ansari's fault as judged by Grace? Possible answers:

First, he was a man. This is always a good answer, if a trifle generic. Men *are* awful, which is obviously why women like Grace pursue them at parties and choose to accept invitations to date them, even though, as we know from her tragic story, she thinks men are all the f@£$ing same, and that same isn't a good same.

Second, he wasn't a mind reader. Well, this is obviously not a defence that can be offered by Mr Ansari at all. *She* knew she wasn't happy with the way things were going (that's why she exchanged kisses with him and hung around his apartment naked), so he obviously had to have known that too.

Third, he was a man and he wasn't a mind reader. A popular choice, combining the virtues of 1 and 2 and thus keeping all options open. Some people might conclude that Ansari's fundamental fault was to have invited this mumbling mannequin on a date in the first place, but we needn't concern ourselves with such an obviously crazy judgement.

As the clickbait headline to her published piece blared, Grace believes that her night of naked naughtiness with Aziz Ansari was the worst night of her life. Well, if that's so, she is to be envied because she must have had an incredibly fortunate life up to the point of her assignation with Ansari. I can think of many things that might reasonably be considered worse than a night out chatting about counter tops and watching *Seinfeld*, bad as that may be, such as acquiring a terminal illness, hearing of the death of a friend or a loved one, having one's cherished possessions stolen, or being the victim of a physical assault resulting in serious bodily injury.

There is a further irony to this already peculiar scenario, which is that Grace herself seems not to have been too sure initially whether what took place between herself and Ansari was just an awkward and unpleasant sexual experience or some form of sexual assault. After a chat with her friends, Grace tells us that she decided to 'validate' [her word] what happened with Ansari as 'a sexual assault'. 'It took a really long time for me to validate this as sexual assault … I was debating if this was an awkward sexual experience or sexual assault. And that's why I confronted [*sic*] so many of my friends and listened to what they had to say, because I wanted validation that it was actually bad.' Hmmm! Let's see. Was I assaulted or was I not? Hard to tell. Let me check with my friends. Yes! What happened is validated as sexual assault.

But does it really require consultation with friends to figure out if you were sexually assaulted or not? Shouldn't that be pretty obvious? Apparently not, if we are to believe the editors of *Everyday Feminism*, who tell us that 'There are a lot of lies out there that can make it hard to know if you were raped.' (see Kirkham) I wonder what those lies could be? Our friends at *Everyday Feminism* are a little coy about telling us. Some obviously unenlightened people might think that if it's really that difficult to know whether you've been the victim of a particular type of crime, our conception of that type of crime might be, just might be, somewhat nebulous. Perhaps after all it wasn't really assault if you want to get technical but something much worse. All this consent/no-consent nonsense is just a male way of thinking of such things. No. The problem is really the deep-rooted sexism that makes even consensual sexual interactions ultimately unsatisfying for women and presumptively illegal for men. Then again, maybe unsatisfactory sex *is* rape or sexual assault (as Germaine Greer now appears to think). Perhaps the distinction between the two is just another example of patriarchal thinking imposed by men on women.

Would it be impertinent to suggest that what Grace felt after her fateful encounter with Mr Ansari—rejection yet again by another one of these f@£$ing-menwhoareallthesame—might perhaps better be characterised as post-bad-date-regret. Whatever about this, there can be little doubt that what she caused to be published anonymously was a classic example of spiteful revenge porn. (see Daum) The pornographic and meretricious detail in her story (which I apologise for having related in part) was clearly intended to hurt and humiliate Ansari, which, it would seem from the reaction it garnered, it succeeded in doing. She may, from her disappointment, have destroyed or, at the very least, damaged Ansari's career, but why should that matter. After all, he's only a f@£$ing-man-who-is-all-the-same but she's a strong and independent woman and women, as we all now know, can do no wrong. In the old dispensation of male-female relationships, it was considered ungentlemanly for a man to bandy a woman's name about. In this age of sexual equality, you might think it unladylike for a woman to bandy a gentleman's name about but apparently it isn't. As Sir Compton Mackenzie remarked, 'Women do not find it difficult nowadays to behave like men, but they often find it extremely difficult to behave like gentlemen.

Baby, it's cold outside

The difference in attitude to the battle of the sexes between the suspicion-laden contemporary world and that of a more innocent or barbarous age (choose your epithet!) can be illustrated by our attitude to Frank Loesser's classic song of seduction, 'Baby, it's cold outside.' Describing the original lyrics as 'aggressive and inappropriate', Lydia Liza and Josiah Lemanski have produced a bowdlerised version, suitable for the neo-Puritanical and infantile world in which it seems we now live. Here are the original lyrics with the Liza/Lemanski version added in italics.

Her: I really can't stay ...
Him: Baby it's cold outside (*Baby I'm fine with that*)
Her: I've got to go away ...
Him: Baby it's cold outside (*Baby I'm cool with that*)
Her: This evening has been ...
Him: Been hoping that you'd drop in (*Been hoping you get home safe*)
Her: So very nice.
Him: I'll hold your hands, they're just like ice (*I'm glad you had a real good time*)
Her: My mother will start to worry ...
Him: Beautiful, what's your hurry (*Call her so she knows that you're coming*)
Her: My father will be pacing the floor ...
Him: Listen to the fireplace roar (*Better get your car a-humming*)
Her: So really I'd better scurry ...
Him: Beautiful, please don't hurry (*No rush*)

It continues...

Her: I ought to say no, no, no, sir ...
Him: Mind if I move a little closer (*You reserve the right to say no*)
Her: At least I'm gonna say that I tried ...
Him: What's the sense in hurting my pride (*You reserve the right to say no*)
Her: I really can't stay ...
Him: Baby don't hold out. (*Well you don't have to*)
Tutti: Ah, but it's cold outside

A little more knowledge of literature on the part of our outraged latter-day Bowdlerisers might have disclosed that the Loesser song is a mid-20th century popular version of the poetic genre called the *Aubade*. The theme of the *Aubade* is that, with the arrival of dawn, lovers who have spent the night together must now part. It usually involves one of the lovers protesting that the light outside the window of the room isn't daybreak, or sometimes just flatly telling the sun to go away and not interfere with our lovers' bliss. A classic—perhaps *the* classic—*Aubade* is John Donne's poem 'The Sunne Rising'. 'Busie old foole, unruly

Sunne/Why does thou thus/Through windowes, and through curtaines call on us?/Must to thy motions lovers seasons run?' Loesser's *Aubade* cleverly inverts the conventional trope and makes the cold outside the lovers' room a reason for staying, instead of the sun's arrival a reason for going. Other writers have taken the subversion of the *Aubade* genre even further. In Philip Larkin's last poem, explicitly called 'Aubade', the arrival of the dawn signals not the parting of lovers but the imminence of death!

What do Liza and Lemanski think is going on in this song? Is it a rhapsody to date rape? If we approach the song without radical feminist preconceptions, we might be able to glean some clues from the lyrics. She came to visit him, not the other way around, and not necessarily at his invitation ('How lucky you dropped in'); she appreciated her stay ('Your welcome has been so nice and warm' and 'You've really been grand'). The man, in traditional *Aubade* style, wants her to stay with him rather than to leave. She sort of, kind of, wants to stay, agreeing on one occasion to accept 'just a half a drink more' and, on another, 'maybe just a cigarette more' but is worried about her reputation—what will her sister, her maiden aunt and the neighbours think ('There's bound to be talk tomorrow'). There is nothing, absolutely nothing, to suggest that she's concerned about being raped or sexually assaulted unless one imports these prejudices into the lyrics. Marya Hannun writing in the *Washington Post*, suggests that, seen in the context of the sexual *mores* of the 1940s, 'the song could be read as an advocacy for women's sexual liberation rather than a tune about date rape.' But such is the power of current feminist orthodoxy that even though Hannun admits that the message of the song might have been progressive and subversive about woman's sexuality when first written, today, she says, 'the song's subtext finds itself at odds with basic notions of consent.' (Hannun) No, Ms Hannun, it doesn't. Read your own piece again and you'll see that you were right the first time round. So, best guess? It's a song of post-seduction or would-be seduction, a situation that on the evidence of the text must have been mutually agreeable.

In any relationship, the person with the power is the person who needs the other person least. In 'Baby it's cold outside', the person with the power is clearly the woman. This song is a reminder to women that they have all the power when it comes to romantic transactions. As such, you would think that our feminist friends would celebrate it. But no! Are Liza and Lemanski paid up members of the Junior Anti-Sex League? 'It was always the women, and above all the young ones, who were the most bigoted adherents of the Party, the swallowers of slogans, the amateur spies and nosers out of unorthodoxy' (*1984*) Have these people ever been in a sexual relationship with anyone? Don't they understand anything about men and women? What world do these deaf-to-literature and blind-to-life people live in? It's seems to be the kind of world the philosopher Thomas Hobbes thought that men occupied in their natural state, a world populated by isolated, unrelated, competitive, aggressive, manipulating and self-centred individuals. But the world we live in is a world of relationships: of brothers, sisters, wives, husbands, lovers, sons and daughters, friends. The 'consentists' treat two people as if they were strangers, meeting for the first time, with no history, no backstory, no context, and sex for them is always polite and Protestant, always Appolonian, never Dionysian. For the consentists, consent, to really be consent, must always be affirmative, continuous and, you've just got to love this one, enthusiastic. And that, ladies and gentlemen, is the very embodiment of foolishness. 'If we all followed a strict code that consent was nothing short of an emphatic repeated "yes"', comments Steve Moxon sardonically, 'then people would have to more or less give up trying to have sex.' (Moxon, 180) Precisely.

Accusation is tantamount to conviction

Nesrine Malik would have us believe that the post-Weinstein #MeToo movement represents a cultural shift that no amount of self-interested complaining by the usual suspects that things have gone too far will do anything to dissipate. The objectors, she thinks, have no reasoned case to bring against the movement. According to her, all we are seeing from them is a brute self-preservationist reaction to the threat to their unearned status, a status that is just the result of biology and social conditioning. Ah yes, I see, Ms Malik, so that's how it works. 'Thank you for applying for the IT specialist position, Mr Johnson. You have the right biology and the right social conditioning—we don't need you to demonstrate any IT competence. God forbid that we should hire a woman who knows what she's doing, when we can hire you, who are a sterling example of an incompetent, unqualified individual, except in the most important respect, which is that you are a man.'

I may be wronging her, but Ms Malik seems to think evidence that might be produced to show that mere accusations are sufficient to ruin the career of pretty much any man accused of sexual harassment is just male hysteria, and we can ignore all that. It's only that pesky patriarchy springing into action, a patriarchy that, according to Ms Malik, is 'a sophisticated system that survives because it creates enough winners who have a vested interest in maintaining it.' (Malik) So, not only do men benefit from the patriarchy, but so do the Auntie Thomashina quislings who are prepared to sell out their sisters for 30 pieces of silver, less, of course, 10-25% to take account of the gender pay gap. Others, while agreeing in part with Ms Malik, are not so sanguine about the nature of the cultural shift that is currently taking place. What we seem to have in either reality or prospect is not only a justified anger against the Weinsteins of this world (if the allegations against him are to be believed), but a counter-revolutionary reaction to certain aspects of the 1960s sexual revolution in which, like all revolutions, original or counter, the boundaries are unclear, the outcomes uncertain, but the casualties inevitable. We have generated a continuum of sexual encounters of the third kind, from the awkward and embarrassing to the unacceptable, the sackable and the criminal, with little clear indication of where one elides into the other.

What sort of world is it in which simply being accused of sexual misbehaviour is enough to get you blacklisted, fired and shunned? Answer: the world of #MeToo. What sort of world is it in which attempting to defend yourself against accusations of sexual misbehaviour is enough to plunge you into the middle of a Twitterstorm (a latter-day form of reputational lynching) and get you blacklisted, fired and shunned. Answer: the world of #MeToo. The #MeToo witch-finders are ever vigilant, ever ready to detect the signs of sin, and attempts at exculpation are just another sign of guilt. If, like the suspected witches of old, you sink when you are thrown into the pond, then you are innocent but dead; if you float, you are alive but guilty. Writing of Konrad von Marburg, the notorious medieval inquisitor, Tom Holland remarks that Konrad's critics 'charged him with believing every accusation that was brought before him; of rushing the process of law; of sentencing the innocent to the flames.' (Holland, 239) *Plus ça change, plus c'est la même chose.*

Emer O'Toole wonders how a woman should respond when a man she likes is accused of sexual harassment. (O'Toole) I shouldn't have thought that this was an unresolvable conundrum, Ms O'Toole. How about suspending judgement until you hear the full facts of the case or is that too radical a suggestion? Indeed, how about suspending judgement even in the case of (or perhaps especially in the case of) men you *don't* like! An infamous case of prejudgement relates to the woman who claimed that, in 2006 at Duke University, three members of the University's lacrosse team beat and raped her. Cue anger and outrage and demonstrations. What was astonishing and disgraceful was that 88 members *of the academic staff* at the university put their names to a piece in the student newspaper, the *Duke Chronicle*, in which they thanked the demonstrators for not waiting to see if the claims were credible. It is true that most of those who put their names to this disgraceful piece of prejudice were teachers in advocacy subjects, such as Women's Studies, African-American Studies and the like, and so only marginally academics, but still they were old enough to have known better.

The intolerance of the #MeToo movement was clearly demonstrated in the response to the Buruma/Ghomeshi/*New York Review of Books* (NYRB) affair. Ian Buruma, the editor of NYRB, published an essay by Jian Ghomeshi who had been acquitted (please note, *acquitted*) in March 2016 of four counts of sexual assault and one of choking. In the essay published by Mr Buruma, Ghomeshi described himself as a victim of 'mass shaming' and said he had endured 'enough humiliation for a lifetime.' He also repeated his claim that the accusations against him made by more than 20 women that he allegedly abused them with slaps, punches, bites and choking, were 'inaccurate', a claim given some substance by his acquittal. Mr Buruma's decision to publish the essay was, it seems, the subject of some controversy within the editorial team of the NYRB, the question being, as Ed Pilkington put it, about 'the extent to which men who had been the subject of #MeToo accusations of inappropriate or abusive sexual conduct should be allowed to rehabilitate themselves into society.' (Pilkington) Mr Buruma added to the controversy when he attempted to defend his decision to publish the essay, remarking of the #MeToo movement, that, 'Like all well-intentioned and good things, there can be undesirable consequences.' His lamentation of what he termed a 'general climate of denunciation' is more than a little ironic inasmuch as he himself then became the object of such denunciation as the result of his publication of the essay and his own attempt to justify it! The editor-in-chief of the *Hufflepuff Post* (sorry, the *HuffPost*) tweeted that 'The Ian Buruma interview [was] even more enraging than the Ghomeshi piece itself'!

Nobody has accused Buruma, at least, not to date, of engaging in any of the proscribed forms of sexual misbehaviour, so why did he end up resigning from his job as editor-in-chief of the *New York Review of Books*, a resignation that bore all the hallmarks of jumping before being pushed? Why, the chap had the infernal gall to publish the Ghomeshi piece that described what it was like to be the target of the fickle fingers of feminist fury! Big mistake, Mr Boruma! The interesting thing about the Ghomeshi piece, as Lionel Shriver acutely notes, is just how self-abasing it and a similar piece by John Hockenberry are. 'My own objection,' writes Shriver, 'is that both essays are so wussy. Choosing to take a stand, these guys might have come out fighting and truly defended themselves—perhaps parsing encounters their accusers recall as violating and the men recall in a more innocent light. Or laying out: I did do this; I didn't do that. But no. Both pieces maunder nauseously on about how the authors have soul-searched, reappraising their disturbed relations with the opposite sex from the year dot. It's not only women who don't have penises.' (Shriver)

What are these men (Ghomeshi and Hockenberry) alleged to have done that is so God-awfully terrible? Murder? Manslaughter? Inflicting grievous bodily harm on random strangers? Stealing the life savings of some poor widow? No, they are reputed to have committed—I can hardly bring myself to say it—a sexual transgression! There! It's out. Now you can understand how shocking it is that these men are not locked up securely in solitary confinement. And yet ... and yet ... as Shriver remarks, 'But — maybe I make a lousy girl—I'd rather be tastelessly propositioned, groped, insulted, subject to workplace abuse of power, than have my legs chopped off or my throat slit. People do scads of horrific things to each other, and in my book sexual offences, especially those that can't even qualify as criminal, don't rise to the top of that dismally long list. John Hockenberry is not Pol Pot. Sleazebag maybe, but Jian Ghomeshi doesn't make lampshades from human skin. Can we get a grip?' (Shriver)

The cautionary tale of Senator Al Franken is one that should be taken to heart by all men. It's a little difficult to feel any sympathy for Senator Franken, who supported the Obamaoid policies that led to the creation of the Title IX bureaucratic inquisitions, but let's be charitable and cut him some slack. He was accused by several women, most prominently Leeann Tweeden, of unwanted attempted kissing and touching. His initial response, incorporating the now usual and nauseatingly pious obeisance to the sacredness of women's feelings, was ambiguous, leaving us in some doubt whether he rejected the charges or accepted them. Under pressure from his colleagues, he resigned just three weeks after the allegations appeared. Mr Franken tells of a late-night meeting with Minority Leader Chuck Schumer, in which he says Mr Schumer issued him with an ultimatum: either quit, or the minority leader would rally the entire Democratic caucus to call for his resignation. Mr Schumer denies that he threatened Mr Franken but agrees that he called upon him to resign. Significantly, Mr Franken goes on to say of his meeting with Mr Schumer: 'I couldn't believe it ... I asked him for due process and he said no.' Now, seven of the thirty six Democrats who demanded his resignation say they regret their decisions. Patrick Leahy, a Democrat from Vermont, described his role in Mr Franken's resignation as 'one of the biggest mistakes I've made' in 45 years in the US Senate. Senator Tammy Duckworth from Illinois concurred with Mr Leahy's regret, saying 'That due process didn't happen is not good for our democracy.' (see Mayer)

Of course, in the new normative environment, it's understandable that an outright and forthright rejection of the charges would have been deemed insensitive. If Franken were to have asserted his innocence, that would have been tantamount to doubting his accuser's truthfulness and, as we now know, you can't do that! Defending yourself is re-attacking and re-victimising the victim. How dare you, sir! How very dare you! Did Franken absorb by a process of intellectual osmosis the advice given to University of Southern California students who are accused of sexual assault, which is to admit that, even if they didn't remember the incident or didn't believe themselves capable of hurting someone, to admit that it's possible that they did? Now, it seems the Senator Franken regrets resigning over the sexual misconduct claims and wishes that his case had been examined by the Senate Ethics Committee. (see BBC 2019) He unambiguously rejects the tale told by his accuser, Ms Tweeden, saying, 'the idea that anybody who accuses someone of something is always right—that's not the case. That isn't reality.'

Where does this leave us? If a man has been accused—accused, note, not convicted—of inappropriate or abusive conduct, he is to lose his job, be expelled from polite society and not allowed to rehabilitate himself. If a man has been tried for offences and acquitted, he is not allowed to publish an account of his mass shaming and humiliation, nor is the editor of a magazine allowed to print it. Are Buruma and Ghomeshi Urban Grandier's for the 21st century? (see Huxley)

#MeToo as toxic femininity

Lying behind much of the #MeToo furore is a barely concealed misandry. It's not just the Harvey Weinsteins of this world (if the allegations against him are to be believed) that are under attack; it is all men, everywhere. It is not just so-called toxic masculinity that is thought to be problematic, but masculinity itself in all its forms. It is not just the actions of certain men that is the problem, but the very being of all men. Second and third wave+ feminism and its daughter #MeToo, all manifest androphobia, the irrational fear and hatred of men, to a greater or lesser extent. A particularly transparent version of the misandric thesis is to be found in a piece by Lisa Wade entitled, 'The Big Picture: Confronting Manhood After Trump.' There, she writes, 'Trump's masculinity is what we call a toxic masculinity. In the pre-Trump era, the modifier was used to differentiate bad masculine ideals from good ones. Toxic masculinities, some claimed, were behind sexual assault, mass shootings, and the weird thing where men refuse to wear sunscreen, but they didn't reflect masculinity generally, so one had to leave that idea alone. But we can only give masculinity so many modifiers for so long before we have to confront the possibility that it is masculinity itself that has become the problem.' (Wade 2017) She endorses a Trump survival strategy for herself and her fellow travellers, one of whose components, perhaps its principal component, is a direct attack on masculinity. 'If we're going to survive both President Trump and the kind of people he has emboldened, we need to attack masculinity directly. I don't mean that we should recuperate masculinity—that is, press men to identify with a kinder, gentler version of it—I mean that we should reject the idea that men have a psychic need to distinguish themselves from women in order to feel good about themselves. This idea is sexist on its face and it's unsettling that we so rarely think of it that way.' (Wade 2017)

As I see it, it is not men's need to distinguish themselves psychically from women that is unsettling, but rather Ms Wade's intemperate tirade. We can make allowances for a certain lack of clarity due to rhetorical heat but, even discounting for that, what Ms Wade says is bizarre. It is always a useful exercise when one element of a binary is attacked, to flip the coin and consider how the attack would look if applied to the other side. Suppose a critic were to complain that the #MeToo movement and its allies are not just expressive of a certain form of toxic femininity but of the very notion of femininity itself, that it is not just the actions of certain women that are problematic but the very being of all women. How do you think such a claim would be received?

What would constitute evidence of 'toxic femininity'? It is, I think, abundantly obvious that women, some women at least, are less constrained by objective notions of justice than are most men, particularly in their apparent willingness to jettison the presumption of innocence when it suits their needs or interests. Susan Brownmiller, for example, doyenne of the feminist movement and the author of *Against Our Will* (1975) in which she gave us the patently idiotic but now ubiquitous 'power' or 'gendered' interpretation of rape, rape as an instrument used by 'all men' against 'all women', isn't worried about the lack of due process in the current furore occasioned by the #MeToo juggernaut. It doesn't bother her that men have been dismissed from their jobs simply on the basis of one woman's word when the allegations made against them have never been proved or even fully explored. If anything were needed to support the thesis that women generally are less prone than men to be constrained by objective notions of justice, the brouhaha over the nomination of Brett Kavanaugh to the United State Supreme Court should be sufficient to demonstrate its cogency. Despite there being no corroborating evidence to support the claim of sexual assault by Christine Blasey Ford, thousands of women (and, alas, some men) marched around shouting, 'I believe her.' Wendy Kaminer makes the incisive point that the #MeToo movement is, in certain respects, a new form of vigilantism. 'Vigilantism is the new black,' she writes, 'and it's not a good look for feminists.' So, toxic femininity anyone?

Sanctifying accusations of sexual misconduct as proof of guilt, effectively blacklisting alleged abusers, #MeToo activists in effect celebrate a form of mob rule. Demanding the unquestioning condemnation of men accused of sexual insensitivity as well as of sexual violence, they endorse regressive notions of feminine frailty. Demonising dissent, including calls for fundamental fairness towards people accused, they risk vindicating caricatures of feminists as misandrist authoritarians.' (Kaminer)

Kaminer identifies a fundamental tension in feminist thought. On the one hand, a desire to free women from constraints; on the other, a desire to protect them by policing men. That tension has been present in feminist thought from the beginning, and it has emerged anew under the banner of #MeToo. On the one hand, the all-the-sex-you-can-consume hook-up culture with no victim-blaming and no slut-shaming; on the other, the condemnation of sexual remarks and sexual advances if unwanted, with shaming and, increasingly, quasi-legal punishment of those deemed to have transgressed. On the one hand, women are men's equal in every way, including in respect of their pursuit of sexual activity—no guff about modesty or chastity will be entertained; on the other hand, women are fragile creatures, continually subjected to male aggression. At the same time, they are morally superior to men, who are rough and uncouth and must be constantly restrained.

In much the same vein as Kaminer, Claire Berlinski believes that the #MeToo and allied movements have now reached a stage of mass hysteria. 'It now takes only one accusation to destroy a man's life,' she writes. 'Just one for him to be tried and sentenced in the court of public opinion, overnight costing him his livelihood and social respectability. We are on a frenzied extrajudicial warlock hunt that does not pause to parse the difference between rape and stupidity. The punishment for sexual harassment is so grave that clearly this crime—like any other serious crime—requires an unambiguous definition. We have nothing of the sort.' (Berlinski)

The accusation of having sexually harassed a woman, whatever may be meant by sexual harassment (don't ask!), is enough to inflict a professional death sentence on any man—note, the mere accusation, not the confirmation of that accusation in a court of law. Some accusations concern matters that, if true, are clearly serious and perhaps even criminal; others, however, are not even social solecisms, let alone criminal offences. In the feminist myth, men are supposed to have all the power, women none. But as I argued earlier, this is simply not true. Whatever about other areas of life, it has never been true of the male-female sexual dynamics that are a permanent and ineradicable feature of the relationship between the sexes where women are, to put it somewhat crudely, in a seller's market. This gives them a psychosexual advantage—a form of erotic capital, to use Catherine Hakim's term—that history shows us repeatedly that they have (understandably) used to their advantage. (see Hakim 2011) Writing of her time in New York in the 1990s, Meghan Daum says of her relationship with an older man, 'I behaved the way I did because in some ways the power imbalance between the two of us was tipped in my favor. I was young and the man was twice my age. He may have had professional power over me, but it was limited and in no way unilateral .... I behaved this way because I must have known on some unconscious level that, at 25, I had more of a certain kind of power than I was ever going to have in my life and that I might as well use it, even if the accompanying rush was laced with shame.' (Daum 2019a)

It is hardly controversial to claim that the consequences of the #MeToo hysteria have been bad for men. But—and here's a point that's often missed—they may well be bad for women too. Relationships between men and women, already fraught, are not likely to become less so in an environment where any man can be accused of some vague offence by any woman, no matter what that supposed offence was, or where and when it happened. It is not unlikely that many men will embrace (pun intended) some form of the Mike Pence strategy, minimising contact with women as much as possible, and certainly not putting themselves in any position in which they would be alone with a woman. In July 2019, a Republican gubernatorial candidate, Robert Foster, refused to allow a female reporter to travel along on his campaign trail without a chaperone. As Berlinski puts it, 'Who could blame a man who does not enjoy the company of women under these circumstances, who would just rather not have women in the workplace at all? This is a world in which the Mike Pence rule seems eminently sensible. Such a world is not good for *women*, however, as many women were quick to point out when we learned of the Mike Pence rule. Our success and advancement relies upon the personal and informal relationships we have with our colleagues and supervisors. In this climate of fear, who could, for example, blame a venerable Oxford don for refusing to take the risk of teaching a young woman, one-on-one, with no witnesses?' Berlinski finishes with a heartfelt plea:

> Women, I'm begging you: Think this through. We are fostering a climate in which men legitimately fear us, where their entire professional and personal lives can be casually destroyed by 'secret lists' compiled by accusers they cannot confront, by rumours on the internet, by thrilled, breathless reporting denouncing one after another of them as a pig, often based only on the allegation that they did something all-too-human and none-too-criminal like making a lewd joke. Why would we even *want* men to be subject to such strenuous, arduous taboos against the display of their sexuality? These taboos, note carefully, resemble in non-trivial ways those that have long oppressed women. In a world with such arduous taboos about male purity and chastity, surely, it *is* rational for men to have as little to do with women as possible. What's in this for *us*? (Berlinski)

It is radically unsettling that the determination of whether an attempt at flirtation or a rude joke constitutes sexual harassment depends entirely upon its perception by its supposed victim. Such a criterion is entirely subjective and not subject to the objective requirement of many laws that what took place would appear so to an unbiased third party, to the mythical woman or man on the street. Tiffany Wright quotes a Twitter correspondent as saying, 'labelling every unpleasant sexual encounter an assault infantilizes women.' To the question 'isn't it enough that this woman felt assaulted', she responds with a burst of common sense, rare in the all too common over-heated discussions, saying: 'Assault is not a feeling. Discomfort is a feeling, embarrassment and hurt and anger are all feelings, but assault has to have an objective definition because of the legal and social ramifications that come with it. When we act as though disrespect, harassment, assault and rape are all different words for the same thing, the conversation starts to lose its legitimacy.' (Wright) If a woman feels that she's been physically assaulted, isn't that conclusive? No! Physical assault is not a feeling, though you will certainly feel it if you're physically assaulted. Shame, disgust, embarrassment, anger—these are all feelings, but physical assault is a public and objective matter that reasonable people have to be convinced happened on the basis of evidence. Some occurrences are obviously physical assault, some obviously not, and some few are borderline. *Nulla poena sine lege*—no punishment without a law—is an ancient legal maxim, but the crime of sexual harassment is so vague that almost any form of conduct can, if subjectively determined, constitute an offence.

Particularly nauseating is the demand for contrition from these alleged harassers. Trying to defend oneself only brings accusations of compounding the felony. Here's an example. 'The only thing that matters is how I made these three women feel,' said Steve Lebsock, a member of the Colorado House of Representatives. As Berlinski notes, 'that is a remarkable thing to say. Why *doesn't* it matter what he thought was happening? Why would we accept as remotely rational the idea that the *only* thing that matters is how the women *felt*? But the confession of such as Lebsock, no matter how abject and humiliating, will not bring forgiveness. Like the confessions of the old Bolsheviks or of those hauled up before the Night Watch Committees of the Cultural Revolution, confession is inevitably followed by execution.' (Berlinski)

Moral panics come, and they come, and then they come again. In earlier times, there were natural brakes on the extent to which such panics could spread. Now, with the speed-of-light-megaphone of the Internet and all forms of social media, the sound of such panics becomes deafening, inhibiting rational thought and reflective consideration. The trajectory of moral panics is always the same. Some form of behaviour or activity comes to public attention. The moral censors of the time—newspaper editors with papers to sell, politicians with axes to grind, the movers and shakers of movements for social change—latch on to the suspect activity and present it as more widespread than it in fact is, and of a far worse character. The sky is falling. In time, but not before much damage has been done to individuals, the panic subsides, but things are never quite the same afterwards.

Individual vs social feminists

One of the amusing (well, amusing to me, at any rate) features of the #MeToo movement is the way it has given rise to an outbreak of woman-on-woman misogyny. All women may be women and, if the transgenderist dogma is to be believed, some men may be women too, but not all women are entitled to their own opinions. Unless you sign up to the #MeToo credo that all men are predators and all women are sainted victims who were, are, or are about to be harassed, sexually abused or raped, then you must hand in your woman union card and do what men are supposed to do in this Age of Aquarius: shut up. That means you, Katie Roiphe, and you Catherine Deneuve, and you Anne Robinson and many others. Why this outbreak of female-led misogyny? Because, as Brendan O'Neill tells us, the #MeToo movement isn't pro-woman, it's pro-a particular set of women: 'well-connected women in culture and the media, who must maintain their alleged victim status at all costs because it is leverage for them in terms both of their career and their moral authority in public discussion.' (O'Neill 2018) Raising doubts of any kind about the aims, purposes and methods of #MeToo endangers jobs and perks for the women who are professional victims and who use their victim status to leverage their individual profiles and careers.

All feminists are feminists, of course, but some feminists are more feminist than others. Yesterday's feminists, no matter how sterling their records, come under condemnation if they don't subscribe to today's feminist orthodoxy. Give way, old women, give way; your ideological purity has rusted with age. Accused variously of internalised misogyny or covert betrayal, many of these older feminists must be wondering just what happened to feminism when they weren't looking! Many 'isms' are objectionable to young feminists—racism, sexism—but ageism seems to be acceptable. These old feminists did good work in their time, their younger sisters suggest, but it's now time for them to step aside. Attempts by these older feminists to moderate righteous youthful fury are seen by some younger activists simply as a gross abuse of their older feminist sisters' power. (What power would that be, then? Can they have younger women locked up? Fired from their jobs? How is this power of feminists of the old guard supposed to be manifested?)

The #MeToo movement that started as a campaign for the vilification of abusive men and then morphed into a campaign against men in general has now gone one step further and provoked wrangling between women of different generations—or so it would seem. Young women are resentful of the comments of some older feminists that seem to disparage the levels of anger and outrage of the #MeToo movement, and they have accused some of their elders, if not their betters, of slut-shaming, victim-shaming and fat-shaming. A favourite target of the more radical radical feminists is the doyenne of feminism (or should that be 'former' doyenne?) Germaine Greer because of her view that trans women are not real women. Well, I should have thought it fairly obvious to those who are not clamped in the vise of transgenderist ideology that so-called trans women are not real women, but I'm only a man, so who cares what I think? Some of the #MeTooers were particularly outraged by Greer's suggestion that women have, on occasion, used sex for career advancement (how could that possibly be true?), and that doing so constituted consent. I never thought I'd say this, but—well said, Ms Greer! On the other hand, no commiserations to you and other feminists of your generation on sowing the wind and now reaping the whirlwind!

Elizabeth Wasserman, writing in early 2015, asks a question that some three years later, in the context of the #MeToo movement, some feminists of an older generation, and a few younger, have been asking: whatever happened to the old confident, progressive feminism? (Wasserman) She wrote then, and how prescient she was, 'The feminism of sexual freedom and against gender stereotyping has given way to one that insists on lumping all women together (#YESALLWOMEN) as a collective victim of sexual assault. The feminism of equality, of toughness, of anti-discrimination, has been overwhelmed by one of victimhood and demands for special treatment. The feminism of solidarity across class divides has been sidelined by an exaggerated concern with the problems of the elite.' (see Wasserman) Somehow, it cannot be doubted that all women are the same, with the same hopes, the same aspirations, the same experiences, the same cultural backgrounds and the same political, philosophical and religious beliefs. The mere possession of two X chromosomes is enough to overwhelm like a tsunami every other factor that might individuate one female person from another.

Margaret Atwood has been accused of 'Aunt Tom-ism' by some of her younger feminist sisters for supporting a male colleague, Steven Galloway, who was accused of sexual assault and was summarily dismissed from his position at the University of British Columbia. Galloway was ultimately cleared of these charges. Atwood was just one of 80 or so people to give her support to Galloway.

Erika Thorkelson wrote, 'If @MargaretAtwood would like to stop warring amongst women, she should stop declaring war against younger, less powerful women and start listening #metoo.' Goodness me! A declaration of war, eh! To which fulmination, Atwood replied with acerbic clarity, 'I have been listening for approx 60 years. Endorsing basic human rights for everyone is not warring against women. In order to have rights for women you have to have rights, period. Me (*sic*) being a blood-drinking monster does not make that untrue.' Another feminist luminary, Laura Krabappel, accused Atwood of betraying the sisterhood by giving priority to her 'powerful male friend over women's pain.' In vain did Atwood point out that she didn't, in fact, know Galloway personally. All to no avail. For defending a man against what she described as a process akin to a Salem witch trial, Atwood has been called a traitor to women and a bad feminist.

Atwood, a veritable if uncanonised saint of feminism because of her dystopian novel *The Handmaid's Tale,* has also attracted criticism for rejecting the idea, the obviously nonsensical idea one would have thought, that all women accusing men of 'sexual misconduct' are automatically to be believed, rather than having their claims taken seriously and investigated. She had the cheek, nay, the temerity, to suggest that women are human beings and, as such, are likely to display behaviour that at times is less than saintly, sometimes reprehensible and perhaps even criminal. Against the juggernaut of the #Me Too movement, she has also insisted on the absolute necessity for due process, an insistence now thought to be provocative! Since when has it been thought provocative to insist on due process? But 'provocative ' is precisely the word Rob Crilly uses to describes Atwood's article in *Globe and Mail* in a piece published in the *Telegraph* in January 2018. (Crilly) Atwood remarks, 'If the legal system is bypassed because it is seen as ineffectual, what will take its place? Who will be the new power brokers? It won't be the Bad Feminists like me.' And she points out the irony that by rejecting due process and the requirement for evidence, the #MeTooers 'are just feeding into the very old narrative that holds women to be incapable of fairness or of considered judgment, and they are giving the opponents of women yet another reason to deny them positions of decision-making in the world.' (Atwood)

Are all women happy to clamber aboard the #MeToo bandwagon? Or is it the case that, as Daphne Merkin writes in the *New York Times*, 'privately, I suspect, many of us, including many longstanding feminists, will be rolling our eyes, having had it with the reflexive and unnuanced sense of outrage that has accompanied this cause from its inception, turning a bona fide moment of moral accountability into a series of ad hoc and sometimes unproven accusations.'

Based on her impressions, she says that while women are publicly reluctant to dissent from the #MeToo orthodoxy, privately, they demur. '"Grow up, this is real life," I hear these same feminist friends say. "What ever happened to flirting?" and "What about the *women* who are the predators?" Some women, including random people I talk to in supermarket lines, have gone so far as to call it an outright witch hunt.' (Merkin)

Not all feminists, then, are gung-ho about the #MeToo moment. Some have argued that by lumping everything from rape and sexual assault to sexual gaucheries together, the focus of legitimate female complaint has been diffused. What disturbs some is the scattergun approach of #MeToo to the accusations that it encourages, accusations that are often radically indiscriminate in differentiating between inappropriate conduct, harassment and outright sexual assault, a lack of discrimination that encompasses a contempt for due process. 'In our current climate,' writes Merkin, 'to be accused is to be convicted. Due process is nowhere to be found .... Expressing sexual interest is inherently messy and, frankly, nonconsensual—one person, typically the man, bites the bullet by expressing interest in the other, typically the woman .... Some are now suggesting that come-ons need to be constricted to a repressive degree. Asking for verbal consent before proceeding with a sexual advance seems both innately clumsy and retrograde, like going back to the childhood game of "Mother, May I?" We are witnessing the re-moralization of sex, not via the Judeo-Christian ethos but via a legalistic, corporate consensus.' (Merkin)

The observation that the #MeToo campaign risked conflating the silly with the serious came quick and fast, and not just from men. Writing in *The Sunday Business Post*, Susan Mitchell remarked that 'this undoubtedly worthy campaign [#MeToo] against sexual assault is being diminished by some of the more trivial contributions. Relatively minor misdemeanours are being conflated with serious sexual assault, while the current discourse is reducing women to innocents who must be shielded from sexual advances and lewd jokes.' She went on to make the point, a discerning point in the context of what was to transpire in the Kavanaugh affair, that 'Assertions are not truths until they are corroborated and established as facts. Due process matters. But as the #MeToo avalanche continues to slide downhill, there is a real risk that innocent people will be buried.' (Mitchell 2017)

A slogan from the heyday of feminism was, 'The personal is political.' Well, no, it's not, unless you're a totalitarian. But what we now witness coming from the #MeToo movement is precisely the inability to distinguish between what is essentially a private matter (how was it for you?) and a public matter (rape or sexual assault). There is a difference in kind, not merely in degree, between assaulting someone and pestering someone, between being raped and just having an unpleasant or unfulfilling sexual experience. One of the deleterious effects of the #MeToo movement has been its characterisation of unsatisfactory sex as lying on a continuum that has sexual violence somewhere along the same line. Sexual violence is one thing; disappointing or regretted sex is quite another.

I suggested earlier that the difference between feminists in their attitudes to #MeToo seems to correspond to a generational divide. On the one hand, we have the older feminists who recommend toughening up, and who are portrayed as if they are outdated, past it, crotchety or just plain afraid; while on the other hand, we have the younger feminists, who are seen either as invested with a legitimate passion for justice, or marred by a naïve idealism, egoism and childishness. But to characterise the difference in approaches between the two sides solely in generational terms may be a little misleading, not least because there are representatives of each generation on each side—or so, argues Moira Donegan. The difference comes down, in the end, to their very different conceptions of what sexism is, and their two very different ideas of how to deal with it; one individual, the other communal; one pragmatic, the other idealistic; one self-sufficient, the other characterised by a sense of female solidarity. One kind of feminism, individual feminism, focuses on the individual, and recommends a pragmatic independence and self-sufficiency; the other kind, social feminism, the feminism of the #MeTooers, focuses on the community of women, and argues for a solidarity based on ideals.

Individual feminists, like Atwood, argue that social feminists fail to respect the individual autonomy of women and to recognise them as moral agents invested with the power to say *no* if *no* is what they want to say. Social feminists, on the other hand, argue that the problem is not an individual one or not *just* an individual one affecting particular women, but a global cultural force that affects every woman, whether that woman has been the object of rape, assault or harassment in her own person. Ms Donegan sums up the division between the disparate feminisms thus: 'There is a greater moral divide between these two strands of thought, because #MeToo and its critics also disagree over where to locate responsibility for sexual abuse: whether it is a woman's responsibility to navigate, withstand and overcome the misogyny that she encounters, or whether it is the shared responsibility of all of us to eliminate sexism, so that she never encounters it in the first place.' (Donegan)

While this particular instance of the division between feminists is contemporary, the divide itself has a history that goes deeper than the quotidian. Instead of mapping primarily onto a generational divide as it appears to at first glance, the two kinds of feminism instead map onto a philosophical divide. Individual feminism is firmly rooted in the broad liberal political tradition, and sees its problems and solutions in individual change and political evolution, whereas social feminism takes its stand solidly in a quasi-Marxist tradition, and partakes of that tradition's propensity to locate a universal enemy, whose evil machinations must be overcome not by evolutionary change but by revolution. What capitalism was to Marxism, sexism (courtesy of the patriarchy) is to social feminism. Sexism can only be overcome by structural and institutional change, not by individual strength and resolution. 'Social feminism,' writes Donegan, 'does not aspire to enable a few women to gain positions of power in patriarchal systems. It's not about giving women "a seat at the table". It's about taking the table apart, so that we can build a new one together.' (Donegan) Social feminism is closely linked to what has come to be known as identity politics. The identity in identity politics can, of course, vary, according to whatever is considered to be the identity marker— sex, race, sexuality or class. In respect of each identity, there is an identity oppressor—men (the patriarchy), whites (whiteness), or straights (hetero-normativity). For the #MeTooers, then, what they perceive as misogyny is not merely the slobbish acts of individuals, but a systemic warping that produces individual effects. Social feminism aims not at a transformation of individual conduct, but at a radical transformation of society as a whole.

Donegan is clear about the weakness of the #MeToo movement, which is that it is not entirely sure what collectivity it is whose interests and concerns and pain and suffering can be collectively identified. Donegan again: 'Women are a varied bunch, and they encounter intersecting oppressions that are not of patriarchy's exclusive making: racism, classism, ability and sexuality. Often, these oppressions are enforced by other women. There are vast gulfs that separate women from one another: gulfs of racism and money, of colonialism, bigotry, history, resentment, defensiveness, ignorance and hurt. It can be very hard to see each other across them.' (Donegan) Women are indeed varied and not just along the lines of intersectional oppression, as Donegan would have it. The fundamental flaw of the #MeTooers is to rely ultimately on a characterisation of women that identifies them by what they are opposed to, much as to many Irishmen of my generation, to be Irish was to be non-British! But women aren't just characterised by being non-X, where X is racism or sexism or classism or any other 'ism'. In fact, the thrust of Donegan's argument, whether she realises it or not, is to undermine the quasi-Marxist leanings of social feminism. She makes a gallant stab at it, however, suggesting that women can be defined as everyone who has experienced misogyny. This appears to make being a woman a matter of a contingent experience. But what if you are a female who *hasn't* experienced misogyny? Does that mean you aren't a woman? Of course not, because *all* women, it seems, experience misogyny. But if that is so, the point of Donegan's attempt at a definition of woman then becomes not a contingent experiential matter but something that is definitionally true, and so completely vacuous.

The issue then is this: are women fully developed moral individual agents with the ability to exercise moral choice and to take responsibility for what they do? Or are they, as it were, elements of a collective who stand together as the victims or potential victims of sexual harassment, sexual assault or rape, so that their suffering is not merely that of any one individual but of the group as a whole? Is a woman's experience of sexual wrongdoing by men merely the experience of that woman, which she can avoid or mitigate by her individual decisions, or is it indicative of a wider cultural force that can be countered only by the collective of women acting together? Despite the general accuracy of her analysis, Donegan's sympathies lie on the side of the collectivity. According to her, '#MeToo's sheer number of testimonies has vindicated theories of sexism as a universal, but not uniform, force—that is, as something that every woman will experience, but that every woman will experience in different ways.' (Donegan) Of course, the sheer number of testimonies does nothing of the kind or, at least, not without some serious begging of the question. The reason that the rabbit comes out of the hat is because it was carefully concealed there in the first place.

They do things differently in France

'They order, said I, this matter better in France.—' With these words, Laurence Sterne begins his 1768 work, *A Sentimental Journey through France and Italy*. As it happens, they order quite a few matters better in France, not least, the relationship between the sexes. At the height of the #MeToo frenzy, some French women published a letter in *Le Monde*, deploring the resultant witch-hunt. Apart from its five principal writers—Catherine Deneuve, Sarah Chiche, Catherine Millet, Catherine Robbe-Grillet and Peggy Sastre—the letter was signed by almost a hundred other French women, whose professions range from marketing consultant through gynaecologist-obstetrician and psychiatrist to architect. They wrote, 'Rape is a crime. But trying to pick up someone, however persistently or clumsily, is not—nor is gallantry an attack of machismo.' (Deneuve *et al.*; see also O'Connell) They note that it is right and proper that the sexual violence that some women were subjected to in their professional lives should be revealed, but they go on to say, 'But what was supposed to liberate voices has now been turned on its head: We are being told what is proper to say and what we must stay silent about—and the women who refuse to fall into line are considered traitors, accomplices!'

Calling a spade a spade instead of a long-handled gardening implement used for digging, they declare that 'what we are once again witnessing here is puritanism in the name of a so-called greater good, claiming to promote the liberation and protection of women, only to enslave them to a status of eternal victim and reduce them to defenceless preys of male chauvinist demons.' They see very clearly that accusations had now become tantamount to convictions, with little attempt to distinguish between the serious and the trivial. 'In fact,' they write, '#MeToo has led to a campaign, in the press and on social media, of public accusations and indictments against individuals who, without being given a chance to respond or defend themselves, are put in the exact same category as sex offenders. This summary justice has already had its victims: men who've been disciplined in the workplace, forced to resign, and so on, when their only crime was to touch a woman's knee, try to steal a kiss, talk about "intimate" things during a work meal, or send sexually-charged messages to women who did not return their interest.'

Many months before the circus of the abuse allegations against Brett Kavanaugh, they foresaw the incipient totalitarianism of the whole fraught business. 'Men, for their part, are called on to embrace their guilt and rack their brains for "inappropriate behavior" that they engaged in 10, 20 or 30 years earlier, and for which they must now repent. These public confessions, and the foray into the private sphere by self-proclaimed prosecutors, have led to a climate of totalitarian society.' Remarkably, given the eternal sexual tension present in male-female relationships, they see a freedom to bother as being indispensable to sexual freedom for men *and* for women. Sexual impulses, they wrote, 'are, by nature, offensive and primitive—but we are also able to tell the difference between an awkward attempt to pick someone up and what constitutes a sexual assault.' They note, as how could they not, that women are not reducible to their bodies, as indeed I might add, men are not reducible to theirs, and they most emphatically do *not* see themselves as the fragile, impotent, eternally put-upon perpetual victims that we see on display in the largely Anglophone media. 'As women, we don't recognise ourselves in this feminism that, beyond the denunciation of abuses of power, takes the face of a hatred of men and sexuality.'

One of the signatories to the Deneuve *et al.* letter, Anne-Elisabeth Moutet, published her own letter in various newspapers. She makes many of the same points that are made in the group letter but adds some elements of her own. She notes that the campaign was at first liberating, but then quickly turned into a social media indulgence. She takes particular exception to the implicit portrayal of women as 'shrinking violets, unable to shake off a bloke trying it on in a bar, traumatised for life the minute someone attempts frottage in a crowded train carriage. She says, 'I find that saying in a calm but VERY LOUD voice, "Will you stop touching my ass!" makes enough commuters laugh that the culprit slinks off at the next stop.' The relationships between men and women, in fact, all human relationships are, she says, 'a complicated skein of trial and error. In America, they tend to live in a black-and-white world, a binary universe of ones and zeroes.' (Moutet)

Commenting on the Deneuve *et al.* letter, Emily Dinsmore remarks, 'The letter's sentiments should resonate with the overwhelming majority of Western women—especially young, working women who have grown up in societies where their chances in education and the workplace are on a par with, and sometimes even better than, those of their male contemporaries. Life for young women is not a continual stream of unwanted sexual advances. Our pay rises or promotions are not contingent on seedy sexual favours.' (Dinsmore) But, as you might expect, the reaction to the French letter has not been entirely positive. Asia Argento tweeted in a resolute *ad feminam* mode that, 'Catherine Deneuve and other French women tell the world how their interiorised misogyny has lobotomised them to the point of no return', a sentiment that, if it had emerged from the mouth or the pen of a man, might itself reasonably have been considered misogynistic!

Women as harassers!

Sexual harassment is supposed to be a sex neutral transgression so that aggressors and victims may, in principle, be either male or female. Be that as it may, the whole world knows that a charge of sexual harassment is a legal tool that is used almost exclusively by females. How gratifying, then, to find that one's prejudgements are, well, prejudices, and that the whole world can mistake mere opinion for knowledge, and that sexual harassment can indeed be female on male. It was reported in August 2018 that a female professor at New York University, Avital Ronell, had been held responsible for the sexual harassment of a former male graduate student. (Alexander) The report describes what it calls 'a host of leading feminists'—a truly terrifying image; picture Valkyries wielding smartphones!—leaping to the defence of the maligned female professor. These are the same feminists, one must suppose, who are normally the cheerleaders for believing any and all accusations of sexual harassment, provided, of course, that it is male on female harassment. Harriet Alexander's report details how Professor Ronell kissed and touched Mr Nimrod Reitman repeatedly (Nimrod! Some raw work pulled at the baptismal font, as P. G. Wodehouse has often remarked), 'slept in his bed with him, demanded he lie in her bed, held his hand, texted, emailed and called him constantly, and refused to work with him if he did not reciprocate.' Avital Ronell is described by one of her colleagues as 'one of the very few philosopher stars of this world.' The light from the star that is Professor Ronell somehow failed to illuminate any dark philosophical places during my 45-year active academic career, so I suspect that this praise is more hyperbolic than veridical. At the end of an investigation that lasted almost a year, the University upheld her victim's claim of sexual harassment and Professor Ronnell was suspended for an academic year.

Ronell has argued that the misconduct against Reitman of which she has been accused would be impossible considering that they are both gay. 'Our communications,' she writes, 'which Reitman now claims constituted sexual harassment ... were between two adults, a gay man and a queer woman, who share an Israeli heritage, as well as a penchant for florid and campy communications arising from our common academic backgrounds and sensibilities ...' Professor Ronell goes on to say that she's heartbroken that her 'fast and loose and exuberant and stupid and childish use of language can somehow be gathered up to be a viable weapon' against her. (see Mangan) With the possible exception of 'exuberant', fast and loose and exuberant and stupid and childish use of language has to be the best description not only of Professor Ronell's emotional effusions vis-à-vis Mr Reitman, but of feminist writing in general.

A letter sent to NYU by Ronell's feminist cheering section, including the somewhat more stellar Judith Butler, described Mr Reitman as someone who had waged a malicious campaign against their sister—not much sympathy for the victim in evidence there!—and demanded that Professor Ronell 'be accorded the dignity rightly deserved by someone of her international standing and reputation.' (see Greenberg 2018) Indeed. Just the sort of dignity routinely denied to males who are accused of sexual harassment.

The Italian actress and filmmaker, Asia Argento, who achieved some prominence in the #MeToo movement after she told the *New Yorker* magazine that Harvey Weinstein had raped her at the Cannes Film Festival when she was 21, has herself received some unfavourable notices for unbecoming sexual misconduct. It seems that she paid almost $400,000 to a young actor who had filed suit against her for sexual assault! Jimmy Bennett, who co-starred with Argento in *The Heart Is Deceitful Above All Things*, claims that he had sex with Argento in a California hotel in 2013 when he was 17 years old, below the age of consent. This encounter apparently traumatised Mr Bennett, affected his mental health and damaged his career. The *Guardian* asked Ms Argento for comment but received no response, so too the *New York Times*, while Bennett, through a representative, declined an interview with the *New York Times*. Perhaps Mr Bennett was too traumatised to respond. (see Anon. 2018)

So, what do #MeTooers do with those victims who may themselves be victimisers? Some voices in the movement are eager to tell us that the accusations against Argento shouldn't discredit the whole movement. Moira Donegan tweeted, 'Cynical people are going to use individual examples of women's bad behaviour to argue that sexual harassment and assault are not part of structural misogyny, even that such abuses have no gender at all ... Ignore these people; they have little interest in justice.' Rose McGowan, another woman who has accused Weinstein of assault, tweeted of Argento that, 'our commonality is the shared pain of being assaulted by Harvey Weinstein. My heart is broken. I will continue my work on behalf of victims everywhere ... None of us know the truth of the situation and I'm sure more will be revealed ... Be gentle.' (see Wong) Indeed, we often know less than the full truth about many interpersonal situations and should await further revelations, but this is not a recommendation we are accustomed to hear from feminists when men are accused of sexual misdemeanours. Still less are we routinely counselled to 'be gentle.' The words 'sauce,' 'goose,' and 'gander' spring to mind.

In February 2018, California Assemblywoman Cristina Garcia, a leading voice in the #MeToo movement, faced accusations that she sexually harassed staffers, including one man who said she fired him after he refused to play a game of spin-the-bottle with her. He was fired two days after questioning the suggestion. But it seems that her spin-the-bottle suggestion wasn't the only thing problematic about Congresswoman Garcia's behaviour. It is alleged that she disparaged staff, telling them they were expendable, used vulgar language, and discussed topics considered to be inappropriate in the workplace, such as her sex life, as well as being vindictive. Garcia, who has been a strident critic of male colleagues who have been accused of sexual misconduct, denies the accusations. 'There have been several claims accusing me of inappropriate conduct in my role as a California State legislator,' she said. 'In each case, these accusations are simply not true and are inconsistent with my personal value system and how I seek to conduct myself as an elected official.' One complainant told the *Washington Post* that Garcia approached him after an assembly softball game in 2014, squeezed his buttocks and tried to touch his crotch. She was, he alleges, visibly intoxicated. Assemblywoman Garcia, who was first elected in 2012, has made women's issues her legislative priority and co-authored a bill that extended the legal definition of rape to include all forms of nonconsensual sexual assault. (Phillips)

The man described as the world's 'most prominent male feminist', Professor Michael Kimmel, is in trouble, accused of sexism and homophobia! A former graduate student, Bethany Coston, now a non-binary assistant professor of gender, sexuality and women's studies, has gone on record to accuse the Stony Brook professor. (see Coston) Coston was, it seems, afraid to speak out while it was a student because it was dependent upon Kimmel's recommendations, and feared retaliation if it did so, but now that it is safely out of Kimmel's orbit, it is free to speak fearlessly about what it thinks is wrong with him. It is outraged by Kimmel's 'benevolent sexist, second-wave feminist, trans-exclusionary frame of reference, which relies so heavily on stereotypical understandings of the gender binary that it also necessitates a homophobic understanding of sexuality', by his explicit sexual talk, by his lack of respect for anyone but cisgendered heterosexual men, by his homophobia, and by his transphobia. The more Professor Coston writes, much of which might seem to an unbiased observer to be inspired by personal pique at not being rewarded or acknowledged in the way it thinks it deserves, the more I sympathise with Kimmel; or at least I might do, if Kimmel hadn't spent his entire professional career telling his fellow men what's wrong with them and how they can be better, in books such as *Angry White Men: American Masculinity at the End of an Era*. 'Hoist with his own petard' is the phrase that springs to mind.

The unalloyed joys of the sexual revolution

One of the consequences of the sexual revolution of the 1960s and the years following was the empowerment of women to engage in sex anytime and with anyone. Happiness all around, then—or perhaps not. Female empowerment, it would seem, has led many young women on university campuses to have casual sexual encounters that they don't really want to have, hooking up, to use Tom Wolfe's term, sex with no strings attached, no relationship, just plain unadorned sex. It might be fun for women to act like this—then again, it might not—but it hardly seems like empowerment. I would go so far as to say that given the difference in sexual dynamics between males and females, a difference futilely denied by feminists, hooking up with men she barely knows is a sure and certain recipe for loss of power for a woman.

Without realising it, raunch feminism has walked young women into the ideal situation for young feckless men to take advantage of them in an environment where there is no dating, no courtship, just a few drinks and Robert is your father's brother. It is little wonder that in this swamp of casual sex, there is increasingly bitterness and disappointment and, in a significant number of cases, accusations of rape, when what probably happened is that two people engaged in a (often drunken) sexual encounter with few or no social constraints, no expectations and, as it used to be thought, no consequences. Writing as long ago as 1993, Roger Kimball noted,

> The demand for excessive freedom is a curious thing. Beginning in wholesale rebellion against restraint, it soon sets about erecting its own restraints—often harsher and more irrational than those it intended to replace. What was meant to shatter the bonds of convention and establish liberty ends up forging a new set of tyrannous conventions, all the more noxious for being imposed in the name of freedom.
>
> The latest access of sexual liberation is a case in point. Born in the 1960s, the movement for sexual liberation has followed a predictable trajectory. It started in naïve abandon—chanting "Down with monogamy, emotional commitment," etc.— and proceeded quickly through shock, disillusionment, bitterness, and rage. Herbert Marcuse, Norman O. Brown, and a thousand lesser gurus foretold the sensual paradise awaiting those who were bold enough to dispense with the repressive trapings of bourgeois morality. (Kimball)

But it seems that all is not well in our latter-day Garden of Eden. The lifting of all restrictions does not seem to have brought us joy unalloyed. As usual, the problem is with the snakes in the garden. There were biological kickbacks—sexually transmitted ailments of various kinds—and psychological kickbacks as well. Sex without strings seemed like a good idea until it was realised that the strings were perhaps a not insignificant part of what made sexual relationships satisfying in the first place. But, like the idiot driver who, upon realising that he is going in the wrong direction, drives even faster to get where he doesn't want to go instead of admitting his mistake and turning around, our free-love zealots, instead of conceding that the old rules that surrounded sex had developed for a reason (*not* the subjugation of women), felt the need to invent new rules which would restore some order to chaos. Rules there will be, one way or another. Will we have rules that have developed over time and have been stress-tested by experience, rules that we assimilate as part of the process of moral and social maturation; or will we have quasi-mechanical rules (for example, affirmative consent), that are incapable of being implemented? The rejection of the former type of rules has lead to the sex harassment industry. Kimball again: 'The restrictiveness and intrusiveness of the sexual-harassment industry have led some to describe it as a "new puritanism." In fact, it is a new marriage of radicalism and intolerance. In this sense, it represents the underside of the movement for sexual liberation: sharing crucial goals and assumptions but differing over questions of implementation and method. Far from signaling a return to traditional sexual scruples (as some commentators have suggested), the sexual-harassment industry is really a kind of guerrilla arm of feminism.' (Kimball)

Van Badham tells us that 'sexual freedom has become another realm of women's experience for patriarchy to conquer.' (Badham) Bad, bad patriarchy! There were all those women, having revolted in the glorious 60s to achieve the right to sexual freedom, and what happens? Men think this means that women have now become more sexually available for *them*! What could possibly have made men think *that*? So it seems to Ms Badham that, despite all the apparent freedoms that women have won for themselves, their lives are still lived in the looming shadow of the patriarchy, a system that is gendered, unequal and unfair. Thank God for sweeping and vague generalisations. However would feminists make an argument without them? We are so lucky to have the CNN reporter Kaitlan Collins to set men straight when she tells them that 'the younger women who work for you don't want to date you; do not want to be your soul mate; do not want to go to ice cream with you; do not want to be your partner.' (Collins) How she knows this is not quite as clear as her ringing statement that it is so, but let that pass. And why she seems to think that these younger women aren't capable of making their feelings about possible relationships with men clear to those pesky men isn't quite clear either, but I suppose it's that pernicious patriarchy at work yet again.

At Christmas 2017, the Police Service of Northern Ireland tweeted, 'If you bump into that special someone under the mistletoe tonight, remember that without consent it is rape #SeasonsGreetings.' If this official utterance is anything to go by, the sexual revolution would appear to have ground to a halt! Just what does the PSNI imagine people *do* under the mistletoe? Is kissing someone now a matter of rape? Bizarre as this incident might be, it is still indicative of an emerging official attitude towards sex that would make it to be presumptively a criminal matter unless rescued from criminality by the magic wand of consent.

The new Puritanism is everywhere. Be careful, Big Sister is Watching You! Come back *1984*, all is forgiven! The Junior Anti-Sex League has been reconstituted and is hard at work; trigger warnings, mandatory sex consent classes for incoming students at university, and the nauseating sancti-moniousness of the #MeToo movement. The new misery-guts approach to sex views the world through the twisted lens of misandry. Anything outside the narrow tramlines of the officially approved, which means outside the pre-contracted, pre-arranged, at all costs not spontaneous approach to human relationships, is *verboten*.

Of course, the new norms on sexuality are not a war on sex on all fronts but rather a war on male sexuality. Sex on a woman's terms is just fine. When can we expect to see a woman being fired from her job for an inappropriate comment or a wayward hug? Imagine what would happen if a man were to report an unwanted advance by a woman to the police. Had a good laugh? I thought so. For years, feminists have been moaning about men's attempts to control their sexuality. There can be little doubt that the new politically correct #MeToo social norms are a well-conceived and well-executed attempt to control men's sexuality. The war on sex is really a war on men, on men having sex, on male sexuality, on just about male everything, except, of course, on men doing all the unpleasant jobs upon which our society depends.

Where are we now?

The #MeToo movement has many charming aspects to it, perhaps too many to list. It is a court of first and last instance with no possible appeal against accusation/conviction. If you are accused, you'll get a fair trial on Twitter and then you'll be hanged. It's view of men, women and sex is distinctly and charmingly retrograde. All men are sexual predators who think of nothing but sex; while all women are innocent victims, actual or potential, for whom sex is essentially a loathsome form of interpersonal communication unless, of course, it is something they momentarily and enthusiastically happen to desire.

There is an inherent danger in attempting to combat irrationality with rationality, and that is that you give the irrational a respect it does not deserve. The proper response to some absurdities is not logical argument but ridicule and contempt. There's an old adage to the effect that you should never wrestle with a pig— the pig likes it and, win or lose, you'll get dirty. The #MeTooers are not into rationality and evidence and argument. They're engaged in a no-holds-barred war against men. Men are sexual predators and women are their prey. Women are frail creatures, likely to faint or have conniptions if approached by a man with dishonourable intentions or even with honourable ones. It is useless to point out that even if some men are sexual predators, most men are not. That is true, but it has no effect on the #MeToo warriors for they believe, in their heart of hearts, that all men are like that, it's just that the men who don't behave that way overtly are either gutless or express their deep-rooted sexism in other ways. For the #MeToo movement, then, it seems that sex is beginning to be perceived as somehow, well, dirty, an unnerving return to what was supposed (wrongly) to be the attitude of the Victorians. 'Lie back and think of England!' Male desire, perhaps at one time necessary to preserve the species, is past its sell-by date now that we have in vitro-fertilisation and soon, we may hope, along with Frances Swiney, artificial wombs. Bring on the Brave New World!

The #MeToo movement is a prime example of a moral panic, predicated on what would seem to be a few well-publicised cases of really bad behaviour by a small number of atypical men, followed by the groundless assertion that this behaviour is typical of men at large. It is carried on by means of a form of mob-hysteria on the suitably idiotically named platform, Twitter. Employers, terrified of being caught in a Twitterstorm, hasten to rid themselves with dispatch of anyone accused of anything that is in any way sexually problematic, lest they too catch the fatal disease by electronic contagion. Any man who dares to criticise the movement is told in a Hironoesque manner to shut up; any woman who dares to criticise the #Metoo movement is likely to be told that she suffers from internalised misogyny! Dissent will not be tolerated!

The #MeToo movement postulates the existence of a continuum of sexual malfeasance that ranges from jokes in bad taste at one end, to gang rape at the other. This supposed continuum demonises the male half of the world's population, while simultaneously trivialising real sexual violence. When it comes to alleged sexual malfeasance, do we distinguish between serious assaults and awkward advances, or are they all the same thing in the end? In its bizarrely puritanical view of sex, in which men are perpetual predators and women are perpetual victims, it demonises men and undermines women's autonomy. Wasn't feminism supposed to be about empowering women, not infantilising them? An irony, one that is largely unnoticed, is that in fact women in the West have every legal protection yet, despite this, or perhaps because of it, they labour under the seemingly irremovable misapprehension that they are disadvantaged and unprotected. As remaining forms of discrimination against women steadily disappear, particularly legal forms of discrimination, so the myth grows that there is an invisible but powerful force, the patriarchy, repressing females, despite there being little or no evidence for this and such evidence as there is indicating that women are, in fact, relatively more privileged than men.

In its assertion of the 'Believe women!' mantra, the #MeToo movement undermines the fundamental legal principle of the presumption of innocence. To be accused is to be convicted. To deny the accusation is itself a further sign of guilt. The fatuousness of the 'Believe women!' mantra is self-evident. *Everything* women say? Even when one woman contradicts another? All women or only some women? All women or only those women who play the victim card? Is there to be any consideration of the intrinsic plausibility of what these women claim, or is it sufficient for them just to make the claim? It now appears that a woman can make an allegation about some purported malfeasance no matter how long ago it was supposed to have taken place, no matter that there is no independent evidence to support the allegation or witnesses to attest to its truth, and that allegation is enough to get a man fired and to suffer public obloquy.

There is an old legal maxim which says that there is no offence without a law—*nulla poena sine lege*. This maxim is often taken to include the provisions that the laws be already published, that is, not retroactive, and also well defined, so that one can know in advance that one is engaging in criminal conduct. What men are being accused of in the #MeToo movement runs the gamut from serious sexual assault, which is a crime, to, well, who knows what? Senator Al Franken was accused of, among other things, squeezing a woman's waist while posing for a photograph! Crikey! What depravity! Everything depends on how a woman feels about something like this, even many, many years later. There is no clear definition of the supposed offence, thus materially violating the maxim of *nulla poena*, and seemingly no statute of limitations on when a charge or accusation may be brought.

The #MeToo movement has the effect of making relations between the sexes intrinsically adversarial. The sheer naked undiscriminating aggression of the #MeToo movement is likely to provoke a reaction so that men, fearing accusations which could cost them their jobs, their reputations or even land them in jail, will avoid contact with women unless chaperoned. This is already happening. (see O'Hanlon) Relations between the sexes are, and have always been, complex and not infrequently messy. Speech is only one means of human communication and not always the most significant. We also communicate with looks, gestures, body postures and the acceptance of socially coded invitations. Shakespeare wrote: 'Sometimes from her eyes I did receive fair speechless messages.' What a pervert!

A little light relief

To make up for all the heavy-duty stuff you've just read, here is a little light relief. Andy Shaw published a piece in the *Spectator* in April 2018 which showed the way forward for all sensitive men who, appalled by the egregious wrongs done to women by men over the ages, wish to atone for those wrongs. Shaw outlines a 7-step programme that no reasonable man could possibly take issue with. I present Shaw's programme here in a re-modelled form since his effort, though a good first shot, isn't sufficiently radical. (see Shaw 2018)

First, we men must realise that the whole idea of sexual attraction is intrinsically demeaning to women. Women's bodies, though taking up space and thus, in one sense, objects, in another, and more important sense, are *not* objects. Being sexually attracted to a woman is always to treat her as an object, and that's bad, very bad. So, repress those vile feelings of attraction and don't look at women as sexual objects. Better still, don't look at women at all. If that proves impossible, ask women to cooperate with you in helping to de-objectify your glances by, perhaps, dressing in potato sacks or wearing bags over their heads. I'm sure they'll appreciate your woke concern and be willing to help you.

Second, remember that as a man you have all the power so that if anything goes wrong in a relationship, it's your fault. It's always your fault, even (and perhaps especially) when it's not your fault. Since unwanted sexual advances are a form of sexual abuse, the best and by far the safest strategy is never to make any sexual advances at all. Flirting, of course, is out, as the Mikado (as portrayed by W. S. Gilbert in the ground-breaking sociological work of that name) so clearly recognised —'so he decreed, in words succinct, that all who flirted, leered or winked (unless connubially linked), should forthwith be beheaded .... and I expect you'll all agree that he was right to so decree'—and attempted seduction must be regarded as equivalent to rape. The only way around these seemingly insurmountable barriers is to have all possible sexual partners draw up a contract encompassing all possible scenarios (in graphic detail), with procedures for agreeing upon the initiation, duration and character of any possible form of sexual interaction. As Shaw puts it, 'A woman must give full and conscious consent to each stage of a liaison. So when you meet a woman for the first time, start by discussing the possible outcomes of the relationship. Jointly draw up a list of possible activities and discuss the various emotional responses that each of you may experience. The list must include all possible communications (talking, Snapchat, phone calls and emails), physical touching (holding hands, kissing, sex, massage, and so on), emotional needs and expectations, as well as long-term hopes for the relationship. When you are both happy with the finalised list, append the official 'standard terms' consent contract and ask one of the bar staff to act as a witness to your joint signatures. You may now engage in early-stage flirtation.' Of course, as Shaw and I both realise, it might be difficult to arrange even this anodyne form of approach by men to women (never the other way around, of course), since even proposing such a contract would itself seem to constitute a form of sexual abuse, but bootstrapping problems can be overcome with a little goodwill on each side. But of course, if any woman disapproves *ex ante* of the proposing of such a proposal, it will constitute sexual harassment or even sexual abuse. But then, with power goes responsibility, so we men must learn to live on the edge.

Third, if, *per impossible*, sexual congress ever occurs, make sure you continue not to objectify your female partner. Think of England or chat about the latest

Paris fashions or discourse on the vagaries of international exchange rates, but do not, repeat *not*, focus on any aspect of your partner's anatomy in a way that could be considered objectifying. At all costs and at all times, you must ensure that her consent is enthusiastic and continuous. Be alert to the slightest sign that consent may have been withdrawn because, should that happen, failure to cease your activities on the instant, even by so much as a microsecond, will constitute rape. As the Ansari episode revealed you must develop the ability to read a woman's mind and the difficulty (even impossibility) of such a task will not be accepted as an excuse for failure. I know you may say that in the heat of sexual congress, your attention might be somewhat distracted, but that also is no excuse. Remember, you have all the power and are responsible for everything. It might be a good idea to record proceedings (sound and vision) so as to have a record to hand in case of disputes or, alternatively, you might bring along a third party to act as a referee who can advise on procedures and remind you of the latest policies as promulgated by the Junior Anti-Sex league.

Fourth, realise the inexpressibly sad fact that you're only a man, so don't talk—listen. Despite the misogynistic canard that women never stop talking, women's voices in fact are never heard. Yes, I know it doesn't seem like that but that's just another example of men's inability to perceive the obvious. Men have talked for aeons; now it's the turn of women. Feminists, who of course speak for all women and not just for themselves, must be listened to respectfully and their pronouncements agreed with. No evidence may be requested to support feminists' pronouncements and counter-arguments are not welcome. As Senator Mazie Hirono very reasonably told us during the Kavanaugh hearings, 'I just want to say to the men in this country, just shut up ...', and who could argue with that?

Fifth, realise just how insidious the patriarchy is. Some women you are acquainted with who seem to like men and appear to have reasonably amicable relations with them are, in fact, victims of false consciousness. They don't know it, poor things, but they have internalised the rampant misogyny embodied in our culture. Make sure you point out to them—respectfully, of course, and without mansplaining—just how oppressed they are, and introduce them to the thoughts of their enlightened and emancipated sisters, who will quickly make their relationships with the men in their lives suitably vitriolic and adversarial.

Sixth, act to bring about real equality for women everywhere, not just in politics or business or law or medicine or in any other well-paid and comfortable positions, but also in the less desirable areas of life which have, of course, been selfishly dominated up to now by men. We need to bring about equal representation for women in drug dealing, car thievery and street crime, in front-line combat and in work-related deaths, and we might need to introduce some specific female-only crimes to bump up women's under-representation in the prison population. One practical strategy would be to arrange a series of job-swaps so that women, for example, could be forced to collect rubbish, fix roofs and work on oil rigs, while men are forced to become primary school teachers and secretaries and social workers. As Shaw says so sapiently and unanswerably, 'Equal representation requires radical action.'

Last of all, admit that feminists are funny. So laugh at them. Also, if you feel charitable, laugh at their jokes.

Finally, I came across this delicious piece of satire on the web. Unfortunately, I forgot to make a note of the source at the time I read it and, despite a reasonably comprehensive subsequent search, I haven't been able to re-find it. Credit to the author whoever he may be. A woman speaks:

> If I have sex and enjoy the experience, that means I exercise autonomy and this is supposed to be very good, but later I remember that I was drunk at the time which sort of kills the idea of autonomy and makes me feel pathetic. I then 'remember' that it was the guy put pressure on me to get wasted and have sex with him. It is clear then that I was raped. On other occasions I dress like a whore and enjoy seeing how my boobs have complete power over men. I feel good because it shows how comfortable with my body I am and how clever I am at dominating men. But the following day I realise that treating yourself like a piece of meat is the opposite of empowering and I feel shit. Fortunately, feminist theory will tell me that I never wanted to exhibit my body, it was the fashion industry, controlled by perverted men that makes us women think we want to be sexy when in fact what we really want is to be Madame Curie. It's clear that I was a victim of a culture of objectifica-tion. We also try really hard to do stuff that fascists think is a man's thing. You know how hard it is to pretend we are interested in car mechanics, boxing, fantasy foot-ball or DIY? Have you any idea how difficult it is to pretend we don't want to have babies or we want to be plumbers or we don't care what our nails look like? I tell you it's torture. Relief only comes when we realise that we don't enjoy those things because we've internalised patriarchal notions that enslave our minds. It's clear we are victims. So please have some compassion. And now I'm off to the hairdresser whilst I pretend to be cleaning the spark plugs of a motorcycle I don't want to have.

Perhaps you are a man and remain unconvinced by what I've written so that, in your heart, you wish to show solidarity with the #MeToo movement. Here's how to do it, gentlemen. (see Reynolds 2018) Call one another out or, in less physically confrontational English, challenge one another. Don't laugh at sexist jokes. If one of your buddies is making a woman uncomfortable, call him ... sorry, challenge him to stop. Don't try to persuade someone to have sex with you who isn't into it. If you're not sure something is acceptable, ask your girlfriend. Ask women if they need support (like Elliot with Allison), but not in a patronising way, of course. Don't run down women with your car. Don't push them under buses. Don't ..... Sorry, I got carried away with a kind of Reynoldian passion. Ignore the stuff about cars and buses. Sorry again! I don't mean that you *should* run down women with your car or push them under buses, just that Reynolds, despite her magnificent condescension, didn't, in fact, manage to include those items in her male not-to-do list.

A Fate Worse than Death

The young have strong passions and tend to gratify them indiscriminately.
Of the bodily desires, it is the sexual by which they are most swayed
and in which they show absence of self-control
—Aristotle

Coito ergo sum
—Anonymous

Historically, the term 'rape' has had at least two quite different senses. In its original signification, rape meant abduction (*raptus*), the removal of an unmarried woman from the custody of her father. Quite often, this was done with the willing cooperation of the woman and constituted what we would today call an elopement. The offence was the flouting of the authority of the *pater familias*, and it often occurred as a way of circumventing the parental prohibition of the marriage of the two parties. Of course, on some occasions, it was simply a form of kidnapping, either as a prelude to a demand for ransom or even for more nefarious purposes. The second sense of rape—forced sexual intercourse with or through violence (*stuprum*)—is generally what people have had in mind when they talked about rape, and most people still do. I believe it is fair to say that the use of violence or the threat of violence by a man against a woman to procure sexual intercourse has been an essential constituent element of *stuprum* for much of Western legal history. On this conception of the crime, rape is essentially a crime of physical violence, actual or threatened. In their *A Natural History of Rape*, Randy Thornhill and Craig Palmer write that 'By one intuitive and relevant definition, rape is copulation resisted to the best of the victim's ability unless such resistance would probably result in death or serious injury to the victim or in death or injury to individuals the victim commonly protects.' (Thornhill & Craig, 1) (NB: the next two sections contain a summary account of the changing definition of rape in common law jurisdictions. Readers not especially interested in legal minutiae might want to skip to the section 'A fate worse than death?' (p.175 ff below), returning to these sections when, and if, necessary.)

The changing definition of rape

During the twentieth century, ideas of what rape consisted in began to change so that it went from being primarily a crime of force or violence to being a violation of the victim's autonomy. It might still involve physical violence but it also might not, nor did it necessarily have to. On this altered conception of rape, for example, a woman who had sex with a man whom she believed to be her husband but who was in fact another man impersonating her husband would be raped, even though there was no physical violence or threat of violence. If what appears to be voluntary consent is vitiated by any factor, not just physical violence or the threat of violence, then the resultant sexual congress is rape. So, for example, deception or intoxication are factors that could vitiate apparent consent. The key trajectory in the changing definitions of rape has been the gradual erosion of the necessity for force or violence, or the threat of force or violence, and its replacement by the idea of consent. Let's take a look at what the law in some common law jurisdictions have to say about rape.

The Irish Criminal Law (Rape) Act 1981 defines rape as occurring when a man has unlawful sexual intercourse with a woman who, at the time of the intercourse, does not consent to it and at that time he knows that she does not consent to the intercourse or he is reckless as to whether she does or does not consent to it. In rape trials, whenever a jury has to consider whether a man believed that a woman was consenting to sexual intercourse, the presence or absence of reasonable grounds for such a belief is a matter to which the jury is to have regard, in conjunction with any other relevant matters, in considering whether he genuinely so believed. The Act goes on to rule out (special circumstances aside) the admissibility of any evidence pertaining to the complainant's sexual experience with persons other than the defendant. It also rules out (special circumstances aside) the publication of anything that would lead the public to identify the complainant or the defendant.

The Criminal Law (Rape) (Amendment) Act, 1990 amended the 1981 Act. Its definition of rape is as follows. Rape is a sexual assault that includes penetration (however slight) of the anus or mouth by the penis, or penetration (however slight) of the vagina by any object held or manipulated by another person. (Sexual assault in turn is defined as the offence of indecent assault upon any male or female person.) The 1981 Act and the 1990 Act are to be construed together. The change from 1981 to 1990 includes the broadening of the definition of rape so that it may be committed by either a man or a woman, inasmuch as the Irish law includes in its definition of rape what is independently considered by English law as assault by penetration. The category of possible victims of rape has also been broadened to include either a woman or a man. As in English law, the Act abolishes any rule of law by which a husband cannot be guilty of the rape of his wife. When a jury comes to consider the question of consent, a failure or omission by the complainant to offer resistance to the penetration does not of itself constitute consent to it.

The Criminal Law (Rape) Amendment Act 1990 was itself amended in respect of the notion of consent by s. 48 of the Criminal Law (Sexual Offences) Act 2017 which reads:

1) A person consents to a sexual act if he or she freely and voluntarily agrees to engage in that act.

2) A person does not consent to a sexual act if—

(a) he or she permits the act to take place or submits to it because of the application of force to him or her or to some other person, or because of the threat of the application of force to him or her or to some other person, or because of a well-founded fear that force may be applied to him or her or to some other person,

(b) he or she is asleep or unconscious,

(c) he or she is incapable of consenting because of the effect of alcohol or some other drug,

(d) he or she is suffering from a physical disability which prevents him or her from communicating whether he or she agrees to the act,

(e) he or she is mistaken as to the nature and purpose of the act,

(f) he or she is mistaken as to the identity of any other person involved in the act,

(g) he or she is being unlawfully detained at the time at which the act takes place,

(h) the only expression or indication of consent or agreement to the act comes from somebody other than the person himself or herself.

3) This section does not limit the circumstances in which it may be established that a person did not consent to a sexual act.

4) Consent to a sexual act may be withdrawn at any time before the act begins, or in the case of a continuing act, while the act is taking place.

5) Any failure or omission on the part of a person to offer resistance to an act does not of itself constitute consent to that act.

In Ireland, those accused of rape can be named only if convicted, but in England, the names of those accused of rape are in the public realm, often for months or even years, while the identity of their accusers remains undisclosed. Some have made the argument that since accusations of rape (false or otherwise) can cause serious damage to those accused, there should be anonymity for all involved in rape trials, the accused as well as the complainant. Some who oppose anonymity for the accused in such cases argue that the interests of open justice trump the possibility of reputational and consequent damage. I might be convinced of the *bona fides* of those who argue in this way if their desire for legal transparency extended to the revelation of the identities of the alleged victims of such crimes as well as that of defendants, but this kind of consistency is not what we get. Instead, we are told, as in a *Times*'s leader, that anonymity for complainants is justified because there are many victims of sex crimes who, because of a fear of humiliation or just not being taken seriously, fail to report them.

It seems to me that there are two coherent positions to take on this matter: anonymity for all (as in Irish law), or anonymity for none—take your pick. The other possibilities are: anonymity for the accused but not for the complainant (no one is advocating this!), and anonymity for the complainant but not for the accused, which is the case at present in English law and which is manifestly incoherent. However, in a subsequent leader, the *Times* changed its tune, arguing that the accused needed protection too. The reason? As Maura McGowan, the Chairman of the Bar Council put it, there is a stigma associated with sex crimes that attaches itself to those accused of perpetrating them, whether they are eventually acquitted or not. I would add that this stigma is aggravated when it is combined, as it has been, with the steady erosion of the principle of the presumption of innocence. In August 2019, the UK's Justice Secretary's proposal that those suspected of criminal activities should be granted anonymity until charged was firmly rejected by both Downing Street and by his own Department! Robert Buckland's proposal was intended to cover not just those accused of sexual offences but *all* crimes. Moreover, if such anonymity had been granted, it would have been granted only until charges had been laid, not until trial and conviction. Mr Buckland had said earlier that he supported a campaign by Sir Cliff Richard to ban the naming of people arrested for rape and other sexual offences, and had added that there was a good case to be made for extending this policy to those accused of other offences where someone's good name stood to be undermined by a mere accusation.

In English law, rape was originally a common law rather than a statutory offence, and it was defined as 'the carnal knowledge of a woman forcibly and against her will.' It was held to be a felony rather than a misdemeanour. (These distinctions are no longer in force—see the Criminal Law Amendment Act 1967.) It eventually morphed into statutory form in the Offences against the Person Act 1828, where it was declared that 'every Person convicted of the Crime of Rape shall suffer death as a Felon.' (§16) To suffer death as a felon meant death by hanging and the confiscation of lands and goods. The death penalty was eventually changed to transportation, then to penal servitude for life, and then imprisonment for life. Because sexual intercourse between a man and a woman is something that is not presumptively criminal (or, at least, it used to be so considered), those who claimed to have been raped were expected to show that they had resisted the act physically and continuously. Moreover, consent was presumed to exist in the matter of sexual relations between husband and wife. As the seventeenth-century jurist, Sir Matthew Hall, noted, 'Rape is an accusation easily to be made and hard to be proved, and harder still to be defended by the party accused, tho' never so innocent.' (Hall, 634)

In English law, an updated statutory definition of rape was given in section 1 of the Sexual Offences (Amendment) Act 1976. This held that a man commits rape if (a) he has unlawful sexual intercourse with a woman who at the time of the intercourse does not consent to it; and (b) at that time he knows that she does not consent to the intercourse or he is reckless as to whether she consents to it. A somewhat broader definition was given in the Criminal Justice and Public Order Act 1994, one key aspect of which is that the victim of a rape is no longer exclusively considered to be a woman, though the perpetrator is exclusively considered to be a man. The Act held that it is an offence for a man to rape a woman or another man, and a man commits rape if (a) he has sexual intercourse with a person (whether vaginal or anal) who at the time of the intercourse does not consent to it; and (b) at the time he knows that the person does not consent to the intercourse or is reckless as to whether that person consents to it. The Act also held that a man commits rape if he induces a married woman to have sexual intercourse with him by impersonating her husband.

Currently in England, rape is defined in the Sexual Offences Act 2003 c. 42 in the following way: a person (A) commits an offence (rape) (i) if he intentionally penetrates the vagina, anus or mouth of another person (B) with his penis, (ii) B does not consent to the penetration, and (iii) A does not reasonably believe that B consents. Whether or not A's belief of B's consent is reasonable is to be determined by taking into account all the circumstances, including any measures that A has taken to ascertain that consent. There are other, lesser, offences: assault by penetration, sexual assault, and causing a person to engage in sexual activity without consent, all of which follow the same basic structure as the definition of rape, the elements being varied appropriately. (see Fig. 1)

DPP v Morgan (1975) had held that an honest belief by a man that a woman with whom he was engaged in sexual intercourse was consenting was a defence to rape, irrespective of whether that belief was based on reasonable grounds.

It remained the law until the enactment of the Sexual Offences Act 2003. This changed the requirements of the defence of mistaken belief in consent, specifically in relation to the matter of its reasonability. A defendant's belief must now be reasonable. His belief is presumed to be unreasonable when violence is used or feared, when the complainant is unconscious or drugged or is unable to communicate a lack of consent by reason of a disability. Unreasonability is also presumed where the complainant is unlawfully detained. The shift in approach in regard to reasonability is essentially a shift from a subjective to an objective test, from what the accused thought, to what he could reasonably be expected to have thought in the circumstances. The 2003 Act also defines as distinct offences: assault by penetration, sexual assault and causing sexual activity without consent. The reasonability conditions for consent for these offences are the same as for rape but the material dimension of the crimes differ. Assault by penetration is the intentional penetration of the vagina or anus of a person by a part of the body or anything else where that penetration is sexual and the other person does not consent. Sexual assault occurs where a person intentionally touches another person and the touching is sexual and the other person does not consent.

Fig.1

Sexual Offences (Amendment) Act 1986	Criminal Justice and Public Order Act 1994	Sexual Offences Act 2003
Unlawful sexual intercourse by a man with a woman	Sexual intercourse by a man with another person (man or woman)	Intentional penile penetration by A of the vagina, anus or mouth of another person B
who at the time does not consent to it	who at the time does not consent to it	B does not consent
the man knows she did not consent or is reckless as to whether she did consent	the man knows that the person did not consent or is reckless as to whether that person did consent	A does not reasonably believe that B consents. The reasonability of B's belief is to be determined by having regard to all the circumstances, including any steps A has taken to ascertain whether B consents

The history of the changing definition of rape in the USA is very similar to what has taken place in the UK and Ireland. For most of the twentieth century, the definition of rape in the USA was that it was 'the carnal knowledge of a female, forcibly and against her will.' That meant that it was an act of rape only if a man forcibly penetrated a unwilling woman through her vagina. It excluded oral and anal penetration, sexual assault of males, and penetration of the vagina and anus with an object or body part other than the penis, and sexual assault of females by females and non-forcible sexual assault. The new definition of rape, updated in 2012, is that rape is the 'penetration, no matter how slight, of the vagina or anus with any body part or object, or oral penetration by a sex organ of another person, without the consent of the victim', a definition which is very close to Irish law as amended in 1990, and the UK from 2003. (see United States Department of Justice Archives) The announcement of the change in the definition began with a statement that, coming from an official source, is bizarrely triumphalistic: 'In a victory for survivors of rape and their advocates, the Attorney General announced a newly revised definition of rape for nationwide data collection .... The change sends an important message to all victims that what happens to them matters, and to perpetrators that they will be held accountable.' On the new definition, a man or a woman can be the victim of a rape, and a man or a woman can be the perpetrator. In addition, there will be circumstances in which consent cannot be given—intoxication or mental incapacity—and the absence of physical resistance cannot be taken to indicate consent. Once again, the similarities to the latest iteration of Irish and UK law is obvious. The definition of rape in all three jurisdictions is convergent.

A typology of forms of rape.
It's not easy to keep all the various factors in mind when considering the matter of rape, so let's see if we can produce a rough typology of forms of rape, using the already-mentioned section 48 list of the Irish Criminal Law (Sexual Offences) Act 2017 as our guide (see above p. 167). While §2a of the 2017 Act repeats the traditional element of the use of force or the threat of the use of force as vitiating any apparent consent (I would include §2g here as well), §§2b-f and §2h significantly widen the factors that can vitiate consent and, as §3 notes, there may be other vitiating factors not as yet listed. §4 is significant in that it holds that even genuine consent may be withdrawn at any time before or during a sexual act, and §5 is applicable to §2a inasmuch as it indicates that a failure to offer resistance to a sexual act does not, in itself, constitute consent to it.

Rape, then, is either a matter essentially involving violence or the threat of violence (RV), or it is not (RnV). Non-violent rape (RnV) can be further divided. It is either a matter where consent *cannot* be given (RnV1) because the alleged victim lacks the *psychic* capacity (temporarily or permanently) to give consent, or from a *physical* incapacity to indicate consent; or (RnV2) where the putative victim is under the influence of drugs or alcohol but is not necessarily unconscious, or is mistaken about the nature and purpose of the act or the identity of other people involved in the act, or where the other person or people involved in the act violate a condition upon which the alleged victim's consent is predicated.

This, then, gives us three broad categories of rape: RV, RnV1 and RnV2. Of these three categories, RV is the original and prototypical kind of rape. It is of rape thus conceived that the crime is rightly regarded with the horror and revulsion that it is. RnV1 contain a list of deplorable scenarios that, in terms of their moral reprobation, range from something close to RV to something somewhat less gross. The only good thing that can be said about sexual intercourse with human beings who are completely unconscious is that at least it doesn't, apart from the act itself, involve the infliction of physical violence upon them. Other than that, the activity is almost as vile and repulsive as the paradigm RV. Much the same estimate can be made of sexual intercourse with those whose mental state removes essential human agency from them. In the category of RnV1, however, sexual intercourse with someone who is asleep may be marginally problematic in that there are degrees of sleepiness ranging from something close to complete unconsciousness through stages of half-sleep to near waking. The scenarios in RnV2 are, with the exception of consent given solely by proxy, less obviously morally problematic than what we have in RV and RnV1.

Laura Perrins tells us that the legal definition of rape and consent is changing. (Perrins) The average woman-in-the-street's conception of rape as a violent encounter between a woman and a stranger to her is, she tells us, not what is usually on offer in rape trials. She is correct in this, though the emotional revulsion still evoked by the term 'rape' is derived primarily from such stereo-typically violent scenarios (RV). It used to be that women who complained of rape were regarded with some suspicion, so much so that a conviction couldn't be obtained on their evidence alone. Those days are long gone. When convictions were first allowed on the basis of the complainant's testimony alone, juries used to be warned about the dangers of conviction on this basis. That warning too has gone the way of the dodo. Although there are some countries such as Finland where violence is still the essential core of rape (though, under pressure from the Council of Europe not, perhaps, for much longer—see Boffey), the juris-prudential momentum in Western countries has been to shift from violence or the threat of violence to consent, from RV to RnV. In July 2019, Greece became the latest European jurisdiction to change its definition of rape from 'a forced sexual act following violence or the threat of severe or direct danger' to 'any non-consensual act.' (See AP; also Oppenheim) We have a list of circumstances in which consent cannot be given or where consent was given but was induced by prohibited means—deception, or failure to carry out the sexual encounter on the terms agreed to, for example, using a condom.

In all these changes, we are moving ever further from the woman-in-the-street's paradigmatic idea of what rape is, which may or may not be a good thing, but is worth bearing in mind. In a case where a man having agreed to use a condom failed to do so, or damaged the condom, or where he agreed to withdraw before ejaculation but did not do so, the Irish High Court has held that rape may have occurred. In 2018, a man was jailed for rape for refusing to put on a condom during sex! The man received a sentence of three and a half years when convicted of raping a woman that he had been dating. The Central Criminal Court in Dublin was told that the woman informed the man that she was not interested in sex without a condom but that he had sex with her anyway. According to a report, the man stopped what he was doing when she told him he was raping her. The judge, Mr Justice Paul Butler, said he had been thinking about the case since it began and it had troubled him deeply. In the 18 years he had been dealing with rape cases, he noted that this case fell into one of the lowest categories he had come across. There had been some consensual sexual activity between the parties and the only clear rule was no unprotected sex. He said this was ignored on this one occasion and that this constituted rape. In her victim impact statement, the woman said the rape had 'destroyed her spirit' and described sleeping with a knife under her pillow for a time afterwards. She said the rape had affected every branch of her life in a profound way. She also said that she was in fear of the accused and afraid of his coming at her with a knife or sledgehammer, but the judge noted that there had been no suggestion of any such violence or any violence at all other than the rape. It may or may not be true that the woman's spirit was broken, though that is somewhat hard to believe. What is not hard to believe is that the man's life is seriously damaged, given that he will serve three and half years in jail and have a permanent record as a sex offender. The paradigm of rape has changed dramatically where a woman has the power to say 'stop, you're raping me,' and the would-be rapist stops!

In a somewhat similar case heard by the UK's High Court, *Assange v Swedish Prosecution Authority* [2011], the defendant, Julian Assange, had sexual intercourse with the alleged victim whose consent to that intercourse was conditional upon Assange's use of a condom that he did not, in fact, use. Did §76 of the Sexual Offences Act 2003 apply? This section holds that where a defendant intentionally deceived the complainant about the nature or purpose of the relevant act, it is to be presumed that the complainant did not consent to the relevant act and that the defendant did not believe that the complainant consented to the relevant act. Was consent vitiated? Yes, said the court, but not by §76 of the Act! The court held that the nature of the act was unaffected by the non-use of a condom, therefore §76 did not apply, but §74 of the Act, which holds that a person consents if he agrees by choice, and has the freedom and capacity to make that choice, was relevant. The reasoning of the judges of the High Court is not immediately perspicuous but interested readers may, if they wish, peruse it for themselves. (High Court 2011)

In relation to cases of alleged rape based on 'conditional consent' such as these condom cases, Ms Perrins asks, 'are these decisions an accurate reflection of the public's understanding of what the offence of rape truly is? Are these cases stretching the definition of rape so far that there is now an insurmountable gap between the Court's understanding of what rape is and that of the public's?' The answer to Ms Perrin's question is, I believe, yes. Once you remove violence or the threat of violence as a constituent element of the crime of rape, you've departed from the understanding that the ordinary person has of it, and the justifiable revulsion with which the act is greeted. The other scenarios, nasty as they may be, do not, when described, have quite the same emotional effect as the original stereotypical scenario.

Ms Perrins continues, 'In the criminal law it is very important that the offence the courts say has been committed is a fair reflection of the public's understanding of it. This is known as the principle of 'fair labelling': the label placed on the offender by the courts must be a fair description in the public's mind—not just a lawyer's mind—of what was done.' So, in many rape trials, the question isn't, 'is this the man who dragged a woman into the bushes and used force or violence to have sex with her?', or even 'did the woman consent to sexual intercourse with this man?', but 'was the act consented to the act that was carried out or something else?' Here, consent is given on certain conditions, and juries are going to be asked whether, on the evidence, the conditions were adhered to. Ms Perrins wonders whether this new idea of 'conditional consent' could include *any* condition being attached to the act? So, for example, if a woman were to consent to sexual intercourse on the condition that she and the person with whom she has intercourse are in a serious relationship, which is what that person has led her to believe but which, in his mind, is not in fact so, would *that* be a possible case of rape? If not, why not?

If a woman tells her partner she is on the pill or has taken some other contraceptive precaution but in fact she hasn't and so has sex that is unprotected, is that rape too or, if not rape, since it doesn't involve penetration by her of him, is it some form of sexual assault? And if indeed she becomes pregnant as a result of this sexual activity, can the man who has been 'sexually assaulted' demand that she abort his child, regardless of her own wishes? On the contrary, it would appear that the man could be liable to provide financial support for that child until it's eighteen years old! Something along these lines actually happened! As reported in the *Irish Times* in 2018, a man came home to Dublin to visit his family and friends for Christmas. On a night out, he was approached by a woman who came on to him and wanted to have sex. She told him she was on the pill. Some weeks later, she told him she was pregnant. When they met up to discuss the situation and he asked her about her statement that she was on the pill, she became angry, telling him she wanted nothing more to do with him and forbidding him from contacting her again. The man says that he is devastated by all of this and has contemplated suicide. (see Murphy)

A fate worse than death?

When we take into account all the relevant changes in the definition of rape, it seems that rape may not, after all, be a fate worse than death, at least not if we are to believe that grande dame of feminism, Germaine Greer. She points out, correctly, that as currently defined, rape is not necessarily a violent crime, and she believes that it should be punished by community service. 'Most rapes don't involve any injury whatsoever,' she writes, and she notes, 'Most rape is just lazy, just careless, just insensitive. Every time a man rolls over on his exhausted wife and insists on enjoying his conjugal right, he is raping her. It will never end up in a court of law.' (Greer 2019) She seems to think that most forms of rape are nothing much out of the ordinary. So, a woman regularly submitting to her husband's late-night advances because she is too tired or apathetic to actively refuse him, or worried about waking the children with the noise if she were to deny him is, she thinks, being raped. She doesn't tell us what she thinks of the situation where a man submits to his wife's late-night advances because *he* is too tired or too apathetic to actively refuse! Do you think this unlikely? Then, consider the strange case of *Willan vs Willan*. [2 All E.R. 463 (1960); 1 WLR 624]

Mr Willan (the plaintiff) and Mrs Willan (defendant) were married. Mr Willan filed a petition for divorce based on cruelty, claiming that Mrs Willan frequently and repeatedly demanded sexual intercourse from him and coerced him to engage in intercourse by a variety of methods, despite his being unwilling to do so. She was often violent toward him, pulling his hair, catching hold of him by the ears and shaking his head violently until he was induced to comply as the only means of getting any rest. Moreover, she would often pester him for intercourse late into the night to the point where the only way he could sleep was to acquiesce in her demands. Mrs Willan argued that Mr Willan's act of engaging in the sexual intercourse with her constituted condonation of her allegedly cruel conduct! The court agreed with her and dismissed Mr Willan's petition for divorce, holding that Mrs Willan's cruelty had been condoned by the husband by the last act of intercourse, which was a distinct act from his wife's preceding acts of cruelty and which in a man must be deemed to be his voluntary act unless induced by fraud. Willan appealed, but while the Lord Justices of Appeal were sympathetic, they rejected his appeal on the grounds that 'an act of intercourse on the part of the husband will operate as a reinstatement of the wife and therefore will be a condonation of her previous misconduct.'

Greer asserts that 'constant "unconsiderate" sex with a partner can be worse than rape by a stranger', and that while rape by a stranger is, as she terms it in her charming antipodean way, 'bloody bad luck', it doesn't necessarily force a woman to reassess her whole life in the way that abuse by loved ones does. Not only does Greer assert that most rapes, so-called, are non-violent, but she also scoffs at the idea that its victims suffer from post-traumatic stress disorder (PTSD). Noting that it has been claimed that 70% of rape victims are reputed to suffer from PTSD while only 20% of military veterans do, she commented, 'At this point you think, what the hell are you saying? That something that leaves no sign, no injury, nothing, is more damaging to women than seeing your best friend blown up by an IED is to a veteran?' She continues, 'Instead of thinking of rape as a spectacularly violent crime—and some rapes are—think about it as non-consensual, that is, bad sex.' So, rape equals bad sex! If that's what rape is, Greer is right not to get too excited about it, but then, why any criminal conviction at all? If bad or inconsiderate sex is to carry a criminal conviction, then many of us are going to be in serious trouble. If rape is just a form of bad or inconsiderate sex, Greer is right to note that it is absurd that rape sentences should be heavier than for attempted murder. The draconian penalties for rape, as distinct from other forms of assault, are based on a conception of female virtue that feminists can scarcely be happy with, loss of virtue being a 'fate worse than death.'

Test your intuitions on the following two hypothetical cases. In the first case, a man threatens a woman with violence unless she agrees to have sex with him. She does. Sexual intercourse takes place, but there is no physical violence other than the sexual congress itself. In the second case, a man bludgeons another man with an iron bar, causing irremediable physical damage resulting in the amputation of the victim's gangrenous leg. How would you begin to compare these two crimes in terms of their seriousness? I quoted Lionel Shriver earlier as saying, 'I'd rather be tastelessly propositioned, groped, insulted, subject to workplace abuse of power, than have my legs chopped off or my throat slit.' (Shriver) When the use of violence or force is removed from the definition of rape, then, radical incapacity to one side, one tends to get accusations of rape due to misunderstood, misinterpreted, disappointed or regretted sex. For men, bad sex is like bad pizza—it's still pizza. For women, despite their supposed liberation, it seems that casual sex and bad sex are never just casual and never just bad or regretted, and so you get women (like Grace) wondering whether the sex they had last night, last week, last month, last year or last decade was rape or not. In a piece published in the *Guardian*, Jane Gilmore is quoted as saying, 'As Greer says, far too often the woman herself is unable to identify what happened as rape when the rapist is a man she knows and perhaps even loves. Not because she wasn't violated—she most definitely was—but because women are accustomed to uncaring behaviour from men, and men are trained to dismiss empathy and thoughtfulness as unmanly.' (Alcorn) If you're going to make sweeping statements, Ms Gilmore, you might as well sweep high and wide. So, women are accustomed to uncaring behaviour from men? Really? From all men? Most men? Some men? One man? And men are trained to dismiss empathy and thoughtfulness as unmanly. Really? All men? Most men? Some men? Or one man? Just how does Ms Gilmore know this extraordinary fact?

What was your honest response to the question I put at the start of the previous paragraph? Which of the two did you consider worse—the threat of violence but no other violence, or the bludgeoning? To try to answer this question non-ideologically, put yourself in the place of the victim in both cases. Which of these two would you consider more traumatic? To ask that question is, I think, to answer it. One might reasonably wonder why an assault by the penetration of a bodily orifice when not accompanied by violence is considered to be so significant as to warrant the severe moral opprobrium and legal sanctions that it does, in contrast to other forms of bodily violation. As Steve Moxon notes, 'A criminal who inflicts life-destroying mutilations can easily receive a lesser sentence than a rapist, yet if we were to crudely ask women if they would rather have parts of their bodies severed than be raped, the reply would not be "which parts are you talking about?" They might express consternation at being presented with such a choice, but they would chose [sic] rape as certainly the lesser of two evils.' (Moxon, 199)

Any hope of drawing a distinction between rape and unsatisfactory sex goes by the board when we are told by Gilmore that, 'Women who have given in but not consented may not necessarily experience this rape as trauma but, as Greer says, they will always suffer damage.' Let's take a closer look at this remarkable claim. First, what does 'giving in but not consenting' mean? Does it mean acquiescence? People can acquiesce either as the result of violence or the threat of violence and then the resultant sexual congress is clearly criminal. But they can, of course, acquiesce for many other reasons that do not result from violence or the threat of violence—tiredness, apathy, and so on—and then the resultant sexual congress, while perhaps not mutually satisfactory, is clearly *not* criminal. We all of us acquiesce in this manner from time to time in many things we'd really rather not do, including, quite often, men to women. Have the women that Greer sees as 'giving in but not consenting' given in as the result of violence or the threat of it? If so, it's rape; if not, it's not rape. Moreover, how do Gilmore (and Greer) know that those women who have 'given in' will suffer damage? Is this a self-evident truth requiring no further evidence, or a somewhat more modest empirical claim? If the latter, what is the evidence for it?

In all cases involving sex resulting from violence or threats of violence, what we have is clearly and unambiguously rape, but what of cases involving sex where the participants are less than fully conscious, whether from sleep or from drink or from drugs? (RnV) Here, matters become more complex. There is a range of possibilities. Consider two lovers in bed asleep. One in a half-asleep state starts to come on to the other—perhaps the man to the woman or perhaps the woman to the man. They have sex. No words are spoken by either party. No explicit consent is sought or granted. Is this rape? And what, if rumour is to be believed, of the drunken hookup scenarios common on university campuses? These may be cases of rape, but to those without an ideological axe to grind, they look rather more like sexual irresponsibility on everyone's part. Part of the problem is with the term *rape* itself, and this is part of what Greer seems to be getting, at even if she's not always entirely clear. The abhorrence we feel for rape derives from the paradigm case of the stranger + violence + sexual penetration (RV). Once violence is taken out of the definition of rape, it opens the floodgates to the expansion of rape claims. It's the absence of violence in much of what is now claimed to be rape that leads people like Greer to say that rape is not that big a deal.

Commenting on Greer's book, Yvonne Roberts makes the interesting and, I believe, accurate point about the notion of consent in the context of sexual relations between men and women, which is that it positions women as subordinate—males act, females are acted upon. (Roberts *et al.*, 2018) On the other hand, she makes another point that is commonly purveyed by feminists but is so wildly inaccurate that you have to wonder what world is inhabited by those who make it. This bizarre point is that 'the whole of the law—not just the treatment of rape—is male interests masquerading as human interests.'

Seriously? What then does Roberts make of the 1828 law: 'Every Person convicted of the Crime of Rape shall suffer death as a Felon.' How would she explain this particular law as serving male interests? This is not the only bizarre comment that Roberts makes. She tells us that sexual relations between males and females are complicated (true!—so far so good!) but then she remarks that 'what's needed is a stronger interrogation by men about the kind of masculinity that still regards the appropriation and possession of a woman— banally or brutally—as what real men are supposed to do; robbing a woman of her self-worth and sexuality in the process.' There may be men who think like this. In a world as varied as ours, every niche, however bizarre, is probably populated by some group or other, but what sane, normal man thinks that the appropriation and possession of a woman is what real men (whatever real man are) are supposed to do?

In the same piece, Afua Hirsch discusses Greer's assertion that we noted above that most rapes 'involve a woman regularly submitting to her husband's late-night advances because she is too tired or apathetic to actively refuse, or worried about waking the children with the noise of confronting him' but Hirsch rejects this by telling us that 'A new generation of anti-rape activists have nailed this, in my opinion, by constructing consent in sex as something that should be ongoing, enthusiastic and active. If men understood this, and sought it, then they wouldn't rape their wives by accident every night, would they?' Rape by accident? Ongoing, enthusiastic and active? Using these criteria, practically every sexual encounter between a man and a woman apart from the first fine careless raptures of early stage romances would qualify as rape!

Greer says she would like to see the law changed so that women are treated as parties in cases relating to their alleged rape or sexual assault. 'The problem,' she says, is that it 'appears to be that women don't count as people in this vast landscape [of rape] ... One of the things that I find really interesting here is the idea that the woman who complains of rape is herself not a party to the action, she is a piece of evidence and she will be examined to find out if the claim she is making that the offence has occurred is true.' This is a reasonable enough point, but what Greer takes issue with in the case of rape holds for all those who are the victims of any criminal action. In a prosecution of a thief, for example, the thief's victim is not a party to the action. So too in the case of non-sexual assaults. If someone hits you in the face while stealing your wallet, it is the state's decision to bring or not bring the assailant to trial. What Greer is describing, and urging a revision of, is a characteristic not just of the criminal law in respect of rape, but of the criminal law as a whole. If you want to be a party to an action, you must take a civil case. As it stands, the operation of the criminal law is more or less the exclusive prerogative of the state and its agents.

To accuse is to convict (again)

We saw above that in the matter of sexual harassment, to accuse is to convict. The situation is similar in the matter of rape except, of course, that the alleged offence, and thus the punishment for it, is substantially more serious. A piece in the *Telegraph* by Cara McGoogan starts with a blazing non sequitur. 'The UK,' she says, 'has a problem with convicting perpetrators of rape.' (McGoogan) Would it be unkind of me to point out that if defendants are acquitted, then they have been judged not guilty *of perpetrating a crime* and so, by definition, they aren't perpetrators. So whatever problem the UK may have, it's not necessarily with convicting perpetrators of rape. Perhaps what McGoogan means is that the UK has a problem convicting men who have been *accused* of rape. That, of course, is an entirely different matter. And if that is so, it could be either because many people who are accused, tried and acquitted, really did commit rape and got away with it, or—wait for it—that many men who are accused, tried and acquitted *didn't* commit rape, and perhaps should never have been charged in the first place.

According to the Crown Prosecution Service (CPS), between 2016 and 2017, almost 42,000 alleged rapes were reported to the police in England and Wales. (That figure rose to just over 54,000 for 2017/18) Of these 42,000 allegations, slightly over 5,000 (11.9%) went to trial, and just under 3,000 of those resulted in a conviction (57.6% of those that went forward to trial, but just 7.2% of those originally reported). That means that almost 92% of reported cases were not actively prosecuted by the police or the CPS, presumably because it was deemed that the evidence didn't warrant proceeding with the case, or that a conviction was judged to be unlikely, or that the putative victim's account was not completely credible. Of those cases that went to trial, slightly more than half resulted in a conviction, slightly less than half in an acquittal. The Victim's Commissioner for England and Wales, Dame Vera Baird, is not happy about this, saying that 'The criminal justice system is letting down current victims and creating new victims by failing to tackle potential serial rapists.' (see Various) In her statement, Dame Vera sometimes describes those who make allegations as 'victims' and at other times as 'complainants'. To describe them as victims is, of course, question begging. Does Dame Vera want the CPS to bring all allegations forward for trial? Given that the conviction rate in the cases that the CPS does bring forward for trial is just over 50%—and these are cases where the CPS presumably has made a judgement that there is a reasonable chance of conviction—one can only imagine how minuscule the conviction rate would be if all allegations went to trial! At the time of writing (September 2019) a report from the CPS reveals that the total number of convictions for rape for 2018/19 was just under 2,000, a drop of over 25% on the previous year. (Davies)

Ann Coffey M.P. suggested that there should be a review of the use of juries in cases of rape so as to improve conviction rates against young men. (Topping) Some of her other suggestions included specialist rape courts and the examination of the role played by expert witnesses in rape cases. In what must be a contender for the Bleedin' Obvious Award of 2018, she said, 'the most common cause of unsuccessful prosecutions in rape cases is jury acquittal.' Well yes, of course it is, just as the most common cause of divorce is marriage! She was especially disturbed by what she saw as the reluctance of juries to convict young men. The reluctance of juries to convict in cases involving young people is, I suggest, that in many if not in most of them, what we have between the parties is a complicated and confused case of 'he said, she said' messy sex, brought about by the confused and confusing state of contemporary sexual morality. Just as juries refused to convict in previous ages for petty offences that, in their view, carried disproportionate penalties of death or transportation, so too juries are reluctant to convict the defendants in many rape cases, given the severity of the sentence.

Rebecca Solnit knows that we know many things. According to her, we know why rape victims don't report rapes; we know that a minority of rapes are reported; we know that of the minority of rapes that are reported, only a small percentage lead to prosecutions; we know that only a small percentage of those prosecutions result in convictions and sentences; we know that women are held to be more responsible for men's actions than men are; we know that we are only just starting to realise that women have been routinely discredited, shamed, blamed, and disbelieved when they speak up about sexual assault; we know who lies about rape, routinely and regularly—rapists; we know that false rape accusations are extremely rare; and above all, we know there is almost nothing a heterosexual white man can do to discredit himself, all the more so if he has social status. And now we know that a groundswell of feminism encapsulated in the #MeToo movement has made it possible for many women to be heard for the first time. (Solnit)

I don't know who the *we* are in Solnit's list of things we know. I, for one, don't know much of what Rebecca Solnit thinks we all know. I don't know why rape victims don't report rapes, if that is indeed what they don't do. I don't know that a minority of rapes are reported, nor does anyone else. I don't know that women are held to be more responsible for men's actions than men are, for the good and sufficient reason that they're not. I don't know that false rape accusations are extremely rare. I don't know that there is almost nothing a heterosexual white man can do to discredit himself. And I certainly don't know that a groundswell of feminism encapsulated in the #MeToo movement has made it possible for many women to be heard for the first time. Looking back over the last 50 years of feminist ululation, it seems that we've been doing little else *but* hearing women during that time.

Chitra Ramaswamy tells us that 'Young men are, quite literally, getting away with rape.' (Ramaswamy) How does Ms Ramaswamy know this? She tells us that less than a third of young men prosecuted for rape in England and Wales are convicted. Despite what she terms 'the juggernaut of #MeToo testimony', women, she says, 'are still not being believed' and 'Men continue to be given a free pass to everything from a woman's body to a Supreme Court nomination.' 'Why,' she asks plaintively, 'are men aged 18-24 being protected by the law? Why are we so desperate to believe men? Because, it seems, that juries are reluctant 'to punish young men at the start of their lives' or are generally unwilling to find them guilty of date rape.

Even by the *Guardian*'s abysmally low standards of reasoning and high levels of emotional incontinence, this is a quite outrageous series of unsupported assertions. First, we're not desperate to believe men in rape cases (once again, who are *we*?) Second, that a majority of men accused of rape are acquitted does not constitute a crisis for the criminal justice system, unless one has independent reasons to think that those who were acquitted were in fact guilty. It might just as easily point (as I think it does) to an overzealousness to initiate prosecutions that are objectively unjustified and that have little or no hope of success, a judgement that recent scandals in the CPS have given some support to. As one commentator remarked, 'It is also of fundamental fairness to the accused that the state does not abuse its might by launching speculative prosecutions based on negligible or inherently unreliable evidence, no matter how sure a complainant professes to be of a defendant's guilt' (Anon. 2019, 150) As it happens, a majority of men accused of rape who are brought to trial are *not* acquitted. Just over half of prosecutions for rape result in a conviction. Third, young men are not, literally, getting away with rape, at least, not those who have been acquitted. If Ms Ramaswamy would care to name the names of those she thinks are rapists who have been acquitted she can do so, if she wishes to lay herself open to defamation proceedings. Fourth, we don't know how many alleged rapes are reported as against alleged cases of rape that are not reported, for the good and sufficient reason that allegations that are not reported are not reported. This is a classic case of the unknowable statistic. Fifth, no men of any age are 'protected by the law', if that means that they are given special privileges. *All* who are accused in criminal cases, male or female, are entitled to the presumption of innocence. And sixth, and last, men are not given a free pass to a woman's body or, if they are, I must have been on my holidays the day those passes were given out because I never got any.

Rape trials today more often than not hinge on a discussion of whether the sexual act was consensual. The stereotype of rape as a woman's being attacked by a stranger and forcibly penetrated accounts for an insignificant proportion of rape trials. 'The legal definitions of what behaviour or actions constitute rape and sexual assault are quite clear, but the definition of consent is less so,' says Dr Hannah Bows, senior lecturer in criminology at Teesside University. (McGoogan) 'There remains a lot of confusion across society about what consent means,' she says. 'We need to rethink our definition of consent to address the current misunderstandings around what consent is.' Dr Bows doesn't tell us what definitional changes she thinks might resolve our problems, and it's not obvious why Dr Bows thinks that the legal definitions of what rape and sexual assault are is quite clear if consent is a constitutive element in the legal definition of rape and that definition is somehow less than clear. In rape trials, the prosecution must prove that consent was absent and that the defendant lacked a reasonable belief in the presence of consent. It is difficult to do this, as it should be, but it is not impossible to prove beyond a reasonable doubt that the person accused of rape knew that there was no consent. The prosecution is entitled to take into account all the circumstances surrounding the alleged rape, including any measures that the accused has taken to ascertain the consent of the alleged victim. As is normal for criminal cases, the burden of proof is on the prosecution but there is pressure to reverse the *onus probandi*. 'Institutional practices should treat victims properly and believe them rather than have them under suspicion,' says our senior lecturer in criminology. This statement by Dr Bows is, of course, massively question begging, as any academic should know. There is no victim if there is no crime, so to talk of a victim in advance of the outcome of a trial is ineluctably to prejudice matters. And if disbelieving those who claim to be victims of rape is inappropriate, so too is believing them, where believing them means not just judging that they are not lying but that, in fact, the content of their assertions is true. In the end, their testimony is what it is: whether it is to be believed is a matter for a jury.

'Rape cases pretty much everywhere reflect the level of sexism and misogyny in that society,' says Professor Liz Kelly, director of the Child and Woman Abuse Studies Unit at London Metropolitan University. 'Any woman who is

After #MeToo

sexually active or has been drinking beforehand is deemed suspect. Those facts are seen to make her account less credible.' (McGoogan) Well, putting to one side Professor Kelly's ritual invocation of sexism and misogyny, the testimony of a witness who has been drinking, whether in cases of rape or other criminal charges, is always open to a credibility check. It must be remembered that in rape trials, the prime, if not the only, witness for the prosecution is the alleged victim, and the jury is attempting to decide whether what that victim is telling them is worthy of credence. That being so, it is important to determine the witness's character and mental condition. Professor Kelly doesn't seem to agree. 'If these facts of everyday life are invalidations of a complaint of rape,' she says, 'then we're not investigating a crime, we're investigating whether someone fits the stereotype of a good victim.' With all due deference to Professor Kelly, no, we're not investigating whether someone fits the stereotype of a good victim; we're attempting to discover whether the witness's testimony is credible, and character is a key component in making a reasonable judgement on that.

Rape on campus

There is an epidemic of sexual violence in British universities. So says Emily Reynolds, writing in the *Guardian*. (Reynolds 2018a). According to Ms Reynolds, almost 10% of female students who responded to a study of sexual violence said they had been raped! She asks, not unnaturally, how did it get like this? The answer to her question is: it more than likely *didn't* get like this. The data come from an entity called Revolt Sexual Assault which hastens to assure us that the statistics contained in this report, and the way in which they are framed, are accurate and validated to professional market research and statistical standards. (see Revolt Sexual Assault) Unfortunately, we are not told what questions were asked and how they were framed. Anyone who has ever conducted a survey knows that the kind of questions asked, and especially the way in which they are framed, will determine to a large extent the kind of answers that are received. In the British version of *House of Cards*, the Prime Minister, Francis Urquhart, recruiting Sarah Harding, asks her why she moved from an academic position at Cambridge to work for a polling company. She answers that it was partly for the money, but also that she wanted to see if it was true that you could get any result you want from a poll. 'And?' inquires Urquhart. 'It's true,' Sarah replies. 'You can make people say anything ... ' (*House of Cards*, second series, episode 1)

Ms Reynolds tells us that being at university should be one of the best times of your life but, alas, 'the majority of students are not having such a good time after all.' I suspect, on the contrary, that what leads to the experiences which are reflected as in a glass darkly in the report is that students are having the best time of their lives as they always have had, but in the messy, unregulated, careless, fraught, sometimes drunken, and often regretted way that is characteristic of 21st century sexual relations. Are female students in constant danger of being sexually harassed or assaulted on university campuses? Some surveys suggest that this is so, but their findings are more than a little suspect. For one thing, the participants in many of these surveys are self-selecting, having an interest in pushing the idea of the prevalence of campus sexual harassment. And for another, what constitutes sexual harassment has suffered from the usual definitional creep, so that it ranges from physical intimidation all the way down to jokes, or banter, or dodgy chat-up lines.

The precarious nature of procedural justice in relation to matters of sexual assault (including rape) can be seen clearly in operation on US campuses. In 2011, under the Obama presidency, the US Department of Education's Office for Civil Rights (OCR) sent a 'Dear Colleague' letter to the USA's almost 5,000 institutions of higher education, outlining new rules for how they were to root out and punish sexual assault. The letter outlawed 'unwelcome sexual advances, requests for sexual favors, and other verbal, nonverbal, or physical conduct of a sexual nature.' Given that much of the money received by third level institutions in the USA comes from the Federal Government, the king's wish is effectively a command. When the funding agencies say jump, those in receipt of funds ask 'how high?' To ensure that they stayed on the right side of the Federal Regulators, many institutions rushed to expand their sexual offence codes. Four ungainsayable points seemed to characterise the Obama administration's 'Dear Colleague' approach to sexual assault on campus: complainants always tell the truth; fair procedures are trumped by the urgency to vindicate victims; criminal acts and boorishness lie along a continuum; and men are natural sexual predators.

The now infamous Title IX of the Education Amendments Act of 1972 states: 'No person in the United States shall, on the basis of sex, be excluded from participation in, be denied the benefits of, or be subjected to discrimination under any education program or activity receiving Federal financial assistance.' If you're an educational establishment in receipt of money from the Federal government, you may not discriminate between men and women. Fair enough, I suppose. What could possibly be controversial about this? Well, quite a lot. Somehow, this short statement of non-discrimination on the basis of sex was, at least until recently, used for purposes for which it would never seem to have been intended, especially the prevention of sexual harassment, which could include what has been called unwelcome verbal conduct. Universities have on their staffs officials called Title IX officers to keep them ideologically neat and tidy, and these officials have increasingly inserted themselves into the relationship between the sexes on campus, something it is hard to see as any of their business. In effect, Title IX is being used as a kind of super-paternalistic device to protect those strong and independent 21st century women who, when it comes to sex, are surprisingly in need of help. These damsels, it seems, are permanently in distress.

Following receipt of the 'Dear Colleague' letter, rules about what has come to be called 'affirmative consent' were put in place on many campuses, requiring that partners engaging in any sexual contact get explicit permission for each touch, every time. It's the law in California, Connecticut and New York. How are these sexual elements to be isolated and distinguished from one another? What makes a touch to be one touch rather than a sequence of shorter touches? The exact position of hands? For how long? What strength of grip? Does consent to a touch for 5.7 seconds allow movement from one location to another or does that move require additional consent? If the touch can move, does it have to be to a contiguous spot? Who is going to arbitrate these complex issues?

In the majority of the cases that have come before college tribunals, it is not unreasonable to judge that we are dealing with messy sex between sexually inexperienced students that usually began consensually and about whose progress the accounts presented by the individuals involved then diverge. But messy sex is not the same thing as rape or sexual assault. It has become quite common for universities to involve themselves in paralegal activities, setting up committees to judge students accused of sexual assault or harassment, the operation of which committees leaves something to be desired in respect of natural justice. (for details on specific cases, see Title IX For All) The interim measures taken against those accused of offences often constitute pre-conviction punishment: exclusion from certain classes or from the campus as a whole or, in the case of those who are in work, suspension or dismissal.

In April 2018, 130 leading law professors, including Professor Janet Hally from Harvard Law School and Denver University Law Professor Dave Kopel, jointly condemned the use of investigative 'victim-centred' practices that undermined the disinterested collection and presentation of evidence, particularly on university campuses. Their letter made the point, one would think the blatantly obvious point, that the ethos of 'believe the victim' presumes the guilt of the accused and amounts to an erosion of due process. In the ever-so-slightly insane and hyperbolically hysterical narratives about on-campus rape and sexual assault, the usual question-begging mantra of 'Believe the Victim!' has become the new orthodoxy. 'Survivors of sexual assault deserve to be believed, not blamed,' Senator Kamala Harris of California tells us, sententiously. And, surprise, surprise, we saw this same mantra enunciated in the Senate confirmation process of Brett Kavanaugh. We have now reached a stage where a demand for evidence to support claims of sexual assault has come to be regarded as somehow biased in favour of sexual assault perpetrators, or even makes one to be a *de facto* rape apologist.

So transparently bad have things become that in August 2017, four Harvard Law professors, feminists to a woman, commented on just how unfair campus procedures in this area have become. (see Bartholet *et al.*) 'Some colleges and universities,' they remark, 'fail even to give students the complaint against them, or notice of the factual basis of charges, the evidence gathered, or the identities of witnesses. Some schools fail to provide hearings or to allow the accused student's lawyer to attend or speak at hearings. Some bar the accused from putting questions to the accuser or witnesses, even through intermediaries. Some schools hold hearings in which the accuser participates while remaining unseen behind a partition. Some schools deny parties the right to see the investigative report or get copies for their lawyers for preparing an appeal. Some schools allow appeals only on very narrow grounds ... providing no meaningful check on the initial decisionmaker.' (Bartholet *et al.*, 2) They note that definitions of sexual wrongdoing on college campuses

> are now seriously overbroad. They go way beyond accepted legal definitions of rape, sexual assault, and sexual harassment. They often include sexual conduct that is merely unwelcome, even if it does not create a hostile environment, even if the person accused had no way of knowing it was unwanted, and even if the accuser's sense that it was unwelcome arose after the encounter. The definitions often include mere speech about sexual matters. They therefore allow students who find class discussion of sexuality offensive to accuse instructors of sexual harassment. They are so broad as to put students engaged in behavior that is overwhelmingly common in the context of romantic relationships to be accused of sexual misconduct. Overbroad definitions of sexual wrongdoing are unfair to all parties, and squander the legitimacy of the system. (Bartholet *et al.*, 2)

Some politicians have acted with a breath-taking contempt for the rights of accused students—male students, of course—and with a complete disregard for the effect that the dodgy procedures employed in the campus kangeroo courts might have on their education and professional prospects. In 2015, at a congressional hearing on campus sexual assault, Congressman Jared Polis of Colorado was of a mind to suggest that anyone *accused* of sexual misconduct should be dismissed without any fact-finding at all. 'If there are 10 people who have been accused,' he said, 'and under a reasonable likelihood standard maybe one or two did it, it seems better to get rid of all 10 people.' (see Reynolds 2015) I see. The principle used to be that it was better for nine guilty to go free, rather than for one innocent to be convicted; now, it seems, it is better for nine innocent to be convicted, rather than for one guilty to go free! O brave, new world, that has such creatures in't! Mr Polis now claims that he misspoke but, as Ashe Schow noted in the *Washington Examiner*, he didn't misspeak, he just didn't like the backlash that followed his outrageous suggestion. (see Schow)

The Trump administration's Education Secretary Betsy DeVos announced in the autumn of 2017 that she was rescinding much of what had been effectively mandated by the 'Dear Colleague' letter, on the grounds that it didn't do justice either to the accuser or the accused and (and this is the really important bit) it deprived the accused, young men for the most part, of their civil rights. The new advice from the Department of Education insisted on impartial and unbiased investigations, the avoidance of sexual stereotypes in respect of both men and women, and interim actions that were proportional to the alleged offence. DeVos's proposal accords to the allegedly delinquent student the presumption of innocence, the right to review all the evidence in the case, and the ability to cross-examine their accusers, although indirectly.

What kind of cases are we talking about? Well, here's one. Drew Sterrett was forced to leave the University of Michigan in 2012 during his sophomore year after a female student's accusation of forced sexual intercourse was upheld. The female student, referred to only as CB, had asked to stay in Sterrett's room. He was surprised when she got into his bed. The rest is not-silence. In fact, so noisy was it that Sterrett's roommate complained about being kept awake. In a statement, this roommate deposed that he would have heard and intervened if CB had objected to what was taking place. While she was at home, CB's mother read in her daughter's diary about her drug-taking, drinking and sexual encounters. She took CB to campus where CB made her accusation, an accusation, by the way, that had not been reported to the police. Sterrett was informed that a student had made an allegation but was not provided in writing with the charges against him or the names of the witnesses interviewed by the university. He eventually received a Sexual Misconduct Investigation Report, which concluded that he was guilty of the accusation made against him.

The bizarre star-chamberish nature of campus sexual assault trials has even made its way on to the small screen, except that they're not presented as bizarre! An episode of *Law & Order: Special Victims Unit* entitled, 'In Loco Parentis', broadcast in March 2018, dealt with this topic. The victim, Mia, who conveniently happens to be the niece of one of the unit's detectives, Carisi, is supposedly raped by another student, Eli. Her uncle is not pleased that Eli received only a one-year suspension and wants to start a police investigation. At this early stage, you might think, conflict of interest? But let us ignore that and plough on. Mia eventually admits to her uncle that she did in fact consent to sex and that there was no rape. He tells her she needs to make things right and apologise to Eli. Mia invites Eli to talk and, wait for it, *now* he rapes her. We have no evidence of this apart from Mia's word, the word of someone who has already admitted to lying about a previous charge of rape. Why does Eli rape Mia? Well, he obligingly tells the court under cross-examination! The prosecution lawyer, Peter Stone, asks,

Stone: What were you studying in college?

Eli: Pre-med.

Stone: You were going to be a doctor?

Eli: I was. A neurosurgeon. But that's gone now.

Stone: You don't think you'll be acquitted?

Eli: You know what? It doesn't matter. I'm already wearing the scarlet R. My friends won't talk to me. You know, since Hudson booted me, I applied to six other colleges. I got 700 on my SATs, and that wasn't good enough. Once the PC police get their fangs into you, your life in polite society is over.

Stone: And that's ... that's what happened to you?

Eli: Sure is. All it takes is one girl to say you looked at her funny, and that's it. Your life's over.

Stone: Yeah, but you did more than look at Mia funny, Eli.

Eli: Why, because she said so? Look, that first time in her dorm, we were in it together. You heard what her uncle, the cop, said. I didn't rape her.

Stone: You were railroaded ... and the bleeding hearts didn't want to hear the truth.

Eli: They wouldn't know the truth if it hit them in the face. They sit there with their self-righteous grins, pointing their fingers at you, whether you did something wrong or not.

Stone: And it pisses you off.

Eli: You're damn right, it does.

Stone: And when you went to Mia's dorm room, you planned on telling her just how much it pissed you off?

Eli: That damn school, they wrap themselves in their political correctness and their honour code, only they don't know the first thing about honour.'

Stone: 'You were accused; therefore, you were guilty?'

Up to this point, Eli's testimony, including his palpable and righteous anger, is believable! Now comes the utterly unbelievable, dramatically unbelievable, and, in real life even more unbelievable *deus ex machina* in which the defendant, for no obvious reason, spectacularly incriminates himself! 'That's right,' Eli says under cross-examination. 'I was already labeled a rapist. What the hell? I might as well be a rapist.' Stone, 'And who better to rape than Mia Marino.' Eli, 'That's right! The bitch ruined me, and I got to ruin her!'

The main thrust of the episode concerns a false allegation of rape against an innocent man and, just as this is discovered and you might expect a conclusion in which the dangers of false allegations are dramatically presented, Eli, conveniently for the script writers (oh wait a minute, they're the ones who wrote this story!) really rapes the supposed victim. And now the whole prior false witnessing and the shafting of the young man is conveniently forgotten about, as is what he correctly says on the stand about having had his life ruined by the false allegation. And, despite his ridiculously unbelievable admission on the stand, he didn't get to ruin Mia; she got to ruin him.

The *Rolling Stone*'s notorious 2014 story about a supposed rape at the University of Virginia consisted of false accusations and fabrications. *Rolling Stone* asked the Columbia University Graduate School of Journalism [CUGSJ] to investigate the magazine's failures. CUGSJ pointed out, not surprisingly, that the magazine's editing procedures were less than perfect, and that its writers and editors had exhibited a lack of scepticism (I would rather say a lack of open-mindedness). But the investigators, in agreement with the writers and editors of the story, kept well away from scepticism about the larger context of the story, namely, the idea that there is something called a 'rape culture' on US campuses. Michael Wolff notes that, 'While almost all of the facts of the U. Va. story were determined to be lies, the central premise of the piece remained, for Columbia and the many journalists analyzing the fallout, unexamined and apparently sound.' (Wolff) The unquestioned central premise—perhaps I should say unquestionable—is that university campuses in the US are dangerous places for women, infested as they are by men who are misogynistic, some-times violently so. It doesn't seem to matter to some that the *Rolling Stone* article was false and based on a source so absurd as to merit derision. It doesn't seem to matter that other similar stories are also groundless (see, for example, the Columbia mattress-girl story). Nothing, it seems, least of all evidence, can shift the belief that campus rape culture is real.

In what must be a supreme irony, much of the opprobrium that *Rolling Stone* received from its publication of this absurd story resulted not from its unjust and ungrounded accusations against the innocent, but because it might cast doubt on others who make similar accusations. In much the same way, as we shall see, it is routine to find in stories of false rape allegations that, instead of expressions of indignation that an innocent person has been falsely accused of a terrible crime, pious warnings are issued that this unfortunate example of a false allegation (always said to be one of very few—enter dubious statistics) might deter other supposed victims from coming forward with their accusations. This nonsense about deterrence is a routine rhetorical response that is about as convincing as the claim that the prosecution of those who make false insurance claims will deter those who have genuine insurance claims from making them.

Absurdities reach new heights when some persist in believing these discredited stories even when their falsity has been demonstrated beyond doubt! So, for example, Jessica Valenti, writing in the *Guardian* says, 'I *choose* to believe Jackie [the woman at the centre of the *Rolling Stone* story]. I lose nothing by doing so, even if I'm later proven wrong—but at least I will still be able to sleep at night for having stood by a young woman who *may* have been through an awful trauma. No matter how the media story ends, or what we come to know, there is a reason that people believed and continue to believe Jackie. There are so many people—too many people—who report similar attacks.' (Valenti 2014; emphasis added) This is an extraordinary thing to write! The important thing is to stand by a young woman who may (note *may*) have been through a trauma, even if she hasn't been through such trauma. And the reason to believe her is that so many people have reported similar attacks. In a later piece, Valenti is militantly unrepentant. She writes, 'Rolling Stone's claim that their mistakes all came out of concern for a young rape victim are [*sic*] irresponsible: in the middle of an all-out backlash against so-called PC culture and anti-rape activism, they shirked their real responsibility both to Jackie and to all the victims of sexual assault, and it will have a resounding impact on those working to end sexual violence. Rolling Stone created a mess for the men and women trying to end sexual violence on campus and off, and it should be the magazine's job to clean it up.' (Valenti 2015) So, you see, it's not Jackie's economy with the truth that is the problem; no, it's *Rolling Stone*'s irresponsibility and the problem that that sort of thing creates for those attempting to end sexual violence. As Michael Wolff comments, 'There is only one side here, one moral cause, one permissible outcome, hence everything bends to that narrative. And even if it's false, it can at least support the greater, undeniable truth.' (Wolff) Falsehood supporting the greater truth—what an extraordinary idea!

Writing about the *Rolling Stone* Jackie story, Lindy West is another person who simply won't give up her prejudices in the face of the evidence. She remarks that 'the "discrepancies" in Jackie's story don't "prove" anything at all—they could very easily be the product of trauma, or the natural elasticity of memory.' The natural elasticity of memory? Moreover, Ms West tells us, 'Jackie's friends did confirm that they believe something horrible happened to her that night, even if the exact details of her experience aren't clear.' Something? What something? Writing some four years before we heard the 'I believe her' chants during the Kavanaugh witchhunt, she wrote 'those words—I believe you, it's not your fault—are aggressively, ubiquitously suppressed in our culture.' (West) Once again, it's not Jackie's fault. It's all the fault of those horrible people at *Rolling Stone*. They, says Ms West, 'threw a rape victim to the misogynist horde in an attempt to distract from their own shoddy journalism ...' While not wishing to exculpate the *Rolling Stone* gang for their shoddy journalism, where does Jackie come into all this? Without her, there couldn't have been any *Rolling Stone* piece and no shoddy journalism to distract from. And you've got to love the idea of a misogynistic horde, bringing to mind images of millions of misogynistic men streaming westwards across the tundra.

Consent

When it comes to sex, men and women have always played games, including verbal games, with each other—what is said is not always what is meant, and what is meant is not always what is said. Since everything I know I learnt from the movies (well, a good deal of it, anyway), here's an example from one of my favourite films that you can use to test your intuitions. In *Tootsie*, Dustin Hoffman plays the role of Michael Dorsey, an unemployed actor and, within the film, the role of a woman, Dorothy Michaels. As Dorothy, he meets Julie (Jessica Lange) and is attracted to her. In a 'woman-to-woman' conversation with Julie, Julie says to Michael, 'It's so complicated, isn't it? All of it! Truthfully, don't you find being a woman in the eighties complicated?' Dorothy replies, ironically and truthfully: 'Extremely!' Julie continues: 'All this role-playing—confusion! Everyone seems so screwed up about who they are. You know what I wish sometimes? That just once a guy would be honest enough to walk up and say, "Listen, I'm confused about all this, too. I could lay a big line on you, we could do a lot of role-playing, but the simple truth is, I find you very interesting and I'd really like to make love with you. It's as simple as that." Wouldn't that be a relief?' Dorothy/Michael gets the message—or thinks he does. Sometime later, Julie is at a party and so too is Michael. Julie is standing alone on a terrace with a drink in her hand, looking at the wonderful view, lost in thought. Michael comes over, leans on the rail next to her and introduces himself. 'Hi. My name's Michael Dorsey.' Julie makes a non-committal go-away noise and no eye contact. Michael persists: 'Great view, huh?' Another eloquent silence from Julie who sips her drink. Michael tries again. Again silence. Michael, give the guy credit for trying, says: 'Can I tell you something?' Julie replies repressively, 'Have I got a choice?' Most men would give up at this point, but not our Michael.

Remembering the lesson he learnt as Dorothy, he says: 'You know, I could lay a big line on you, but the simple truth is—I find you very attractive, and I'd really like to go to bed with you.' Julie turns and hurls her drink into his face.

As the *Tootsie* extract shows, whether and how one person expresses sexual interest in another is not always straightforward. Asking a total stranger 'Can I have sex with you?' as Michael Dorsey does, is not, it would seem, socially acceptable even in our era of supposedly open and transparent discussions about sex between the sexes. I've tried the Dorsey strategy many times and it's never worked for me. (Joke! Not really!) If anything is to happen between a man and a woman, someone has to start somewhere and the consensuality cannot go all the way down, like the elephants that hold up the world. Someone, usually the man (once again, isn't it amazing how much the initiative, whether it's a privilege or burden, still resides with men in this area) indicates his interest in some way or another—by indirect suggestion, by invitation to some nominally neutral shared activity (most of these coded and understood as such by socially aware participants), somewhere or another—a bar, or a party. If the initiator—let's not be coy, the man—needs permission to initiate a sexual advance, does he need permission to seek such permission and so on *ad infinitum*, like *Dad's Army*'s Corporal Jones's 'Permission to speak, sir' which, paradoxically, can only be expressed by speaking, the very act for which the soldier is asking permission? Sexual intercourse is the kind of human activity that is not normally explicitly negotiated. A series of events takes place between a couple in which there is (eventually) a rebuttable presumption that consent is given. It is a rebuttable presumption because 'Stop', 'Take a hike, Buster', 'F@£$ off' and similar forceful expressions will unambiguously establish the lack of relevant consent.

In our contemporary world, if sex isn't to be rape, then it must be consensual, but in the rough and tumble of sexual relations, who's going to ask for and receive explicit consent, even more unrealistically, who's going to validate affirmative, continuous and enthusiastic consent? *You* are, if you are a man and if you don't want to be charged with rape. Are we then to carry forms around with us that we sign before engaging in sexual activity? And what would such a form say? Would it permit all and every form of sexual activity or only some? Would it be signed in stages as the relationship progresses? Would it have emergency stop clauses that could be used when necessary or would you have to agree on some trigger word like 'Basingstoke' to bring matters to a halt? But this is the 21st century—who has a pen? Surely there must be an app somewhere that would give our tempestuous lovers what they need at the touch of a key? And sure enough, there is! Gunner Technology has produced a consent app (snappily called uConsent) for the smartphone-using modern lover, eventually to be equipped with a panic button so that there'll be no need to shout out 'Basingstoke' when you want things to come to a dead stop. And it doesn't just allow you to grant global consent to unspecified sex; you can use it to detail the approved acts before you engage in them. And yet, despite this, there are those cynics who say that romance is dead! (For a prescient comedic approach to this way of doing things, see Stephen Fry & Hugh Laurie's 1990s comedy sketch, 'Pre-Coital Agreement'. In the 1990s, this was parody, now it is beyond parody.)

Imagine the possible items you might be asked to check. 'I hereby grant you permission to hold my hand/put your arm around me/kiss me.' But you might need to go into more detail on each item, so, for example: 'I hereby grant you permission to hold my hand (a) for 10 seconds or less; (b) for up to 5 minutes; (c) until our hands drop off; (d) other.' Or perhaps: 'You have permission to touch my left breast or my right breast but not both at the same time.' The possibilities are multitudinous and are restricted only by the limits of our imagination and our ability to enter all this data on the app, while continuing to interact romantically with our willing (up to a point) partners. Will this solve all those messy disputes about whether he or she consented? (I say *he* but funnily enough, it's rarely or never a matter of *his* consent.) Alas no. Feelings, moods and minds can change so rapidly that consent may have been withdrawn before ever anyone can register the change on the convenient app. So don't produce the app in court when you've been charged with rape; it's not very likely to be accepted as proof of consent.

Sexual relations are usually an aspect of intimacy. In intimate relations, one of the advantages is, or at least it was, that you don't have to talk all the time. The 'explicit' or 'affirmative' consent model treats lovers as if they were perpetual strangers to each other. Moreover, when we achieve intimacy in a relationship, certain things are taken as being in order unless explicitly rejected, for example, a kiss, a hug and, yes, even sex. When it comes to so-called 'affirmative consent,' consent has to be obtained at every stage of the interaction to all instances of sexual interaction, not just globally at the start. The problem with this, as I've just mentioned, but it's worth mentioning again, is figuring out how to define the 'atomic elements' of the interaction. Do I ask 'May I touch your leg' or should the question be, 'may I touch the lower part of your leg?' Do I have to specify for how long and how tight or how hard the touching is to be? If not, why not? How is this consent to be manifested? Should it be in writing? If in writing, should it be witnessed? Should those contemplating sexual action be accompanied by a Commissioner for Oaths at all times?

The real effect of laws based on this completely inoperable notion of consent is to place the burden of proof on the person who is likely to be accused of sexual assault to prove that he (always he) obtained this peculiar form of consent at every stage and micro-stage of the sexual interaction. Such affirmative consent laws might appear to be equally applicable to both participants in sexual relationships, but those of us who are men probably suspect that these laws are directed at us and not at women. I wait with bated breath to read reports of women being prosecuted for sundry kinds of sexual assault on the grounds that they didn't ask for and receive continuous, affirmative and enthusiastic consent from their male partners. The retrograde sexist nature of the affirmative consent laws appears to have escaped the normally eagle-eyed quick-to-take-offence radical feminists, for these laws encapsulate a picture of women as weak and vulnerable, so much so that they need the protection of these essentially paternalistic laws to protect them from all powerful predatory men.

The law has long recognised that a contract can be formed by means of a course of conduct. A man walks into a restaurant (this is not the start of a joke!), orders a meal, consumes it and, by so doing, contracts to pay for it. I suppose it is just about conceivable that someone from an alien culture or an alien planet seeing food being dispensed might mistake the restaurant for some kind of upmarket food bank and be surprised when presented with a bill when he gets up to leave. But, such bizarreries to one side, you order, you eat, and you pay. There's no verbal agreement to exchange money for food, still less a signed contract. Similarly, while talking to your stockbroker on your mobile phone, you pick up a copy of the *Financial Times* at your newsagents, take it to the counter, hand over a £5 note, the shop assistant takes it, hands you your change and off you go. Not a word spoken, nothing signed. Consent (indeed contract) can be given by a course of conduct. If explicit, affirmative consent is always required for entering upon contractual relations then, upon ordering a meal, you should be required to sign a contract or, when buying the *Irish Times*, the assistant should ask you, 'Do you consent to buy this paper from me now at the price of €1.90, and you should answer in your best Meg Ryan manner, 'Yes! Yes! Yes! Oh God, Yes! (affirmative and enthusiastic consent) I do.' After the subsidence of the initial rapture, the would-be purchaser would then ask the vendor: do you consent to sell it to me? The shop assistant, with perhaps modified rapture, will, in ideal circumstances, also answer 'Yes!'

In a sex education class, it was reported that some boys suggested that if you're having sex and the other person doesn't stop you then that could constitute consent. One of the instructors offers the counterexample of someone getting mugged to show that in some situations people are too scared to say stop. But there are differences. Unless there is force or the threat of force, as in the case of the mugging, why would a person be too scared to say stop when in a sexual situation with another that they didn't want to be in? And it is only if there is force or a threat of force that the mugging analogy holds. Some years ago a headline appeared in an online site claiming that 27% of Germans believed that rape could sometimes be justified! Shock! Horror! The report was high on indignation and low on analysis, but a closer reading revealed not that a significant percentage of Germans believed that rape was justified, but rather that having sexual intercourse without explicit verbal consent may be justified in certain circumstances.

The simple-minded and facile notion of affirmative consent seems to overlook the fact that much sex takes place in circumstances where what occurs is neither obviously consensual nor obviously non-consensual. Consider the following scenarios. *Movie*. The apartment door slams. We see a couple engaged in a passionate embrace up against the door, lots of clothes being ripped off by both parties. Fade to a shot of naked bodies engaged in sexual intercourse, then to a couple lying side by side in bed. Lots of noise but no words spoken. Rape? If so, of whom by whom? *Real life*. A couple in a long term loving relationship in bed together. Early morning. One party, half-asleep, makes sexual contact with the other. Coitus results. No words spoken. Rape? If the man made the initial contact, would you judge it to be rape? Yes? But what if it was the woman? If in either of these scenarios the so-called affirmative consent rule is applied, then one or other of the parties (perhaps both) has been raped or, at the very least, sexually assaulted, which, of course, is nonsense.

If you bring your wife up a cup of tea and some toast in the morning and kiss her awake, is that a case of sexual assault? Well, if you're Kristin Bell, the woman who provided the voice of Princess Anna in Disney's *Frozen*, the answer it would seem is yes. She asks, 'don't you think that it's weird that the Prince kisses Snow White without her permission? *Because you cannot kiss someone if they're sleeping!*' (Allen; emphasis added) So I reckon we'll have to revise the lyrics to Leonard Cohen's 'Alexandra Leaving'—'Even though she sleeps upon your satin; Even though she wakes you with a kiss.' If men can't kiss sleeping women, it's hard to see how you can justify a woman kissing a sleeping man. Did Alexandra seek permission? I think not! Arrest that woman!

We've already seen that the notion of consent now deemed relevant to sexual encounters is not only just a matter of a woman's saying *yes* but her doing so freely and enthusiastically. Such free and enthusiastic consent must be given not just initially but must be ongoing. 'Did I really give ongoing free and enthusiastic consent?', a woman might muse, several weeks after the original encounter. If, after a chat with her friends (like Grace), she's convinced that she didn't, then, even if, at the time, she *appeared* to give consent, she really didn't. Even the existence of evidence that suggests otherwise—post-coital text messages refuting the claim that what happened was against the woman's will (as in the case of Liam Allan), or photographs showing myself and my now-deemed assailant cuddling together (as happened in the trial of Samson Makele)—cannot be allowed to count against my revised and refined judgement.

Can you agree to have sex when you have alcohol on board, or can no agreement or consent possibly be held to obtain in such circumstances? Well, first it must be said that whatever the answer to this question is, what's sauce for the goose is sauce for the gander. If drunkenness removes responsible moral agency, then someone who assaults another while he is drunk, would thereby appear to be absolved from the agency necessarily required to be responsible for the act. On the other hand, if drunkenness does not remove moral agency, then it would appear to make possible consent to sexual activity, whether one is male or female. A woman has 4 vodka shots, 10 pints of lager, gets drunk, has sex with a man who is not drunk. Is she a victim of sexual assault? Now, a man has 4 vodka shots, 10 pints of lager, and has sex with a woman who is not drunk. Is *he* a victim of sexual assault? If you think she is but he isn't, please explain the difference. Does it have to do with anatomical equipment?—he has a penis and she doesn't, in which case there might be a relevant difference; if not, however, and if the matter is really about consent, then either both are sexually assaulted or neither is. Drunken sex, regretted sex and unwanted sex (unwanted in the sense that the sex was not particularly desired by one or other party but was still consented to) is not rape.

When it comes to alcohol, the reality is that women who are drunk get a free pass. It is a man's responsibility, and only a man's responsibility, to determine the extent of his female companion's inebriation, and it is his responsibility, and only his responsibility, to get the consent required to prevent the sexual activity from being rape. In 2013, two students at Occidental College had consensual sex while both were drunk. At the time, both agreed that the sex was consensual. Some months later, the woman filed a Title IX complaint against the man and he was expelled. Why? Because the university's policy forbids students from having sexual contact with anyone who is 'incapacitated' by drugs or alcohol. Putting to one side the appropriateness of this policy, a question naturally arises: why wasn't the woman expelled too? After all, she had precisely as much sexual contact with a person who was incapacitated by alcohol as he did. But I suppose it is too much to expect consistency in these matters.

In very many of the alleged cases of rape where the participants are known to each other, alcohol is involved. One or both of the parties is likely to have imbibed a significant quantity of drink. In 2017, a 24-year old man was cleared of a charge of rape. The alleged victim had taken six bottles of Blue WKD, three Sour shots and two vodka Red Bulls before she met the alleged rapist. The accused man had taken three pints of Carlsberg, three triple vodkas and cokes. Defending counsel said the case should serve as a 'warning to every man who goes back to a woman's room for a one-night stand and the repercussions when that woman later regrets it.' In the 19th century, *Punch* magazine had a two-panel piece of relationship advice. One panel read: 'Advice to a young man contemplating marriage.' When you turned over the page, the other panel read: 'Don't!' Today, we might mirror this: 'Advice to a young man contemplating sexual congress with a young woman: don't!—unless you have a notarised statement permitting you to do so (a young woman, however, doesn't need one from you, oddly enough) stating the precise terms and conditions of contact, start and finish times, duration, range of permitted positions, types of sexual contact, and a clear and unambiguous method of indicating that permission has been withdrawn. I have suggested already a trigger word such as 'Basingstoke'; otherwise you risk public obloquy and a gaol sentence even if you are acquitted. To repeat, when it comes to the explosive mixture of alcohol and sex, it seems that it is men's responsibility, and only men's responsibility, to monitor inebriation levels. Men must judge the level of their female companion's sobriety. It's as if women, strong, independent adult women, were their wards. But that can't possibly be the case!

Radically, some feminists—think Andrea Dworkin—argue that structural social features of coercion and female subordination under what they see as the malignant effects of the patriarchy, make genuine consent either very difficult or even impossible. If this were so, most, if not *all*, sexual intercourse between a man and a woman would be rape. In their *Rape Investigation Handbook*, John O. Savino and Brent E. Turvey discuss what they call 'Political Definitions' of rape, which they characterise as seeking to advance the agenda of a particular group rather than assisting justice or clinical treatment. In a class taught by one of the authors, a student argued that 'it is not possible for females to engage in consensual sexual activity in any context with a male.' According to her, the power structure of society has eliminated the ability of a woman to choose whether or not to have sex, because of the economic dependence of many women on men, and their greater physical and political power.' That being so, it follows that 'Sex under such circumstances is necessarily pressured at best, and therefore must be considered a form of rape.' (Savino & Turvey, 8) Somewhat less comprehensive but still remarkably wide-ranging is the argument made by Robin Morgan, the editor of *Ms* magazine, that you have rape 'any time sexual intercourse occurs when it has not been initiated by the woman, out of her own genuine affection and desire.' (see Savino & Turvey, 8) We can hear echoes of the Dworkin/Morgan line in the recently emergent idea of affirmative consent and, in particular, in the idea that a female's consent to sexual intercourse with a male must be ongoing and enthusiastic.

In the aftermath of the trial of the Belfast 4 (see below, p. 219 ff), one Roe McDermott gave an interview to the *Irish Times*. At the time of the interview, Ms McDermott was studying for an MA in Sexuality Studies in San Francisco. A lesson she takes from the Belfast 4 affair is that our understanding of what consent consists in is unclear, so much so that in fact 'it is possible for one person to leave a sexual encounter believing it was consensual, while another person can leave believing it was rape.' (McDermott) If this is so—and I believe she is correct to think it is so—this is very troubling, as consent is what makes the difference between a perfectly legal act and one that carries frightful consequences. (see Criminal Law (Sexual Offences) Act 2017.) Ms McDermott is particularly critical of the 'No means No' framework as a criterion for the revocation or non-granting of consent, arguing that to require it is to place the burden on a potential victim to stop an unwanted sexual encounter instead of, as she sees it, demanding that a person asks for and receives consent before pursuing any form of sexual interaction. Given what she sees as the typical forms of female socialisation that prioritise deference and politeness, she believes that it can be unsafe or perhaps dangerous even when possible for women to say 'No' in the context of sexual violence. To require verbal or physical resistance from women in such contexts is unhelpful. On the other hand, a 'Yes Means Yes' framework provides a much safer option for women. On this criterion, consent must not only be given freely but—you know the story by now—must be enthusiastic and active and ongoing throughout the whole sexual process.

It is curious that Ms McDermott's views seem to embody certain bizarrely anti-feminist assumptions in respect of sexual relations between men and women. First, it would appear that sex is something men do to women, rather than something that occurs mutually between men and women, so that consent is something that men require from women but not women from men. If sexual assault is essentially a matter of non-consent, then that can apply equally to males or females. If a man isn't explicitly asked for consent and sex occurs, *he* has been sexually assaulted! Second, from Ms McDermott's perspective, women don't seem to possess moral autonomy. They are essentially passive and reactive in their relationships with possible sexual partners. One must not expect a woman to resist, to say *no* in a loud and affirmative way or to make it clear that she is withdrawing consent. It's the man's job to ascertain all this. If she gives consent, it is up to the male to scrutinize that consent and make sure that it is real and freely given. The woman seems to bear no responsibility in this matter. Men shoulder the unique burden of responsibility when it comes to sex. Why is this? Because men, it would appear, are always in a position of privilege and power vis-à-vis women. Because they are powerful and privileged, men have to accept complete responsibility for everything that does or does not happen in relations between the sexes. Whenever anything goes wrong, it is always the fault, sometimes the criminal fault, of the man. Asking for evidence to justify this claim is indicative of sexism and misogyny. An obvious objection might be that it is utterly unrealistic to the messy reality of most sexual encounters to demand that a woman's consent be free, active, enthusiastic and ongoing. Her interviewer asked, 'can we really expect people to constantly ask "is this okay?" during sex?' Yes, says Ms McDermott, 'we can, we should, and with the slightest bit of practice, asking for consent will soon feel like a natural part of sex. And not just sex—good sex.' Really, Ms McDermott? Really? At the risk of repeating myself I must ask, asking for consent for what, precisely? How specific do we have to be about location, timing, and so on? And who does the asking; just the man, or the woman, or both?

What is Ms McDermott's approach to the asymmetry between male and female roles in respect of alcohol or drugs, discussed a little earlier? Alcohol, and drugs seem to remove the capacity of the woman to give consent, but not the responsibility of the man to obtain such consent. A woman's ability to give 'real' consent may be legally and literally impaired by the consumption of alcohol, but men with a similar level of inebriation are likely to end up in a court of law if they misread the signals. Here, interestingly, Ms McDermott remarks that 'alcohol is not a lobotomy. Alcohol does not make people do things; it merely lowers their inhibitions so they are more likely to act on their own pre-existing impulses.'

Ms McDermott, disappointingly but not unexpectedly, echoes the usual feminist pablum when it comes to her account of the justice system as a whole. For her, as for many feminists, 'the justice system was never designed to protect victims of sexual violence—because historically, victims have always been assumed to be women' and as we all know, our legal systems were built by and for the support of patriarchal societies. What kind of evidence does Ms McDermott cite to support this astonishing claim? Well, she notes that a patriarchal society is one in which the few dominate over the many, and the few were not women. It doesn't seem to occur to her that while the few were usually men, most men, almost all men, were not among the few either, and that the kind of society she is describing is one in which almost everybody—women *and* men—were dominated by a small number of people. We still operate under the same basic political structures and now, increasingly, women are among the few who dominate, but that makes no difference to every other woman *and man* who is not part of the few.

Another point McDermott makes, aligning herself on this point with Germaine Greer, is that rape is taken to be an offence against the state rather than a wrong done to another person. It's not the woman's day in court. The rapist has broken the state's law and the victim is merely a witness for the state. I have some sympathy for this point except that it doesn't establish what it sets out to establish in any interesting way. As I mentioned when discussed Germaine Greer's little book on rape, the side-lining of the victim happens in the prosecution of *all* crimes. We're unlikely to be surprised to find Ms McDermott calling for a radical shakeup of the entire justice system. We must acknowledge, she says, that 'it may be necessary to completely transform and rebuild the system, rather than trying to add a few protections onto a fundamentally flawed foundation.' Just what radical transformation she has in mind she doesn't confide to us. I hope I may not be considered paranoid if I fear that the presumption of innocence may be on the hit list of things to be disposed of.

What would a world in which women can feel safe look like? Will it be a sanitised world with all possible moves on the sexual chessboard programmed in advance? Will contracts be drawn up and notarised? Will physical contact be monitored to ensure that it stays within contractual bounds? As I already mentioned, Fry and Laurie's 'Pre-Coital Agreement' is a perfectly ludicrous (and very funny) comedy sketch in which lawyers cold-bloodedly discuss the intimate details of male-female sexual interactions as if they were discussing the details of a contract for the production and supply of widgets. Here's some advice for you men before you head off into the quagmire of possible sexual interaction with a woman.

First, meet a woman. Second, after the initial 'what's your name' and 'where are you from?', discuss and agree all possible outcomes of a potential relationship. This can take some time and should not be rushed. When agreement has been reached, it should be noted in writing. It's not absolutely necessary to employ legal assistance à la Fry & Laurie but it might be advisable. Third, list all possible joint and mutual activities. This list should be comprehensive and include all possible physical forms of contact (in detail), all permissible forms of communication, all emotional needs and interests, again in detail—the man's list will normally be shorter than the woman's but that's to be expected—and all possible future contingencies. Fourth, the joint lists emerging from steps 2 & 3 should be notarised. Fifth, flirtation may now begin, but only under strict supervision. Sixth, the material on the lists is indicative only and any sexual contact must be enthusiastic and affirmative and must manifest continuing consent (from *both* parties), the consent duly witnessed and attested and, if at all possible, the interaction should the observed by a neutral observer to make sure that all conditions are adhered to at all times—otherwise, spontaneity might break out and that's the last thing anyone would want!

One of the consequences of the increasingly poisonous atmosphere created by the hysteria of the #MeToo movement and its adherents is that the relationship between the sexes, already tense, had become increasingly fraught. Women are being taught to regard all male interactions with them as possibly suspect, and men are becoming paralysed in their approaches to women lest their words or actions be misconstrued and they're outed on the Twittersphere, accused of sexual harassment or misogyny or both, and fired from their jobs by employers who are terrified of being seen to be associated with anything that might remotely be construed as anti-woman. Will the brave new world of sanitised sexual relations be a world in which men increasingly reduce or eliminate contact with women as they would with an infection-ridden geographical zone? Helen Smith in her book, *Men on Strike: Why Men Are Boycotting Marriage, Fatherhood, and the American Dream—and Why It Matters*, envisions an American society where 'men are sensing the backlash and are consciously and unconsciously "going on strike". They are dropping out of college, leaving the workforce and avoiding marriage and fatherhood at alarming rates.' One solution, admittedly a radical solution, to the contemporary sex war is to separate the sides by means of the equivalent of a sexual de-militarised zone. So, we might get first, a complete separation of men and women in public, in work, and in school—parallel tracks all the way along; second, chaperonage in any situation in which men and women must of necessity interact; and third, sex finally permitted but only under the supervision and direction of a third party, and only if validated as affirmative, continuing and enthusiastic.

In the toxic environment that now subsists where unsubstantiated allegations can cost a man his job and his reputation, it would make sense to disintegrate workplaces. If this isn't going to happen (and it is perhaps unlikely to happen), the very least that will happen is that workplaces may become covertly less woman-friendly, thus making real the feminist fantasy of female oppression. If I am an employer and two candidates present themselves for a position I'm offering, A and B, and A is endowed with state-sanctioned victim status with all that that entails while B is not, I am more likely to hire B than A. We've seen something like this already in the USA in respect of workers with disabilities. The presumably well-intentioned 'Americans with Disabilities Act' in fact increased the cost of hiring disabled workers so that we witnessed a steep decline in their employment. It is not unimaginable that something similar may happen when it comes to considering the employment of women.

Victim-blaming

Victim blaming is a very bad thing, a Very Bad Thing indeed, especially in the case or cases of alleged rape. But when it comes to home protection and personal safety, it seems that police forces engage in this very dubious activity! How else is one to understand the kind of advice that they offer to potential crime victims! Don't they realise that in offering this advice, they are implicitly condoning burglary and assault?

On their website, the Irish police force, *An Garda Síochána*, offers extensive advice on personal and property protection. In respect of *property* protection, they advocate locks, reinforced glass, wide-angled viewers, door chains, automatic light timers, recording serial numbers of valuable items, checking identity of servicemen, keeping tools and ladders inaccessible, and arranging for your lawn to be mowed if you're going to be away from home for any length of time. In respect of *personal* protection, they advise you to be aware of your vulnerability (man/woman, old/young, able bodied/disabled, alone/in company, a local/a stranger, confident/timid); to be aware of your environment (busy places attract thieves; isolated places attract muggers and robbers), and in respect of your individual behaviour, to be wary of strangers, to avoid confrontation, to get off your phone, conceal your wallet or purse, not to struggle with a thief, to avoid darkly-lit places and to avoid waiting alone at bus stops and on train platforms.

Regardless of what you do or don't do, no one has a right to enter your home and walk off with your property. You should be able to walk out of your house, leave your front door and windows open and, in an ideal world, expect to find everything in order when you return. Similarly, you should be able to go anywhere at any time in any condition and expect to be unmolested, to walk around the dodgier areas of the city on your own, late at night, with your wallet sticking conspicuously out of your back pocket and, in an ideal world, expect nothing untoward to happen. In offering the advice they do, especially in respect of your personal behaviour, are *An Garda Síochána* suggesting that failure to take these measures renders you blameworthy if you're robbed or assaulted? Is this antecedent victim-blaming?

Would it be too radical to suggest that we need to make a simple distinction between what is *justifiable* and what is *prudent*? Robbery and theft are never justifiable. Rape, assault (sexual or otherwise) and mugging are also never *justifiable*. But it doesn't follow from this that one shouldn't be *prudent* in acting so as to pre-emptively prevent robbery, theft, rape, assault and mugging. And if one is careless about taking measures to protect oneself, then one is, *in that respect*, blameworthy, while it still remains the cases that robbery, theft, rape, assault and mugging are *not* thereby somehow justified by your carelessness.

And so to the demonisation of George Hook. On his radio programme (*The Right Hook*) coming from the Irish radio station *Newstalk*, Mr Hook made some remarks that were widely interpreted as victim blaming. What he in fact said was: ' ... but when you then look deeper into the story you have to ask certain questions. Why does a girl who just meets a fella in a bar go back to a hotel room? She's only just barely met him. She has no idea of his health conditions, she has no idea who he is, no idea what dangers he might pose. But is there no blame now to the person who puts themselves in danger? You then of course read that she passed out on the toilet and when she woke up the guy was trying to rape her. There is personal responsibility because it's your daughter and my daughter.' Allowing for a certain clumsiness in phrasing, it's fairly clear that Hook was talking about the blame that might reasonably be attached to a lack of prudence and he was *not* justifying rape. He was doing just what *An Garda Síochána* do on their website. If George deserves to be demonised, then so too do *An Garda Síochána*; if *An Garda Síochána* is blameless, then George is, if you'll pardon the pun, off the hook. In a similar vein, in 2017, when sentencing a man to six years in gaol for rape, Judge Lindsey Kushner QC said that while women were entitled to drink themselves into the ground, they should be aware that their 'disinhibited behaviour' could endanger them. 'Judge's warning to drunk women "will stop reporting of rape"' was a fairly typical Guardianesque reaction to Judge Kushner's comments. (Anon. 2017a) She was accused of 'blaming the victims' by, among others, Dame Vera Baird, the then Northumbria Police and Crime Commissioner (and ex-Labour MP— what a surprise!) Of course, this is nonsense. What the judge said is no more victim blaming than if police offer advice on measures to prevent burglaries and assaults.

Let's envision a Q&A session with a feminist 'victim-blaming' dogmatist:

Q. Would you be willing to answer a few questions about crime?
A. Sure.
Q. Excellent. If Tom is mugged by Sandra while walking around a notoriously dodgy part of town, late at night, with his bulging wallet hanging out of his back pocket, who has committed a crime? Tom or Sandra?
A. Why Sandra, obviously!

Q. Very good. Now if Tom were your brother or son, what advice would you offer him in respect of walking around that part of town at night and displaying his wallet for all to see? Remember, you've promised to answer truthfully!

A. Do I have to answer this question?

Q. Well, how about this. Accepting that criminality is criminality regardless of whether or not the victim of that criminality has or has not taken reasonable precautions against its occurrence, would you think our late-night-walking wallet-displaying, dodgy-part-of-town inhabiting Tom had acted wisely or foolishly?

A. I suppose I'd have to say that he had acted foolishly—but that doesn't give anyone the right to mug him!

Q. Well, of course. Who in his right mind thinks that advising Tom (or Deirdre or Harriet) to take sensible precautions against being a victim of crime is thereby justifying the actions of the criminal?

A. Aha! I see where you're going with this. You're trying to fool me into accepting that it's right to blame rape victims for being raped.

Q. No. I'm not adopting a CathyNewmanesque strategy of asserting: 'So what you're really saying is ... ' I'm simply trying to get you to see that in a perfect world, precautions against aggression would not be necessary. But this is not a perfect world, and being reckless about your personal safety for ideological reasons is not really a very sensible decision. In no other part of our lives would we object to being offered sensible advice on how to protect ourselves against aggression. I recently heard a public-service announcement from the police advising homeowners on how to protect themselves against burglars. I suppose you'd interpret that as blaming the victims of burglary for the loss of their goods?

A. The situations are entirely different. Rape is rape is rape, and you're just trying to justify the rapist and blame the victim.

Q. (Sigh.....)

Unbelievable as it seems, Dame Angela Lansbury is a victim-blamer! We know that victim blaming is one of the new seven deadly sins. How could the motherly star of *Murder, She Wrote* have committed such a sin? More to the point, how did she do it? By uttering the words, 'There are two sides to this coin.' But we know that there are never two sides to a story when one side is a woman and a victim and the repository of all the virtues, including epistemological purity. Women are to be believed, always and everywhere; men are vile and, if accused, are guilty without the need for a trial. Let's have no nonsense about *audi alteram partem*. Yet another little bit of procedural justice bites the dust

A big fuss broke out in late 2018 in a rape trial in Cork, Ireland, when it was revealed that counsel for the defendant in a case of alleged rape asked the jurors to take into account the kind of underwear the complainant was wearing.

The jury took just ninety minutes to find the defendant not guilty. If you paid attention to the shock/horror stories that reported this event, you might be forgiven for thinking that that was the only consideration the jury had to bear in mind. It seems to have escaped the attention of the terminally outraged that there must have been other evidence and testimony that was presented to the jury, apart from that relating to the intimate garment in question. But who cares about that when we can have a reason-free attention-grabber to make hay with? Incidentally, the verdict of the jury, who had heard all the evidence and testimony in the trial, was unanimous. Some of the commentary presented the suggestion of the defendant's counsel as a case of victim blaming. I suppose it's pointless to say that since the jury acquitted the defendant, and determined in so doing that no rape took place, there was no victim so that, *a fortiori*, there can be no victim-blaming.

Whenever the discussion turns to whether it would make sense for women to take some modest precautions to help prevent rape or sexual assault, the instantaneous reaction is to shout 'victim-blaming'! But the cry of 'victim-blaming' has other implications, not least that women, just as women, are essentially victims, as it were, victims by nature and should be referred to as such in court cases even before there is any determination of wrongdoing on the part of another. Those who have easy recourse to the cry of 'victim blaming' also implicitly characterise women as passively irresponsible and essentially childlike in their innocence. But women are human beings, just as men are. And as men are sometimes idiotic, so too are women. And as men sometimes lie, so too do women. And as men are sometimes irresponsible, so too are women. Unless, of course, you have been out of touch with reality for some time and think that women, as women, are the pink of perfection and flawless. Let me know when visiting hours are and I'll come to see you.

A Presumption of Guilt

I tell my clients 'innocent before proven guilty' is not reality.
It's more of a marketing slogan to promote faith in our justice system;
without that premise, the system would fall apart
—Xavier Donaldson

Where was the Judge whom he had never seen?
Where was the High Court, to which he had never penetrated?
He raised his hands and spread out all his fingers.
But the hands of one of the partners were already at K.'s throat,
while the other thrust the knife deep into his heart and turned it there twice
—Kafka

We must believe those who say they've been raped! This statement may mean either that the substantive content of what is claimed by those who make the claim is true, that is, that they have in fact been raped and that we should therefore believe what they say; or it may mean that we should believe that those who make such claims believe what they claim—a belief about a belief, a meta-belief. It is perfectly possible to assent to the latter without necessarily assenting to former. It might seem that unless we assent to the truth of the substantive claim, we are obliged to believe that those who make such claims do *not* in fact believe what they claim, that they are, in fact, lying, but, of course, we are under no such obligation. In ordinary circumstances, it is perfectly possible for a person to hold a belief without that belief's being true, and their holding such a belief may be either a mistake, or a matter of self-deception, or a lie. The situation is not essentially different when it comes to claims about rape. Persons making claims that are substantively false may be mistaken, self-deceived, or lying.

Suspension of judgement
From the point of view of persons adjudicating such claims, the issue is often presented as if there were only two options; either those who make such claims

must be believed, unless and until there is good reason to doubt their claims; or they should be doubted, unless and until there is good reason to believe their claims. But these are not the only options. There is a third possibility, which is, that the claim should neither be believed nor doubted, but rather taken seriously and investigated. Belief or disbelief in the substantive claim should not be arrived at until evidence other than the bare assertion of the claim is produced.

Suspension of judgement is very difficult for us human beings, especially when our emotions are engaged. Much seemingly inexplicable human irrationality, not least, our rush to make snap judgements, is explicable by reference to the facts of our evolution. For most of human existence, when we needed to make life or death judgements, we needed to make them quickly. Inaction and suspension of judgement is not usually an effective evolutionary option. It is better to do something and possibly get it wrong, rather than do nothing and certainly get it wrong! Our residual physical instincts (such as stretching out our arms when we fall), allow us to react without thought to some immediate physical dangers; our beliefs function more or less as culturally formed quasi-instincts that serve similar survival functions at a cognitive level. (see Casey 2011)

Those who make the case for the presumptive substantive belief of claims of rape argue that it is better for some liars and fantasists to get away with their lies and their fantasies than that those with genuine claims should be discouraged from coming forward with their complaints, but this is to ignore the devastating effects of false accusations on those who are falsely accused. Rarely, if ever, is the same publicity given to the rebuttal of false claims as it is to their initial assertion, and even if that happens, the stain on the character of those falsely accused is never completely washed away. Carolyn Hoyle and her fellow investigators write,

> during and following all these processes, accused individuals and their families do indeed suffer enormously from the stigma and revulsion associated with sexual abuse, from the deprivations during the investigation and the lifelong suspicion (that they "got away with it") that is likely to follow. [The present study] finds that even if such allegations do not lead to criminal proceedings, they are likely to have life-changing effects. Formal investigations, whether in a civil or criminal context, are harrowing for the accused person, and may result in immediate suspension from work and temporary restrictions on contact with children, and a record of having been reported and investigated, which can cause longer term damage to employment prospects and relationships.' (Hoyle *et al.*, 5)

There is strong pressure to shift the onus of proof onto the accused in rape and sexual assault cases, which would require those accused to prove that they are innocent rather than requiring the prosecution to prove them guilty. Edward

Greer quotes Linda Brookover Bourque, the author of a definitive 1989 study, *Defining Rape*, as claiming that, 'the ultimate objective of rape reform is to shift "the burden of proof from the victim to the offender".' (Greer 2000, 948) To repeat a point I made earlier, Susan Brownmiller, doyenne of the feminist movement and the author of *Against Our Will* (1975) isn't worried about the lack of due process in the current furore occasioned by the #MeToo juggernaut. It doesn't seem to bother her that men have been dismissed from their jobs simply on the basis of one woman's word, when the allegations made against them have never been proved or even fully explored. I wonder if Brownmiller would be as sanguine about the absence of due process if she were ever to find herself arraigned on a criminal charge and she herself were to be denied it. But only men are on the receiving end of the #MeToo witchhunt, so why should Brownmiller care?

Due process

The notion of due process seems to be a dry and technical and rather boring concept. Who could possibly get excited about it? Well, I could, for one, and so could all those men on US university campuses, such as John Doe who, having been denied anything resembling due process, find themselves accused, convicted and sentenced in the marsupial investigative process that passes for a quasi-judicial campus hearing. John Doe, for example, was tried in a case of supposed campus sexual assault and was suspended for five years. A real court reinstated him and, if the recommendation of a federal magistrate is accepted, James Madison University may be required to pay him almost $1,000,000 to cover his legal expenses. The magistrate held that Doe's suspension was unfair, inasmuch as the assault was alleged but not proved. The story follows what is, by now, a familiar pattern. Doe and Roe had sex and then, several months later, Roe alleged that she had been too drunk to give her consent to the act. The initial campus tribunal held that Doe wasn't guilty on a charge of sexual misconduct. Roe, however, filed an appeal and, in the light of the Obama administration's now infamous 'Dear Colleague' letter, which resulted in the weakening of the already-on-life-support due-process protections, a three-professor board overruled, without explanation, the decision of the original tribunal. The board would not allow Doe to be represented by a lawyer or to cross-examine his accuser, and would not permit him to see additional evidence supplied to them by Roe. Part of this evidence was a voicemail purporting to show that Roe was intoxicated on the night of the alleged assault but, in fact, that voicemail had been sent on the night *before* the event, something that one of the appeal board members said she didn't realise until Doe took his legal action.

What are the elements of due process? In criminal cases, the first and by far the most important element of due process, described as 'the golden thread running through the web of English criminal law', is the presumption of innocence of the defendant. (see *Woolmington v DPP* [1935]) It is *not* that the defendant *is* innocent until proved guilty; he is simply *presumed* to be innocent. This is merely a presumption, of course, and it is one that can be overturned by evidence and testimony. It is the prosecution's task to do the overturning— it is not the defence's task to establish the defendant's innocence.

A habit has developed of referring to those who report rape as 'victims', as if the genuineness of their claims was already established. This practice slyly undermines investigative and judicial impartiality. In 2017, the UK's Justice Secretary, Liz Truss, announced new measures to spare alleged rape victims from having to face live cross-examination in court. If these measures were to be implemented, victims would be able to give their evidence in pre-recorded videos that the jury would see after the trial began. Ms Truss said, 'the changes to rape trials would prevent victims facing the trauma of confronting their attackers without reducing the right to a fair trial.' (Summers 2017) At the risk of repeating myself, let me just say that a moment's reflection will show the glaring problem with this ostensibly compassionate move. In using the term 'victim', and thus assuming that there *is* in fact a victim, the procedure pre-judges the outcome of the trial. During the course of the trial, all that we have, legally speaking, is an *alleged* attacker and an *alleged* victim. Until the jury brings in a guilty verdict, we don't know, legally, whether we have a victim or not, so that the measures proposed by Ms Truss, though no doubt well-intentioned, are prejudicial to the trial process.

The proposed new measures, then, involve a none-too-subtle overturning of the presumption of innocence. Moreover, since most of the alleged attackers are men, the move is, even if only inadvertently, sexist. It is perhaps not too much to see the Truss move as an example of legal misandry. There may be a victim; there may not; a woman may tell the truth; a woman may tell what she believes to be the truth but which isn't the truth; a woman may lie. A man accused of rape may tell the truth when he denies the charge of rape or he may lie but, in the UK, he will not have the benefit of anonymity that the alleged victim has. If complainants are allowed to give their evidence via video, this already indicates that the justice system regards their evidence as more worthy of protection than that of the defendant. If the cross-examination is also allowed to be pre-recorded, that exacerbates an already very dangerous prejudicial tendency.

In a report on the Metropolitan Police Service's handling of historic sexual offence investigations, Operation Midland, the author of the report, Sir Richard Henriques, recommended that during the investigative and the judicial process, those who make complaints should be referred to as *complainants* and not as *victims*. He also said, 'There is plain evidence, in the cases that I have reviewed, that an instruction to believe complainants has over ridden a duty to investigate cases objectively and effectively. An instruction to remain objective and impartial while interviewing a complainant will not detract from the obligation to support complainants through the criminal justice process nor deprive any complainants of rights under the Victims Charter.' (Henriques 2016, §1.25, 16-17) He went on:

> I have a clear and concluded view. All 'complainants' are not 'victims'. Some complaints are false and thus those 'complainants' are not 'victims'. Throughout the judicial process the word 'complainant' is deployed up to the moment of conviction where after a 'complainant' is properly referred to as a 'victim'. Since the entire judicial process, up to that point, is engaged in determining whether or not a 'complainant' is indeed a 'victim', such an approach cannot be questioned. No Crown Court judge will permit a 'complainant' to be referred to as a 'victim' prior to conviction. Since the investigative process is similarly engaged in ascertaining facts that will, if proven, establish guilt, the use of the word 'victim' at the commencement of an investigation is simply inaccurate and should cease. (Henriques 2016, §1.12, 7-8)

Astonishingly, in the 2019 redaction of Sir Richard's report, the Metropolitan Police Service said that it had *not* accepted his recommendation that those who make complaints should be referred to as complainants and not as victims! The reason it offered for its refusal is that the term 'victim' is 'a commonly accepted term across a wide range of guidance, policy and legislation.' In a sentence that I find hard to credit, the Met go on to say, 'The use of the word victim is not intrinsically linked to the issue of belief.' (Henriques 2019, 384; see also Evans 2019, and Murphy & Vikram) In rejecting some aspects of Sir Richard's report, specifically those relating to the behaviour of some of the police officers who conducted the investigation in Operation Midland, the Director General of the Independent Office for Police Conduct (IOPC), Michael Lockwood, said, apparently without any trace of irony, that, in relation to the conduct of the investigating officers, 'the presumption of innocence until proven guilty must prevail ...', a presumption of innocence that would seem to have been in much shorter supply for those who were the targets of Operation Midland. (Lockwood) Sir Richard said that, a year after he made his recommendations in his report, they still had not been adopted. 'These problems are entirely down to the instructions that police must believe "victims" as they call them. Everything flows from that viewpoint because officers do not then bother to check messages or make basic inquiries.' What he called an 'artificial mindset' was, he said, 'imposed upon them [the police] by the College of Policing which says victims must be believed.' (Henriques 2016)

The chairman of the Criminal Bar Association, Angela Rafferty QC, made the eminently sensible and, one would have thought, obvious remark that 'it is not the job of the police or CPS to judge the truthfulness or otherwise of any allegation made.' (see Evans 2017) Dominic Grieve, a former UK Attorney General, said that he found 'the use of the term victim for a person making a complaint unfortunate because it creates a distortion in the process as police carry out an investigation. The police must stop referring to complainants as victims. They must be welcoming to complainants and take them seriously, but must always keep an open mind about complaints.' (Evans) Alison Levitt, the former principal legal advisor to the UK's Director of Public Prosecutions, said that the police 'must approach these cases with an open mind. It is their duty to investigate whether or not it leads towards the suspect or indeed away from the suspect.' (see Evans 2017) This is a statement straight out of the Big Book of the Bleedin' Blatantly obvious, one would have thought but, in our new, supposedly 'victim-centred' normative environment, apparently not! In the more complete (2019) version of Sir Richard's report, the Metropolitan Police Service says that it now fully accepts Sir Richard's recommendation that the instruction to 'believe the victim' should cease, adding that it 'supports the view that allegations should be investigated impartially and with an open mind.' (Henriques 2019, 385)

The presumption of innocence is attacked not only by the state and its agencies when they play the 'victim' card, but also by moral panics such as #MeToo and other online campaigns. As I have already shown, in the #MeToo world, due process takes a battering: accusation equals conviction. End of story. No defence will be accepted. There is no need for trials, no need for evidence; all we need is an accusation: *vox populi, vox diaboli.* The people have spoken, now let the lynching commence. In old films, one sometimes sees the villagers appear with lighted torches in their hands, ready to deal with the villains. (Do they keep those torches permanently lit and conveniently placed just inside their front doors?) Another familiar trope is the angry mob in old-fashioned Westerns, ever ready to deal with the low-life villain in jail, without the necessity for the expensive and unnecessary luxury of a trial. The latter-day equivalent of the villagers and the angry lynch mob is the wittering of the Twitterati. The casual dismissal of the presumption of innocence is particularly grating in accusations of rape or sexual abuse, where there are very often no witnesses to the alleged crime apart from the complainant and the accused, and where, more often than not, there is a complex and messy relation between the two parties. Because of a deplorable history of past failures to take rape and sexual abuse claims seriously, there is a tendency to give the benefit of the doubt to the accusers rather than to those accused. Carolyn Hoyle writes, 'Even in cases where the evidence only consists of testimony from the alleged victim and is strongly rebutted by the alleged perpetrator, the moral imperative not to "let down another victim" or to leave a possible sex offender free to cause further harm may be compelling. While this must, logically, reduce the chances of guilty persons avoiding prosecution ("false negatives"), it also risks increasing the likelihood of innocent people being presumed or found guilty ("false positives"). (Hoyle *et al.*, 4)

While the presumption of innocence is by far the most important element of due process, it is not the only one. Another aspect of due process is that *all* the evidence pertinent to the charge, whether it supports the prosecution case or strengthens the defence case, must be produced and not 'edited', and the prosecution must hand over to the defence any such evidence pertinent to their case. Danny Kay (no, not *that* Danny Kaye!) was jailed in 2013, having received a four and one half year sentence for rape. After he had been incarcerated, Facebook messages were uncovered that supported his side of the story. Defence lawyers at the Court of Appeal said that the prosecution had given an 'edited and misleading' outline of the online interactions between Kay and the person who accused him of a crime.

The right to silence and the prohibition of double jeopardy are yet other aspects of due process. The right to silence entails that no one should be obliged in a criminal trial to incriminate himself. This right used to be more or less absolute. In fact, at one stage, a defendant in criminal cases was not permitted to testify! Now, a refusal to answer questions from the inquisitors requires one to be cautioned that adverse inferences can be drawn from that refusal. The prohibition of double jeopardy requires the prosecution to make up its mind whether it thinks there's a case to answer before proceeding to trial. Now, as the result of the Criminal Justice Act 2003, double jeopardy is a thing of the past for murder and rape, and there is nothing, in principle, to prevent the prosecution from 'giving it a try'. If the initial prosecution fails, they can always come back for a second go. Given the disparity in power and in financial resources between the state and the typical criminal defendant, this is a disturbing development.

I mentioned that some feminists, such as Susan Brownmiller, don't seem to be too bothered by the possible erosion of due process in matters of rape, sexual assault or sexual harassment. Other women, however, take a different view. In an interview she gave in 2017, Christine Hoff Sommers said, 'Feminism has to be aware of the importance of due process. And not presuming guilt—guilty because accused is not only morally wrong, it's socially corrosive. Men and women do work together, we are working together. And, for the most part, it's good. I was thinking last night, what is going to be the outcome of all of this #MeToo panic? And, I just think it's going to be a lot of isolation and loneliness. It's going to be frightening for many people, for a while, to interact in the workplace—certainly if you're not supervised. Because any woman now has the power to destroy a man with one accusation, even a false one.' (Sommers 2017)

The Kavanaugh contention

'I believe her' was the mantra of choice during the Brett Kavanaugh Supreme Court confirmation hearings. It seemed that if one wasn't prepared to believe Christine Margaret Blasey Ford, one had to disbelieve her. It didn't seem to occur to many people to suspend judgement until the evidence was heard in full. Bill Burr, the TV stand-up comic, says in one of his routines, 'Believe women? What, all of 'em? I'll give you 87%. But that last 13% that keys your car, lights your shit on fire and puts a family pet in a pot of stew! Yeah, due process. Somebody says something happened and somebody else says, "it happened this way". Now it's frontier justice. [He pauses] Did you see just how nervous everybody got in here just because I suggested there should be due process?' (Burr) Lionel Shriver remarks, self-referentially, 'one exceptionally idiotic meme runs, 'BELIEVE WOMEN'. With closing on four billion females, that's right next door to 'BELIEVE EVERYBODY'. I'm a woman, and I'd not want you to buy everything I told you without my making a convincing case. Like men, women can be stupid, self-justifying, desperate for attention, dishonest and delusional.' (Shriver)

In the Kavanaugh hearings, we witnessed amazing scenes of people (mainly women) running around after Senators, buttonholing them in lifts and along corridors. Now, where else have we heard of women running around in feral packs, tearing men to non-metaphorical pieces. Let me see ... hmmmm. Ah yes, the Maenads! The Maenads—their name means the 'raving ones'—were the female followers of Dionysus. If you think the Maenads are to be found only in classical times, think again. We've all seen the footage of the Beatles being pursued by hordes of young women and screamed at so loudly at concerts that their music was inaudible. George Harrison lamented, 'The more fame we got, the more girls came to see us, everybody making a noise so that nobody could hear us.' But Beatlemania is not an isolated instance of this phenomenon. The same screaming and fainting happened to Frank Sinatra, Dean Martin, Elvis and many others. In the 19th century, the pianist Franz Liszt inspired the same kind of maniacal attention from women. This form of behaviour seems to be a purely female phenomenon with no male equivalent; the Spice Girls and the Sugababes were not screamed at by hordes of pubescent young males. Was Beatlemania (and the other similar manifestations) a 'modern incarnation of female hysteria', as Paul Johnson described it in the *New Statesman*, a description that has drawn criticism over the years; or was it simply, as it was described in the *British Journal of Clinical Psychology*, 'the passing reaction of predominantly young adolescent females to group pressures of such a kind that meet their special emotional needs.' You watch the footage and decide. On reflection, perhaps the Senator-chasing women could better be thought of as part-Maenad, part Violet Elizabeth Bott. Violet Elizabeth who? Don't you remember—the sweet, adorable little girl in Richmal Crompton's *William* stories who used emotional terrorism to get her own way by lisping, 'I'll thcream and I'll thcream 'til I'm thick. I can you know.' (For a definitive account of the Kavanaugh confirmation process, see Hemingway & Severino 2019)

During the Maenad mania of the Kavanaugh hearings, Senator Mazie Hirono said, 'I just want to say to the men in this country, just shut up and step up. Do the right thing—for a change. Not only do women like Dr Ford, who bravely comes (*sic*) forward need to be heard but they need to be believed.' Can you imagine any male Senator or any man in public office saying: 'I just want to say to the women in this country, just shut up and step up. Do the right thing— for a change.' Incidentally, Senator Hirono doesn't always seem to have held the position the women need to be believed. When Lenore Kwock, the hairdresser of Hirono's political mentor, Senator Daniel Inouye, claimed she had been forced into non-consensual sex by Inouye and had suffered persistent groping by him, Hirono, who was then a member of the State House and was regarded as a protégé of Inouye, was conspicuously silent on the matter. Didn't she think that Kwock needed to be believed? If she did, she doesn't appear to have said so.

An interviewer on TV asked the Senator, 'Doesn't Kavanaugh have the same presumption of innocence as anyone in America?' Hirono responded, 'I put his denial in the context of everything that I know about how he approaches his cases.' You will notice—it's hard not to notice—that Hirono doesn't answer the question that she is asked. Just how difficult was it to say, 'Yes, he is entitled to the presumption of innocence' in response to this question? Instead, she made the point that her disbelief in his protestations of innocence was linked to her disagreement with his judicial rulings! This elliptical non-answer was made even more clearly in her appearance on CNN when she said, 'He's very outcome-driven, he has an ideological agenda, and I can sit here and talk to you about some of the cases that exemplify his, in my view, inability to be fair.' It appears that Hirono thought that Kavanaugh's judicial decisions (with which she disagrees) somehow undermined his credibility *tout court*. Another questioner on TV asked Senator Hirono: 'can you clarify what you meant? Do you believe

Judge Kavanaugh does deserve the presumption of innocence or not?' Once again, Senator Hirono conspicuously refused to say, 'Yes, he deserves to enjoy the presumption of innocence as does everyone else.' Instead, she replied, 'we're not in a court of law. We're actually in a court of credibility at this point and, without having the FBI report or some semblance of trying to get corroboration, we are left with the credibility of the two witnesses.' I don't know what a court of credibility is, but I'd hate to be dragged before one, especially if Senator Hirono were sitting on its bench!

It could be argued, as Senator Hirono seems to argue, that the confirmation hearings for the ratification of a nomination of a judge to the United States Supreme Court isn't a court proceeding and so the presumption of innocence rule doesn't apply. This indeed is the very point made by Lisa Graves, who was chief counsel for nominations for Senator Patrick Leahy (Democrat) of Vermont, when he was the ranking member of the Senate Judiciary Committee. Her reason for so thinking is that if Ford were to be believed, Kavanaugh wouldn't go to jail, but would simply not be appointed to the Supreme Court. But this argument is utterly disingenuous. First, it's not at all clear that believing Ford wouldn't at some time in the future lead to a jail sentence for Kavanaugh, even if that were unlikely. And second, and most importantly, going to jail isn't the only punishment that can be inflicted on a person. Those men—and it's almost always men—who have been the victim of campus kangaroo courts by being convicted and expelled from university on the basis of accusations to which they have had no adequate opportunity to respond, or those men—and it's almost always men—who have been fired from their jobs because of mere allegations, have been the victims of a violation of the principles of natural justice. And natural justice applies across the board, not just in the rarefied context of criminal proceedings.

A bit of common sense was supplied by Jonathan Turley from George Washington University Law School who remarked that Senators 'should not be publicly stating that they believe or disbelieve these witnesses. They should be affirming that they keep an open mind as to the allegation, and that there is some standard of review.' Keeping an open mind! Now, there's a revolutionary sentiment. It is revealing that in the heat of the Kavanaugh controversy, the *Christian Science Monitor* ran a piece entitled 'What Kavanaugh case means for "innocent until proven guilty"' The author of the piece, Francine Kiefer, described the situation as one in which 'two paradigms are hurtling toward each other in a clash: the age-old legal standard that someone must be presumed innocent until proven guilty, and the new #MeToo social norm that accusers of sexual assault should be believed.'

Senator Hirono was not alone in demonstrating contempt for procedural justice. Here is what her Democratic Party colleague, Senator Richard Blumenthal had to say on TV: 'These allegations are serious and credible and now the person with the most knowledge about them, namely Judge Brett Kavanaugh has a responsibility to come forward with evidence to rebut them.' Yet another principle of due process takes a hit, this time, the right not to have to incriminate yourself by being forced to give evidence in your trial. No criminal defendant can be obliged to give testimony or to answer any questions nor, until recently, could failure so to do allow the drawing of adverse inferences.

In the Brett Kavanaugh imbroglio, much was made of the memories, or rather lack of memories, of his accuser, Dr Ford. Our memories are not simple mechanisms that we can access as routinely and as uncomplicatedly as we can access records on a computer. Memories are constructed and reconstructed. There are few things easier to do than to induce false memories. Discussing the notorious 1984 Fells Acres Day Care Center case of alleged child abuse, Julia Shaw, author of *The Memory Illusion*, reports one of the teachers at the Center saying, 'they scared the hell out of me ... The whole thing was geared toward convicting them [the accused], no one was asking, "Do you think this really happened?" No one wanted to hear anything that was common sense.' (Shaw 2016, 221-22) Shaw notes that in this case, 'there was a shocking lack of evidence', no scars, no injuries. (Shaw 2016, 222) The children always denied the abuse in the first instance, but suggestive interviewing techniques and encouragement with toys eventually led them to give answers that suggested abuse. (see also Anon. 2011a) In a similar vein, Barbara Hewson writes that it is very easy 'to implant false memories, which may be quite vivid and detailed.' She continues:

> A study published by members of the Department of Psychology in Utrecht University, in May this year [2013], found that subtle misinformation conveyed to normal people could create false memories. This follows the same findings in earlier research by US psychologists such as Elizabeth Loftus in the 1970s. The 2013 Dutch study also references an earlier Dutch study in 1996, after an aircraft crashed into an apartment block. The media reported that videos of the crash were made, though no such footage actually existed. Yet a survey found that over half of those interviewed later on claimed to have seen the non-existent video material, and some proceeded to give details of what happened when the plane hit the building. In the 2013 study, 249 soldiers deployed in Afghanistan were interviewed about stressors in deployment. After the interview, 213 were given subtle misinformation about an imaginary but plausible event, namely, a harmless missile attack on their base on New Year's Eve. They were asked if they recalled such an event, but denied it. Seven months later, they were retested. Twenty-six per cent of participants (55) were now

recalling this fictional event, which previously they had denied experiencing. What this shows is that memory is malleable, and that memory for a potentially traumatic event is not immutable. As the 2013 study authors wrote: 'New information, from whatever source, can be incorporated into existing memories and can change the way people remember events.' (Hewson; emphasis added)

Memories, to be credible, require external validation. Laura Kipnis, in her book *Unwanted Advances*, notes that 'One problem with retroactive accusations is that memory doesn't exactly sharpen over time. In fact, most memory research demonstrates that subsequent events reshape and distort our memories, and the more we recall a given memory, the less accurate it becomes. These revisions accumulate, and can come to seem just as "true" as what actually happened.' (Kipnis, 95) She also writes, chillingly, 'Sexual consent can now be retroactively withdrawn (with official sanction) years later, based on changing feelings or residual ambivalence, or new circumstances. Please note that this makes anyone who's ever had sex a potential rapist.' (Kipnis, 91)

One important point that needs to be made immediately is that those who come to believe that they have certain memories as the result of dubious investigative strategies, and even more dubious and unscientific therapeutic methods (hypnosis and regression), really *do* believe that they have these memories. They are not lying; that is, they are not claiming something to be true knowing it to be false. The unbiased observer will often be impressed by the patent sincerity of the post-investigative reports. Carolyn Hoyle and her fellow researchers are careful to note that they do *not* suggest that 'all false claims are made with deliberate ill intent. Indeed, we consider it likely that many untrue allegations are instead constructed through therapy, retrospective reflection or rumour, or through the suggestibility of some witnesses during investigative interviews, and are believed by their authors to be true.' (Hoyle *et al.*, 5)

In some forms of psychotherapy, the idea of repressed memory is suggested to the client by the therapist, and she is told that this memory needs to be uncovered or recovered if healing is to take place. Then the suggestive questioning begins. Sometimes, details of certain kinds of trauma are given to patients, and 'the patient is told to visualise them in line with a memory script. "Just picture a trauma happening, and the memory should start to come back to you".' (Shaw 2016, 232) The following passage from Shaw is particularly relevant when read in the context of the Kavanaugh savaging.

> Another problematic attitude that we see influencing cases involving alleged abuse is the logical fallacy that 'Where there is smoke there is fire.' I shudder at the blithe certainty contained in that statement every time I hear it. I cannot help but wonder at the mental gymnastics the person in front of me must be doing to reconcile such

a view with modern notions of justice. They are twisting innocent until proven guilty into guilty until proven innocent; the assumption of that statement clearly being that when individuals are accused of a crime they are probably guilty. Even when a person is exonerated, popular notions that the alleged crimes must have occurred often persist. Even if no evidence is found, no scars are revealed, and alibis are solid, accusations can override our better sense of justice. (Shaw 2016, 233)

It should be noted that Shaw is extremely keen to establish her woke credentials, asserting, 'No social scientist would ever argue against the notion … that most people who approach the police with historical abuse cases are accurate.' She goes on to say, 'most cases of sexual abuse *are* valid, there is gross underreporting of it, and we desperately need victims' voices to be heard.' (Shaw 2016, 235; emphasis in original) How does Shaw (or indeed, most social scientists) know that most cases of sexual abuse are valid? How does she know that there is gross under-reporting of it? What's the evidence for these assertions? Given the overall tenor of her book, it is more than a little odd that Shaw should make these assertions, but the oddness becomes somewhat more explicable when one realises just how toxic the situation can become for anyone who is deemed to depart from, or even to call into question, current victim orthodoxy. However, having made her obeisance to right thinking, Shaw recovers her intellectual poise. 'Opponents of false memory research often claim that we are silencing victims and defending the guilty. There is, of course, a legitimate concern here— it would be an awful thing for someone who has had any kind of traumatic experience to be disbelieved. But given that there is empirical evidence that false memories do exist—and can be created—any conception of justice must surely also be concerned with trying to protect the innocent from false conviction.' (Shaw 2016, 237-38)

Not guilty but guilty anyway
In 2018, professional rugby players Paddy Jackson and Stuart Olding were tried for rape and, eventually, acquitted. In the same trial, two other men, Blane McIlroy and Rory Harrison, were acquitted on related charges. Following their acquittal, Jackson and Olding were fired by their employer! 'The jury settled the legal formality of their guilt,' wrote Sarah Ditum, 'but, as with myriad other men, the case to answer doesn't end with an acquittal.' (Ditum) What case is there to answer that hasn't been answered? Is there another law beyond the law? From the accounts of the trial reported in the media, it is unlikely that there will be many people who will be impressed with the moral probity of the defendants or even, if it comes to that, with the moral probity of the complainant, but that's an entirely different matter from assessing the defendants'

responsibility for criminal actions. If we all have a criminal case to answer because of our supposed moral defects, then the criminal courts are going to be even busier than they already are.

In the aftermath of the extensively reported trial of the Belfast 4, the *Irish Independent* reported that thousands of people had attended rallies nationwide expressing solidarity with the woman at the centre of the Belfast rape trial. Let it be clear understood that they were expressing solidarity with the woman that the jury determined had *not* been raped! The events were advertised using the hash tag #IBelieveHer, something the jury, who had heard all the evidence, had conspicuously failed to do. But, of course, our ralliers had the advantage over the jury of not having had their minds contaminated by evidence and witnessing the examinations and cross-examinations at the trial. The ralliers, on the other hand, believed her, presumably because women are never confused, never ambivalent, never vindictive, and they never ever exaggerate, misrepresent or lie. One rallier said, 'It's time change is made', although it's not entirely clear what kinds of change she had in mind (that's if she had anything in mind at all), unless it was the advantage attached to going straight to conviction upon accusation, and dispensing with the expensive triviality of a trial. Some of the ralliers were of the opinion that we should now concern ourselves with how people who make claims of rape and sexual assault are treated. Indeed—I agree! I am inclined to say that at the moment, they are treated with excessive gullibility, with lots of loud encouragement from the misandrist authorities, with public outbursts of sympathy from the media and the useful idiots of rent-a-rally, and with no serious consequences to anyone except to the reputations and finances of the defendants if the charges are unsustained. The ralliers appeared to be incensed that the now-21-year-old complainant at the centre of the Belfast case spent eight days on the stand. Well, yes. What did they expect? She was the principal witness for the prosecution. Without her evidence, there would have been no case to answer. What do they suggest the defence should do? Is it their suggestion that she shouldn't give evidence, shouldn't have that evidence cross-examined, and that her deposition simply be taken as gospel and the accused convicted forthwith? Silly question! Of course it is. Steve Moxon might have been writing of the Belfast 4 when he wrote, 'The vitriol expressed for the men accused—whether subsequently found guilty or innocent—is on a par with that reserved for murderers (and sometimes worse).' (Moxon, 179)

One newspaper reported that 'after the verdict collective anger was unleashed across the internet and across the island, with demonstrations in the Irish Republic and in Northern Ireland.' Goodness me! Not just anger, but collective anger! And according to another rallier, not just collective anger but palpable anger. The Twitterati went on the march. The hashtaggers (#IBelieveHer) came out in force. Activists, we were told, ominously, were lobbying for change to the criminal justice system. Which criminal justice system needed to change and in what way we weren't informed. 'Our arcane legal system,' it seems, 'is not fit for purpose. It is a system invented by privileged men to further privilege privileged men', lacking 'compassion and understanding and it is not victim-centric.'

Why is it not fit for purpose? If it is a system invented by privileged men to further privilege already privileged men, how is it that anyone ever gets convicted of rape? Why is it that the defendants' names are public property and, even in the event of acquittal, their reputations remain trashed? Why is it that the complainant's name must remain secret? In the particular case in question, how did our 'not-fit-for-purpose legal system treat our supposedly privileged men, Jackson and Olding? They were publicly accused of rape, had their names and faces constantly in the media, lost their jobs, and incurred enormous legal bills to defend themselves on charges of which they were eventually acquitted. What man would want to be privileged in this way!

If the Ulster Rape trial has shown anything, it has shown that in today's toxic #MeToo-infected social environment, one can be guilty even if acquitted! At the time of the French Revolution, a law passed by the National Convention stated that '*Le Tribunal révolutionnaire est institué pour punir les ennemis du peuple.*' And who were the enemy of the people? Well, pretty much anybody the new political elite didn't like. As one might expect, the accused didn't have many rights. Today, in the #MeToo environment, to be accused is *de facto* to be guilty. Conviction is a legal nicety that is unnecessary. It is ironic that the French law, which had been proposed by Robespierre and Couthon, ended with the execution of around 1,300 people, including, in a delightful twist of fate, Robespierre and Couthon. Would it be uncharitable to hope that something similar might happen to the holier-than-thou Twitter-ranters; that they, some of them at least, might find themselves accused of a crime, suffer obloquy and be deemed to be guilty even if acquitted? Yes, it would be uncharitable, and the better half of my nature wouldn't wish this on anyone, not even on the insufferable holier-than-thou Twitterati.

The 'not guilty but not innocent' fate of Paddy Jackson and Stuart Olding had an earlier incarnation in the case of the footballer Ched Evans. Evans, who played football (soccer) for Sheffield United, was convicted of rape and served half of his sentence before finally being released. In April 2016, the Court be of Appeal quashed the original conviction and, following a retrial at Cardiff

Crown Court, he was acquitted. Before his acquittal on a retrial, but after his release in 2014, he wanted to go back to playing for Sheffield United and Sheffield United wanted him back. But no! The Furies didn't want Evans to be able to restart his life. He hadn't been punished enough. He was a rapist, and rapists cannot ever be sufficiently punished. Under pressure from the *Erinyes*, United withdrew the contract offer to Evans, and Oldham Athletic did likewise a few months later. It took two years for Evans to find a club down in the depths of League Division 2, but that only happened after his conviction had been quashed and a retrial ordered. But even his acquittal upon retrial was not good enough for vengeful furies. Some of these acted as if the judge and jury at the retrial had misbehaved! The Northumbria Police and Crime Commissioner, Vera Baird, complained that the acquittal set the justice system back 30 years, while the Rape Crisis people whined that the acquittal would—you know what's coming here—prevent complainants from reporting their complaints to the police. None of these seemed to think that spending years in prison, losing his job and acquiring an evil reputation for a crime he didn't commit was something that they might sympathise with Evans for. And why is that, I wonder? If a woman had been sent to jail and lost her job and reputation in similar circumstances, would Ms Baird and the Rape Crisis people have been so blasé? When it comes right down to it, it seems that Evans's real crime was that he was a man, and that's something that, in these times, is hard to forgive.

False allegations

Liam Allan, a student, was charged with 12 counts of rape and sexual assault. In 2017, his trial was discontinued when it turned out that the investigating officer had failed to reveal evidence from the complainant's phone that effectively undermined the case for the prosecution. It seems that the officer felt that the texts were, as he put it, 'too personal'! What was in those texts? Nothing much, except that the complainant had requested casual sex from Allan and had fantasised about rough sex with him! Allan spent two years on bail before the trial was discontinued. During this time, the police had in their possession the evidence that eventually exonerated him! Was this just a matter of normal incompetence, or an oversight resulting from a too-heavy caseload? Not quite. Some issues of principle are involved here, in particular, a culture of 'believe the victim'. Judge Peter Gower said that Mr Allan would not have been charged if these messages had been seen.

The complainant is to be investigated for attempting to pervert the course of justice. She told police that she hated sex, but she wrote hundreds of text messages to friends discussing in detail her enjoyment of sex, and saying she was devastated when Mr Allan said that they could not meet again. The Crown Prosecution Service and the police are reviewing why 40,000 text and Whats-App messages weren't handed over until *after* Mr Allan's trial had begun. Edited excerpts from these messages were produced in court. In one message to one of her friends, the complainant described how she had called Mr Allan in a panic and begged him to see her, writing: 'Honestly I was just a mess and I was like I'm asking for one last chance to show you how much you mean to me.' Writing to another friend about having sex with a man (not Mr Allan) she said, 'After the initial pain of the train getting into the tunnel it's not that bad, after a while it's alright and it's fun ... everyone knows I enjoy it but it still hurts me to this day but no pain no gain. It's worth it ....' One of the crucial text messages from the alleged victim that *wasn't* disclosed to the defence stated, 'It was not against my will.' (see Robins, passim)

Mr Allan's case is not an isolated one. Inspectors reviewing 146 similar cases found that there were obvious disclosure issues in them. (see HMCPSI/HMIC) In over a third of these cases, the prosecution didn't deal with these issues at all. Take the case of Richard Holden who, in May 2018, was acquitted on charges of sexual assault. Mr Holden, who used to be a special adviser to Sir Michael Fallon, accused the UK Police and the Crown Prosecution Service of having subjected him to a 'cruel public shaming'. The judge told him that he left the court without a stain on his character but, while that may be true legally, in terms of public perception, he will forever be stained by having had his name connected to a disgraceful act that he, in fact, didn't commit. Mr Holden tweeted, 'Police investigation appalling. They consistently failed to pursue ANY reasonable line of inquiry that wasn't in line with the initial allegation. Disclosure was delayed and incomplete throughout, including denying evidence the police had collected and knew existed.' Mr Holden lost his job and had to wait 15 months for his case to come to trial. During this time, the police interviewed only the witnesses for the prosecution but not other witnesses who told a different story. During this time, the police also failed to inspect the complainant's phone. The trial, when it eventually came on, took five days but the prosecution's case was so threadbare that the jury took just ten minutes to clear Mr Holden! So, let's add up the pluses and minuses for Mr Holden: on the plus side, he has been cleared of a criminal charge and has no legal 'black mark' against him; on the minus side, he has lost his job and salary, has had to pay his own legal defence bills and has suffered reputational damage from which he will find it difficult to recover. Justice has clearly been done.

If Mr Holden is correct in his assertions, then the police failed to observe two requirements of the Code of Practice detailed under the Criminal Procedure and Investigations Act 1996. These elements are, in respect of investigations, that 'in conducting an investigation, the investigator should pursue *all* reasonable lines of inquiry, whether these point towards *or away from* the suspect. What is reasonable in each case will depend on the particular circumstances.' (see Ministry of Justice, §3.5 Emphasis added) And in respect of disclosure, the Code of Practice mandates that, 'In every case, irrespective of the anticipated plea, if there is material known to the disclosure officer that might assist the defence with the early preparation of their case or at a bail hearing (for example, a key prosecution witness has relevant previous convictions or a witness has withdrawn his or her statement), a note must be made on the MG5 (or other format agreed under the National File Standards). The material must be disclosed to the prosecutor who will disclose it to the defence if he thinks it meets this Common Law test.' (see Ministry of Justice, §6.6) As I write (October 2019), the UK's Attorney General has taken the unusual but sensible step of suggesting that police and prosecutors could ask the legal team of alleged rapists for possible lines of inquiry about alleged victims, so that evidence leading away from suspects could be identified. According to a report, this could 'help prosecutors and police investigators identify search terms for data on mobile phone, computers and social media that could reveal "undermining material' enabling weak cases to be closed at an early stage.' (Hymas)

Retired fire chief, David Bryant, had his conviction for rape overturned in the Court of Appeal. (see Mendick) He had been in jail for three years. In 2012, his accuser, Danny Day, claimed that Mr Bryant had raped him some 35 years earlier. Before reporting this alleged rape to the police, Mr Day sent Mr Bryant a letter in which he threatened to make him pay one way or another, and further threatened that, unless Mr Bryant got in touch with him, he would go to the newspapers and to the police. Rather than follow-up a possible case of attempted blackmail against Mr Day, the police pursued Mr Bryant who was convicted in 2013 on the basis of Mr Day's testimony alone, receiving a sentence of eight and a half years. In the High Court judgement, Master Gary Thornett said that Mr Day's letter to Mr Bryant 'would not strike any reasonable person as anything other than a blackmail note. It is clearly threatening. The invitation to make contact seems well away from a need to discuss and elicit an apology but instead seeks either a financial payment or retribution through the threat of police involvement and publicity.' Mr Thornett also held that Mr Day had deliberately used the police and Crown Prosecution Service to wage a 'campaign of self-aggrandisement'.

Mr Bryant was eventually freed in 2016 when the Court of Appeal quashed his conviction, after it emerged that Mr Day had sought medical help for being a serial liar! One of his more piquant lies was that he was a champion boxer who would have fought at the Los Angeles Olympics if he hadn't been so traumatised by the rape! Mr Bryant's lawyer pointed out that Bryant was lucky in that Day's lies were, in the end, easily exposed. He said, 'If he [Day] had been a really good psychopath Dave would still be in prison ... How many Dave's are there wrongly locked up? I am guessing it is in the hundreds—that's the scandal and it is only getting worse.' Two significant factors in this appalling case are worthy of note: first, the alleged rape took place 35 years before it was reported, and second, Mr Bryant was convicted on the basis of Mr Day's testimony alone. The temporal distance of the alleged rape from its report is a feature of what are known as cases of 'historic sex abuse' and, given the issues of memory already discussed, this makes such claims extremely problematic. The conviction of one person on the sole testimony of another is, independently of issues of temporal distance, also problematic.

Louis Richardson, a former University of Durham student, went through 15 months of forensic anguish before he was cleared in 2016 of all charges of rape and sexual assault. His accuser continued to send him suggestive messages long after the alleged rape had occurred. This didn't, it seems, raise any issues with the police or the CPS. Will Richardson ever be able to erase the stigma resulting from the 15-month long investigation? Probably not. This can have practical as well as psychological consequences. Angela Epstein wrote, 'Imagine future employers Googling names of prospective candidates to assess suitability. Sure the newspaper cuttings record Richardson's innocence. But when you've got a waiting room full of hungry and equally capable students desperate for work, why take a punt on this one?' (Epstein)

The disparity between what happens to the acquitted accused and the anonymous alleged victim is striking. What are the costs to the woman who makes a false accusation, one that can be determined not just to be a matter of disputed interpretation but one that is outright false and known to be so by the complainant? Very little, as it turns out. What are the costs to those accused by false accusations? Quite a lot. Jay Chesire who was falsely accused of rape was discovered hanged in a park. He was 17 years old. The alleged victim withdrew the allegation two weeks before his death but Chesire was, as his mother recounts, distraught as a result of the charges made against him. Angela Epstein writes, 'when rape accusations prove false and the defendant is acquitted, that cloak of anonymity should immediately be rescinded. The law fails to take into account what happens when a boozy young woman, remorseful at playing away from a jealous boyfriend, salves her conscience by going after the innocent young man with whom she had consensual sex. Nor does it address the manifest injustice to men in the approximately 40 per cent of rape cases where they are acquitted.' (Epstein).

Samuel Armstrong, a former chief of staff to the Conservative MP Craig Mackinlay, was eventually cleared of raping a woman in his boss's office. Once again, crucial evidence was disclosed just days before trial. Armstrong was cleared unanimously by after a seven-day trial. The alleged victim's phone records also showed that hours after the alleged attack, she contacted a tabloid newspaper so that a sympathetic account of her supposed ordeal might be published. It emerged that the woman had not wanted to release medical records showing she suffered depression and anxiety. In a text related to the records, she said she wanted to conceal them so as to have 'more leeway to hide certain aspects and mould what comes out.' As the result of this woman's allegations, Mr Armstrong was suspended from the Conservative Party and lost what he described as his dream job.

The cases of Allan, Holden, Bryant, Richardson, Chesire and Armstrong are striking examples of false accusations. But things sometimes can get even stranger. In England, prosecutors charged a man with rape even though the woman who was allegedly raped insisted that he had committed no crime! Police failed to list her statement—in which she made it clear that she did not believe the man had raped her—in a schedule of unused evidence that could help the defence. The accused man's barrister was unaware of this woman's statement, which only emerged on the opening day of the trial. She was having sex with two men and when she shouted 'Stop', the accused man stopped but the other man didn't. Not only did the accused man stop, he pulled the other man away from the woman. Her statement read: 'I do not believe Male Two should be charged. I do not believe he did anything wrong on the night. I am thankful that Male Two was there as without him I do not know how long Male One would have continued to have sex with me.' Despite having her statement, the Crown Prosecution Service (CPS) charged both men. In the circumstances, the judge, not unnaturally, indicated that the prosecution might like to reconsider its decision to prosecute, which they duly did. In a further twist, the woman ultimately withdrew her support for the prosecution of the man she believed had raped her because her trust in the system had been eroded.

Sometimes, the criminal justice system's approach to the problem of false allegations results in something that would be farcical if a man's freedom and reputation weren't at stake. Take the case of Mrs A who accused her husband of rape, then changed her mind and retracted the allegation. Despite her retraction, the CPS carried on with the prosecution because crimes are considered to be offences against the state and not just transactions between the parties involved.

In any event, Mrs A said she had lied in her original statement and that no rape took place, whereupon, she found herself charged with perverting the course of justice, and then, changing her mind again, she said that the original allegation was true! The CPS now resumed the prosecution of her husband *and* she was charged with falsely retracting a true allegation for which she received a sentence of 8 months reduced, on appeal, to a community order. You couldn't make this stuff up!

In January 2018, the UK's Attorney General, Jeremy Wright, requested the Crown Prosecution Service to review all live cases to see whether they might be compromised by a failure to disclose vital evidence before the trial. Mr Wright was of the opinion that there was a substantial problem with the way in which police followed disclosure procedure in cases of rape. Mr Wright made his comments after four rape cases collapsed within a short space of time when it was discovered that, just days before the trials, the prosecution had released vital information that would have cleared the defendants.

The Crown Prosecution Service has admitted that there are systemic disclosure issues in criminal cases, revealing that 900 criminal cases were dropped in 2017 for that very reason. Some commentators have speculated that the disclosure problems were the result of under-resourcing. A report on CPS Rape and Serious Sexual Offences Units published in 2016 by HM Crown Prosecution Service Inspectorate warned of what it called a 'vicious circle' in which police sometimes handed incomplete case files to CPS lawyers who then, instead of demanding more evidence, chose to charge suspects because they were under pressure to do so. The Report noted that 'there is considerable pressure on the CPS to improve on success rates and to prosecute more cases, which may lead to some cases being pursued even though there is little chance of obtaining a conviction after a trial.' According to the UK's shadow attorney general, Shami Chakrabarti, the collapse of two rape cases is a result of austerity (lack of government spending) in the criminal justice system. (Chakrabarti) However, the real attorney general, Jeremy Wright, said that while resourcing was part of the problem, it wasn't the most significant part. The principal problem was simply the failure of the police and the Crown Prosecution Service to disclose pertinent evidence. In the words of one critic, 'The wrongly accused wait until the day of trial, or perhaps for eternity, for the state to disclose material that fatally undermines the prosecution case.' (Anon. 2019, 13) Mr Wright firmly rejected the speculation that lack of government spending lay at the root of the problem, noting that over the three year period from 2015 to 2018, the number of special prosecutors specifically dealing with rape and sexual offences had increased by 40%.

Given the scandal in the UK over the failure of the prosecution in some rape cases to disclose relevant evidence, the Criminal Cases Review Commission (CCRC) announced in 2018 that it would revisit over three hundred cases to see if critical evidence was missed during the original trial. Following the spectacular collapse of some high profile cases, when it was revealed that the investigators and the prosecution had failed to disclose vital evidence that proved the defendant's innocence, concerns were expressed about the safety of convictions already obtained. But it turns out that the CCRC will not, in fact, examine all 300+ cases but only 61 of them. A 2017 joint report from Her Majesty's Crown Prosecution Service Inspectorate and Her Majesty's Inspectorate of Constabulary concluded that 'Non-compliance with the disclosure process is not new and has been common knowledge amongst those engaged within the criminal justice system for many years and it is difficult to justify why progress has not previously been made in volume crime cases. Until the police and CPS take their responsibilities in dealing with disclosure in volume cases more seriously, no improvement will result and the likelihood of a fair trial can be jeopardised.' (HMCPSI/HMIC, §11.4)

Of course, there are those who will make light of the significance of the collapsed rape trials. One such person is Charlotte Proudman, who describes the problems around the lack of disclosure in the trials of Allan and Itiary as a 'media frenzy.' (Proudman) While conceding the potential such trials have to cause injustice for defendants and complainants alike, she pooh-poohs what she regards as the disproportionate focus on failed rape prosecutions to the exclusion of collapsed trials for other crimes. She then goes on to claim that 'the microscopic reporting of collapsed rape trials is part of a broader backlash against the Harvey Weinstein allegations and the #MeToo movement, which, she says, 'exposed endemic sexual harassment and even rape. The reporting of the Allan and Itiary cases has the power to regress, not progress, gender equality.' She wants more to be done to encourage women to report cases of rape but states, without giving any reason, that this doesn't entail 'granting defendants anonymity.' But why not? She appears to have absolutely no idea of the opprobrium in which rape is held in society (and rightly so), so much so that to be accused of rape even if subsequently cleared, leaves an indelible stain on a man's reputation. As we saw on the Allan case, the judge said that 'Mr Allan leaves the courtroom an innocent man without a stain on his character' but that, while legally so, is manifestly not so in terms of the public's perception. Ms Proudman believes that the reporting on the Allan case and other similar cases sends a message to women that their allegations of rape might not be believed if they claim that a sexual encounter was consensual and later report rape, or that it might not be believed if they ever discussed rape fantasies and later report rape. Really! How shocking! When one considers that the principal, often the only, evidence in rape trials is the testimony of the complainant, her credibility is paramount, so that conceding consensuality and then subsequently changing her story might affect how her evidence is received by a jury; likewise with reports of her fantasies.

Are false accusations of rape really all that significant? Isn't the apprehension and conviction of rapists what really matters? If some men are falsely accused along the way, well, that's unfortunate but really little more than collateral damage. In England, James (not his real name) was arrested on a charge of rape on the day of his daughter's third birthday. The arrest took place in his home, in front of his new wife, his family and his friends. His accuser was his ex-wife. Within a week, he was entertaining thoughts of suicide. James's new wife recounts how severely he deteriorated after the accusation, frequently crying, and planning to kill himself. The shame of the accusation—a false accusation, as it turns out—was almost too much to bear. Luckily for him, his name, unlike the name of many men accused of rape, was not published. Still, it was eight months before the charges were dropped and he was free to pick up the shattered pieces of his life.

The usual pious low figure of false rape reports is trotted out by Ms Proudman: this time, it's 3%. But as long ago as the year 2000, Edward Greer noted: 'It is indisputably true that, largely through the efforts of legal dominance feminists, there now exists a consensus among legal academics that only two percent of rape complaints are false. This purportedly empirical statement is ubiquitously repeated in legal literature. Dozens of law review articles reiterate that no more than one in fifty rape complaints is false. This empirical fact, however, is an ideological fabrication.' (Greer 2000, 949) The likeliest source of the 2% claim is Susan Brownmiller. This is what Edward Greer has to say about this source. It is worth quoting his account in full:

> Despite the plethora of pyramided citations, it turns out that there is one, and only one, underlying source—feminist publicist Susan Browmiller's interpretation of some data, now a quarter-century old, of unknown provenance from a single police department unit. There are no other published studies that this author could find. All of the sources cited at the outset of this [that is, Greer's] article trace back to Ms. Brownmiller.
>
> Susan Brownmiller set forth the following in her book [Brownmiller 1976]: "When New York City created a special Rape Analysis Squad commanded by policewomen, the female police officers found that only 2 percent of all rape complaints were false—about the same false-report rate that is usual for other kinds

of felonies." When one looks at her "Source Notes" for this proposition, she states it to be: "NYC Rape Analysis Squad found only 2 percent of complaints were false: Remarks of Lawrence H. Cooke, Appellate Division Justice, before the Association of the Bar of the City of New York, Jan. 16, 1974 (mimeo), p. 6."

Ms. Brownmiller, who is a very meticulous and organized writer, very kindly on my request located and sent me a copy of this xeroxed speech. In relevant part, the judge's speech reads: "In fact, according to the Commander of New York City's Rape Analysis Squad, only about 2 percent of all rape and related sex charges are determined to be false and this is about the same as the rate of false charges of other felonies."

These judicial remarks do not suffice to determine whether or not there was an underlying written report, although the locution used is suggestive of being based on a quotation from a newspaper article rather than a formally written text. When I contacted the then-judge's clerk, and he made inquiry of all those directly involved in the preparation of Judge Cooke's speech, their best recollections are that they did not rely upon any report but cannot remember precisely how they did obtain the two percent figure. Of course, it remains possible that some such report was generated, but as of this date, no one is able to adduce it. Without the document, one cannot analyze the underlying data, the protocol used in evaluating it, or even whether it met minimum criteria of accuracy. (Greer 2000, 955-57)

Earlier, I mentioned that, according to the UK's Crown Prosecution Service (CPS), 42,000 alleged rapes were reported to the police in England and Wales for the year 2016-2017. Of these 42,000 allegations, just over 5,000 (11.9%) went to trial and just under 3,000 of those resulted in a conviction. That 3,000 is 57.6% of those that went forward to trial but just 7.2% of the allegations originally reported. It should be borne in mind that these convictions were produced under the rubric of the new, consent-based definition of rape so that an even smaller percentage of these convictions pertain to violent rapes. (RV) What all this means is that almost 92.8% of reported cases were not prosecuted by the police or the CPS, presumably because it was deemed that the evidence didn't warrant proceeding with the case, or that a conviction was judged to be unlikely, or that the putative victim's account was not completely credible, or a combination of all three. If 42.4% of cases that the CPS believed had a reasonable chance of producing a conviction were rejected by juries, it's not unreasonable to think that *at least* the same percentage of the cases that the CPS did *not* think had a reasonable chance of success would have been rejected by juries and, given that even the CPS did not think them likely candidates, probably a much greater percentage. We may conclude from this that the percentage of false reported allegations lies somewhere in the region between the extremes of 48.2% and 92.8%! Whatever the truth of the matter about the level of false accusations, even one malicious false accusation is one too many. Some falsely accused men may be able to put their lives back together, others may not, but the notion of there being any significant number of false accusations of rape is routinely dismissed by rape-prevention advocates.

Feminists will sometimes argue that there is no reason for a woman to make an accusation of rape unless it really happened, especially since, according to them, the process of investigation and prosecution is so traumatic as to amount to a 'second rape'. Karen Smith, the executive director of the Sexual Assault Centre of Edmonton, for example said 'Nobody would report sexual assault needlessly because it is a gruelling process to go through.' But they would, Ms Smith, and they do because there *are* reasons: rejection after a single-incident sexual encounter; shame and self-loathing after regretted sex; the use of the rape accusation as a way of displacing responsibility when the sexual encounter becomes known to others (parents, boyfriends); spite; mental derangement and, as I already mentioned Angela Epstein noting, a boozy young woman, remorseful at playing away from a jealous boyfriend, salves her conscience by going after the innocent young man with whom she had consensual sex. (Epstein; see also Morris)

There is much evidence of sympathy and compassion for those who complain of rape and sexual assault, but where is the compassion for those who suffer as the result of false accusations? A common cry of caution when it comes to dealing with false allegations is that we don't want to make too much of them in case it discourages genuine victims from coming forward. The idea is that a failure to convict might open the complainant to perjury charges or wasting police time. But this doesn't necessarily follow. There's an important difference between lying, which is deliberately claiming that something is true which you know to be false, and telling a factual untruth, which can be a matter of you saying what you believe to be true but which is not in fact true or which others do not believe. False allegations can be either lying or just factual untruths. That's for juries to decide. Ms Proudman tells us of a friend of hers who was deterred from coming forward because she might not be believed and so could be prosecuted. (Proudman) If a case were taken and the accused found not guilty, it wouldn't necessarily follow that the CPS would conclude that the complainant had been guilty of perjury. An acquittal on a charge of rape doesn't necessarily imply that the legal system *must* regard the complainant as lying or as perverting the course of justice? Malicious cases such as that of James may not be frequent (but then again, who can tell for sure?), but accounts of alleged rapes in which a jury is not convinced of the truth of all the claims made by the complainant must be reasonably common if the statistics are anything to go by.

In many cases where no conviction ensues, I suspect that it's because the jury, given the presumption of innocence, didn't believe that the complainant was telling the truth, or the whole truth, or nothing but the truth. It doesn't follow from this that they believed that she was lying. A jury is quite capable of coming to the conclusion that a complainant believes the version of the story that she is telling, but that the story is not in fact true or not true in relevant respects. That X% of claims are patently false doesn't mean that 100-X% of claims are true. Similarly, that Z% of rape cases result in conviction, doesn't mean that 100-Z% of cases that result in acquittal were without some foundation. Sometimes, what happened cannot be determined beyond a reasonable doubt.

Some accusations of rape are malicious and without any foundation, and are made by women who, for one reason or another, are seemingly quite happy to see innocent men pilloried and sent to jail. It says something about the times in which we live that we are more disposed to believe that a significant number of men are disposed to rape women than that it is conceivable that a significant number of women are willing to lie about being raped. Women who bring these knowingly false accusations should receive punishment proportionate to that which would be meted out to their supposed attackers had they been convicted, but don't hold your breath while waiting for this to happen.

Other accusations lie in a grey area between truth and falsity. It may be true that rape trials in such cases are traumatic for women who are genuinely convinced, however groundlessly, that they've been victims of rape, but they are nowhere near as traumatic as they are for the men who are falsely accused. If convicted, they face a lengthy jail term and the effective ruination of their lives. But even if acquitted, they are exposed (in the UK) to publicity and sometimes to informal sanctions. To repeat, there's a difference between lying, on the one hand, and, on the other, making a statement that is judged not to be true. Where it is clear that the alleged victim was lying, then she should be prosecuted.

Those who think that women never lie about being sexually assaulted or raped should acquaint themselves with the truly extraordinary case of Claire Morgan. In 2017, Ms Morgan claimed that a taxi driver had sexually assaulted her. She told a detailed story about the assault. The driver spent three hours in police custody and faced the prospect of sexual assault charges. In addition, he was forced to surrender his taxi permit during the six-week investigation, thereby being unable to work. The police spent sixty hours checking out Morgan's story. In the end, the diligence of the investigators, together with CCTV-revealed inconsistencies in Morgan's account, spared him prosecution. So far, a depressingly familiar tale. But now comes the twist. Morgan had also set up a Facebook profile under an assumed name, Sarah Jenkins, claiming (as Jenkins) that she had witnessed the attack! She reported bogus details to Crimestoppers anonymously. Suspicion was aroused when Morgan gave different accounts of the supposed attack to her friends. She received a sentence of two-and–a half years for perverting the course of justice. In an ironic twist, the newspaper article reporting this bizarre story contained an inset panel advertising phone numbers that victims of sexual assault could call for help and support. What's ironic about this you might wonder! Well, the story in which it was inset was a story precisely *not* about sexual assault but about a spectacularly *false* allegation of sexual assault. One might have expected the inset to contain phone numbers that those who had been falsely accused of sexual assault might call for support, but no, not so.

If we are to believe all those women who make accusations of sexual assault or harassment, what are we to make of the case of five high school girls in Pennsylvania (reported October 2018) who confessed to targeting a boy with false accusations simply because they didn't like him? The boy was sacked from his job at a swimming pool and underwent multiple court appearances, in addition to being detained in a juvenile facility. Girl 1 accused the boy of assaulting her in July 2017, but later admitted that she had made up the allegation, explaining, 'I just don't like him!' The boy was charged with indecent assault and two counts of harassment. He pleaded not guilty but was put on probation. Later, another accusation of sexual assault was made when a friend of Girl 1 told a school official that he had sexually assaulted her at her home. These allegations were supported by two other girls. As a result, the boy was charged with indecent assault, criminal trespass and simple assault. A month later, the three girls recanted their allegations and admitted lying about the sexual assault. The boy's parents are suing the parents of the girls, the school district and the local District Attorney. According to them, the girls who made the false accusations have suffered no repercussions. (see Heidt)

The *Belfast Telegraph* reported in 2013 that 23 year-old Natasha Foster, who falsely accused a former boyfriend of rape when he ended their on-again/off-again relationship, was sent to jail by the judge who declared that such accusations could be perceived as an attack on the criminal justice system. (Kilpatrick) Her defence lawyer had described Ms Foster as a 'woman scorned' whose behaviour was a mixture of 'impulsivity, anger and hurt and a sense of rejection.' Her wounded feelings resulted in Mr X's being arrested and spending 12 hours in custody. During the trial, the judge made what are now the ritual politically correct comments to the effect that those making such false accusations undermine claims made by those who have genuinely been raped. Well, of course he did. This is the standard line. I note there is nothing in the report to say that the judge talked about it as an attack on the defendant.

So, concern for the justice system—tick; concern for genuine rape victims—tick; concern for the defendant—? Ms Foster was sentenced to three months in prison. Well, that's proportionate, isn't it? If the man she accused had been convicted, he would have received a prison sentence of substantially more than three months. She gets three months for doing something that could have had catastrophic consequences for the man she falsely accused! The judge took into account in his sentencing what he described as her genuine remorse and the fact that she was a young mother. Ah, I see; that makes all the difference. (see Anon. 2013) Ms Foster is not the only woman in Northern Ireland to have been convicted of making false claims. Another woman was jailed for nine months, while a third received a suspended sentence of 2 years plus a fine of £1,000. Once again, it might be worth noting that these penalties are trivial compared to what the men who were falsely accused would have received if the falsity of the claims hadn't mercifully been revealed.

In 2018, Anna Costin was jailed for four years for falsely accusing four men of sexual assault. She had originally been given a three-year community order after she pleaded guilty in January to perverting the course of justice. The judge in the Court of Appeal who jailed Costin said that the judge who had imposed the community order on Ms Costin had been somewhat too concerned with *her* problems. Incidentally, the lenient judge was male and the judge who imposed the four-year jail sentence was female! Lady Justice Hallett remarked that 'All of the allegations were thoroughly investigated and, thank goodness for the men concerned, they were able to prove their innocence and the falsity of the allegations but, obviously, with devastating consequences for them.' (see BBC 2018)

In 2014, a woman alleged to the Irish police that she was raped by a foreign national after socialising in the early hours of the morning after a football match. At her trial in 2018, she denied that she knowingly made a false report and that she wasted police time. It took the jury four days to return a unanimous verdict of guilty. Because the judge determined that she had no previous convictions and was, in his judgement, unlikely to re-offend, and because she was since married, was working and had brought stability to her life, he imposed a sentence of 30 months which he immediately suspended, this, despite his acknowledgement that she had put an innocent person at risk with her false report and had wasted a substantial amount of police time! Oh well, what she did wasn't all that serious. It only had the potential to ruin a man's life. (Lucey)

Warren Blackwell spent almost three and a half years in prison for a crime he didn't commit. The whole graphic and detailed story of the sexual assault he was alleged to have perpetrated was a fiction from start to finish. What is most distressing about this case is that the police suspected as much from the start, as they knew that the complainant had not only convictions for offences of dishonesty but was also a serial complainant. In respect of her earlier complaints, the police investigation resulted in the judgement that the allegations of assault were untrue and that the supposedly corroborative physical injuries were self-inflicted. None of this information was disclosed to Mr Blackwell's defence team. (see *R. v. Blackwell*)

The *New Zealand Herald* reported that a man who had been incarcerated for ten months as the result of a false rape accusation would receive no compensation. (Anon. 2017) On the first day of the trial, the complainant admitted she had lied. Compensation, however, is available only for wrongful conviction and Christopher Ferguson was merely on remand. He had denied the charges but was denied bail. Of course, we got the usual invocations from the usual suspects at the end of the trial. Anna Hoek-Sims, who was described as the Dunedin Rape Crisis's community educator said, parroting the usual party line, that 'false allegations made it harder for real sexual-abuse victims to come forward because most feared they would not be believed.' This endlessly repeated solemn warning that false allegations can result in the possible deterrence of real victims is a routine rhetorical ritual response that is quite unconvincing. Ms Hoek-Sims stressed only about 2% of cases that made it to court were based on fabricated claims and said it was important to consider why it happened. (Only 2% of cases are fabricated, eh! Where have we heard this before? Thank you, Ms Brownmiller, for the gift that keeps on giving.)

So you see, the real problem isn't that a man spent ten months in custody on false allegations and had his name smeared, but that real victims will find it harder to come forward! To repeat what I wrote earlier, the common cry of caution when it comes to dealing with false allegations is that we don't want to make too much of them lest it discourage genuine victims from coming forward. The idea is that a failure to convict might open the complainant to charges of perjury or of wasting police time but, of course, this doesn't necessarily follow. There's a big difference between lying, which is deliberately claiming that something is true which you know to be false, and telling an untruth, which can be a matter of your saying what you believe to be true but which is not in fact true or which others do not believe. False allegations can be either lying or just factually untrue. That's for juries to decide.

Ms Hoek-Sims has a tender heart—for those who make false allegations! She said, 'I think we need to keep in mind that people who make false complaints often make them for another reason, such as personal issues, health issues or even past history of sexual violence and often when something like this happens, the person can be forgotten in the fury that follows a false accusation ... I hope that in this case, the person receives the support they need.' That's quite a bit of understanding and compassion for the liar but not quite so much for the chap who sat in jail for ten months as the result of the lie. 'False rape' culprits, writes Steve Moxon, 'are usually not prosecuted, and frequently not even cautioned, and consequently remain protected by legal anonymity.' He continues:

> If jailed, the sentencing is feather-light—usually just three months or at the most six. This is even when a man has been falsely named and lives in fear of being seriously injured in reprisals .... Tracey Rowe named a man she'd never had contact with as her 'stranger' rapist, to cover having sex with someone else. As a result, he was fired from his job and attacked, whilst his wife lost her own job .... Rowe did not admit the truth for three weeks .... With many instances of 'false rape', there is at least one male victim who not only may spend weeks or months in prison, but he then goes through months or years of hell, including losing partner/wife/ children/job/friends/home/life, and ongoing community hostility against which he has no defence, such is the impossibility of convincing a gossip network and proving a negative. This makes fabricated rape the most heinous form of 'indirect aggression'. Indeed, many people have called for sentences equivalent to what the accused man would have received had he been convicted; not least as a long-overdue deterrent measure to start to reduce the prevalence of this crime. (Moxon, 182-3)

Given the reluctance of the criminal law system to prosecute those who make false rape allegations, should those who believe they've been falsely and maliciously accused of that crime try the civil law route as a means of redress? Take the case of Brian Banks who was falsely accused of raping a classmate, Wanetta Gibson, in 2002 when he was just seventeen years old. He spent five years in jail and he wasn't exonerated until, extraordinarily, he managed to record his accuser on tape admitting to lying about the incident. Instead of pleading not guilty when charged, Mr Banks took a plea bargain because, as he put it himself, 'I was a big black teenager, and no jury would believe anything I said.' His accuser, Wanetta Gibson, had won a settlement against the Long Beach Unified School District, and after Mr Banks's exoneration they sued her in return. The courts ordered her to return the money she had been awarded. (see Kandel) Other men who have been falsely accused have considered the route of a civil action, but it is not something that can be routinely advised. As Xavier Donaldson, who is a defence lawyer and former assistant District Attorney in New York said, 'these suits should be extremely case specific, extremely rare. ... You can't win these cases, too much backlash ... I tell my clients innocent before proven guilty is not reality. It's more of a marketing slogan to promote faith in our justice system; without that premise, the system would fall apart.'

Coda

• The #MeToo Movement exploded onto the social scene in 2017 in the wake of the Harvey Weinstein scandal, re-invigorating a feminism that had for some time been overtaken in the radical charts by even more radical forms of victimology. Suddenly, all men, everywhere, were under attack for contributing, directly or indirectly, to the sexual harassment of women, and a barely concealed misandry, latent in much of the latest wave feminism, found a new and virulent mode of expression.

• Feminism is either the claim that men and women should be treated equally by the law, a claim that almost everyone fully accepts, or else it is a particular form of radical transformative ideology that neither I, nor anyone else, is obliged to accept on the basis of the principles of natural justice.

• In the matter of women and work, legally enforced special privileges or policies that favour women (or, indeed, any other group) cannot be justified, nor should a spurious notion of representation be used to further the interests of an elite group of women. The gender pay gap, to the extent that it exists at all (and then usually in the form of a gender *earnings* gap) is not the outcome of some form of unjust discrimination but primarily the result of individual choice.

• Subject to the constraints of reality, there should be no *state-imposed* discriminatory legal policies that favour either women or men. On the other hand, subject to the zero aggression principle (*No one may initiate physical violence against the person or property of another*), individuals or groups of individuals should be free to do as they wish with their property, including favouring one sex over another when it comes to its disposal, if that is their choice. Such decisions, of course, have consequences, and those who make them must be prepared to live with negative non-aggressive responses, including criticism or boycotting.

•Women and men should be free to make the social and career choices that they wish to make, whether others approve of those choices or not. As long as such choices involve no violation of the zero aggression principle, others are obliged to tolerate such choices, but there is no obligation on others to facilitate them, nor should they be obliged to approve of them on pain of legal sanctions.

• The patriarchy is portrayed by feminists as a malign social force that supposedly engages in the universal oppression of women and systematically privileges men at their expense. There is, of course, no such ghostly entity—if there were, it would be a singularly and spectacularly ineffectual force, inasmuch as women, on the whole, are not only *not* oppressed in comparison to men but are rather the beneficiaries of legal and social privileges.

• The obnoxiously offensive notion of toxic masculinity is just the latest weapon to be wielded in the war on men, a thinly disguised form of misandry that every man, and every fair-minded woman, should reject.

• The #MeToo movement is a classic case of leaping from the particular to the universal, taking its point of departure from a very specific context, the world of entertainment, a world hardly representative of the wider society. It is a prime example of a moral panic, predicated on what would seem to be a few well-publicised cases of really bad behaviour by a small number of atypical men, followed by the groundless assertion that this behaviour is typical of men at large. The #MeToo movment is carried on by means of a form of mob-hysteria on the suitably idiotically named platform, Twitter.

• The #MeTooers view of men, women and sex is distinctly and charmingly retrograde. All men are sexual predators who think of nothing but sex; all women are innocent victims, actual or potential, for whom sex is a loathsome form of interpersonal interaction unless, of course, it is something they momentarily and enthusiastically happen to desire.

• Apart from legitimating an indiscriminate attack on men and masculinity, the #MeToo movement has also exposed a conceptual fault-line in radical feminist anthropology. Are women fully-developed moral agents, able to exercise moral choice and to take responsibility for their actions? Or are they moral infants, elements of a collective made up of the victims of sexual harassment, sexual assault or rape, whose suffering is not just that of any one individual woman but of the group as a whole, and which can be alleviated only by women acting together to counter the sinister cultural force that produces it?

• In its chanting of the 'Believe women!' mantra, the #MeToo movement undermines the fundamental legal principle of the presumption of innocence. To be accused is to be convicted. To deny the accusation is itself a further sign of guilt.

• The #MeToo movement makes already fraught relations between the sexes even more adversarial than they already are. The sheer naked undiscriminating aggression of the #MeToo movement is likely to provoke a reaction so that men, fearing accusations which could cost them their jobs, their reputations or even land them in jail, will avoid contact with women unless they are suitably chaperoned.

• The changing legal definition of rape has largely negative implications for relations between the sexes. For most of our legal history, rape has been taken to be essentially a crime of violence. In the common law systems of England & Wales, Ireland and the USA, the concept of consent is now central to the definition of rape. As currently interpreted, that concept is unworkable, at once infantilising women and, at the same time, potentially criminalising every sexual encounter in which a man is involved. The changing legal definition of rape also has implications for issues of procedural justice, not least, the danger it presents to an erosion of the presumption of innocence.

References

Agencies in Berlin. (2018) 'Politics and science need more women, says Angela Merkel.' *The Guardian*. (12 November).

Alcorn, Gay. (2018) 'Germaine Greer's On Rape: provocative, victim-shaming, compelling, ambivalent.' *The Guardian*. (6 September) .

Alexander, Harriet. (2018) 'Female professor suspended after sexually harassing male student.' *The Telegraph*. (14 August).

Allen, Nick. (2018) 'Frozen star Kristen Bell speaks out over "weird" prince's inappropriate kiss in Snow White.' *The Telegraph*. (18 October).

Angier, Natalie. (1999/2014) *Woman: An Intimate Geography*. London: Virago.

Anon. (2011) 'Women and Men in Ireland,' *Central Statistics Office Report*, available at http://www.cso.ie/en/media/csoie/releasespublications/documents/otherreleases/2011/Women,and,Men,in,Ireland,2011.pdf.

Anon. (2011a) 'The Cleveland Report: by Judge Elizabeth Butler-Sloss.' *The Therapeutic Care Journal*. Available at https://www.thetcj.org/child-care-history-policy/the-cleveland-report-by-judge-elizabeth-butler-sloss.

Anon. (2013) '"Wicked" Natasha foster to spend Christmas in jail for "crying rape".' *The Belfast Telegraph*. (25 November).

Anon. (2014) 'Feminism & astrophysics.' *The New Criterion*. (December).

Anon. (2017) '13yo admits lying in rape case after defendant spent 10 months in jail.' *New Zealand Herald*. (30 March).

Anon. (2017a) 'Judge's warning to drunk women "will stop reporting of rape".' *The Guardian*. (11 March).

Anon. (2018) '#MeToo activist Asia Argento settles own sexual assault complaint.' *The Irish Times*. (20 August).

Anon. (2018a) 'Feminising the Curriculum? No Thank You.' *The Oxford Student*. Available at https://www.oxfordstudent.com/2018/03/24/feminising-the-curriculum-no-thank-you/.

Anon. (2019) *The Secret Barrister. Stories of the Law and How It's Broken*. London: Picador.

AP. (2019) 'After criticism, Greece toughens rape law.' (6 June).

APA. (2018) 'APA Guidelines for Psychological Practice with Boys and Men.' Available at https://www.apa.org/about/policy/boys-men-practice-guidelines.pdf.

Arnt, Bettina. (2019) *#MenToo*. Melbourne, Victoria: Wilkinson Publishing Pty Ltd.

Atwood, Margaret. (2018) 'Am I a bad feminist?' *The Globe and Mail*. (13 January)

Badham, Van. (2018) 'That's patriarchy: how female sexual liberation led to male sexual entitlement.' *The Guardian*. (2 February).

Badinter, Elisabeth. (2006/2003) *Dead End Feminism* (trans. Julia Barossa). Cambridge: Polity Press.

Barekat, Houman. (2019) 'Mask Off by JJ Bola—masculinity redefined.' *The Guardian*. (12 September).

Barnes, Brook. (2019) ' Harvey Weinstein: Ashley Judd sexual harassment lawsuit dismissed by judge. *The Irish Times*. (10 January).

Barnes, Terry. (2018) 'The feminist revolution is already over. Men lost.' *The Spectator*. (March).

Bartholet, Elizabeth, Nancy Gertner, Janet Hally & Jeannie Suk Gersen. (2017) 'Fairness for All Students under Title IX.' Available at https://dash.harvard.edu/bitstream/handle/1/33789434/Fairness%20for%20All%20Students.pdf?sequence=1&isAllowed=y.

Baskerville, Stephen. (2017) *The New Politics of Sex: The Sexual Revolution, Civil Liberties and the Growth of Governmental Power*. Kettering, Ohio: Angelico Press.

Bastiat, Claude Frédéric. (2007 [2011]) *The Bastiat Collection*. 2nd edition. Auburn, Alabama: The Ludwig von Mises Institute.

BBC. (2018) 'Shrewsbury woman jailed over false sexual assault claims.' (23 May).

BBC. (2019) 'Ex-US Senator Al Franken regrets resigning over sexual misconduct claims.' (22 July).

BBC. (2019a.) 'Harvey Weinstein timeline: How the scandal unfolded.' (24 May).

Berlatsky, Noah. (2019) 'Psychologists – and Gillette are right about "traditional masculinity".' *CNN Opinion*. (15 January.)

Berlinski, Claire. (2019) '#MeToo Eats Itself.' *The American Interest*. (27 April).

Bindel, Julie. (2018) 'A war on women is raging in the UK – the femicide statistics prove it.' *The Guardian*. (18 December).

Boffey, Daniel. (2019) 'Finland under pressure to criminalise lack of consent in rape laws.' *The Guardian*. (2 September).

Boorse, Christopher. (2012) 'Premenstrual Syndrome and Criminal

Responsibility,' in Benson E. Ginsburg and Bonnie Frank Carter, *Premenstrual Syndrome: Ethical and Legal Implications in a Biomedical Perspective*, New York: Springer, 81-124.

Bourke, Linda Brookover. (1989) *Defining Rape*. Durham, North Carolina: Duke University Press.

Britton, Alexander. (2018) 'Women launch £4BILLION lawsuit against Tesco for equal pay.' *The Mirror*. (7 February).

Brockmann, Hikle, Anne Maren Koch, Adele Diederich and Christofer Edling. (2017) 'Why Managerial Women are Less Happy Than Managerial Men.' *Journal of Happiness Studies*, Vol. 9, No. 3, 755-779.

Brook, Erynn. (2018) 'Is the term "mansplaining" sexist? You asked Google—here's the answer.' *The Guardian*. (6 June).

Brookman, Fiona and Jane Nolan. (2006) 'The Dark Figure of Infanticide in England and Wales: Complexities of Diagnosis.' *Journal of Interpersonal Violence*. Vol. 21, No. 7, 869-889.

Brownmiller, Susan. (1975) *Against Our Will: Men, Women, and Rape*. New York: Simon and Schuster.

Burnett, Ros. (ed.) (2016) *Wrongful Allegations of Sexual and Child Abuse*. Oxford: Oxford University Press.

Burr, Bill. (2018) 'Bill Burr thinks women are overrated.' Conan interview. Available at https://l7world.com/2018/08/women-overrated-bill-burr-conan.html.

Butler, Sarah. (2018) 'Tesco equal pay claim could cost supermarket up to £4bn.' *The Guardian*. (7 February).

California Department of Education. (2019) 'Model Curriculum Projects.' Available at https://www.cde.ca.gov/ci/cr/cf/modelcurriculumprojects.asp.

Carey, Nessa. (2012 [2011]) *The Epigenetics Revolution: How Modern Biology is Rewriting Our Understanding of Genetics, Disease and Inheritance*. London: Icon Books.

Casey, Gerard. (2011) 'Thinking Critically about Critical Thinking,' in *Critical Thinking and Higher Order Thinking*, (ed.) Mike Shaughnessy. New York, Hauppauge: Nova Science Publishers, 23-39.

Casey, Gerard. (2017) *Freedom's Progress?* Exeter: Imprint Academic.

Casey, Gerard. (2019) *ZAP: Free Speech and Tolerance in the Light of the Zero Aggression Principle*. Exeter: Imprint Academic.

Catlin, George. (1996 [1875]) *Life among the Indians*. London: Bracken Books.

Chakrabarti, Shami. (2017) 'Collapse of rape cases is result of austerity, says Shami Chakrabarti.' *The Guardian*. (23 December).

Channel 4. (2018) 'Interview: Cathy Newman and Jordan Peterson.' Available at https://www.youtube.com/watch?v=aMcjxSThD54.

Charen, Mona. (2018) *Sex Matters: How Modern Feminism Lost Touch with Science, Love, and Common Sense*. New York: Crown Forum.

Chesler, Phyllis. (2009) *Woman's Inhumanity to Woman*. Chicago: Chicago Review Press.

Christodoulou, Holly. (2018) 'Cops and Sobbers. Police force brings in "crying rooms" for female officers going through the menopause.' *The Sun*. (28 January).

Clark, Robert C. (25 October 1995) 'Harvard Law School Memorandum: Sexual Harassment Guidelines.' Available at The 'Lectric Law Library at https://www.lectlaw.com/files/edu01.htm.

Cocks, Richard. (2019) 'When One Sex Attacks the Other, Both Lose.' *Voegelinview*. Available at https://voegelinview.com/when-one-sex-attacks-the-other-both-lose/

Cohen, Stanley. (2011) *Folk Devils and Moral Panics*. London: Routledge.

Collins, Kaitlan. (2018) 'CNN reporter to male bosses: We don't want to date you.' (25 January).

Cook, Cody, Rebecca Diamond, Jonathan Hall et al. (2019) 'The Gender earnings Gap in the Gig Economy: Evidence from over a Million Rideshare Drivers.' Working Paper No. 3637, Stanford Graduate School of Business, 2018.

Copson, Gary. (2018) 'Sex abuse police were told to believe the victims—but that's not their job.' *The Guardian*. (6 July).

Corston, Jean. (2007) *A Report by Baroness Jean Corston of a Review of Women with Particular Vulnerabilities in the Criminal Justice System. The Need for a Distinct, Radically Different, Visibly-led, Strategic Proportionate, Holistic, woman-Centred, Integrated Approach*. The Home Office.

COSC.(no date) 'Male Victims of Domestic Violence.' Available at http://www.cosc.ie/en/COSC/Pages/WP09000005.

Cosslett, Rhiannon. (2017) 'At last men are joining our conversation about toxic masculinity.' *The Guardian*. (6 September).

Coston, Bethany M. 'Reclaiming my fear: I will no longer stay silent about Michael Kimmel.' *#MeTooSociology*.

Cott, Nancy F. "Feminist Theory and Feminist Movements: The Past Before Us," in Mitchell and Oakley, pp. 49-62.

Crilly, Rob. (2018) 'Margaret Atwood triggers online row with criticism of #MeToo movement.' *The Telegraph*. (16 January).

Dalrymple, Theodore. (2005) *Our Culture, What's Left of It: The Mandarins and the Masses*. Chicago: Ivan R. Dee.

Daum, Meghan. (2019a) 'Team older feminist: am I allowed nuanced feelings about #MeToo?' *The Guardian*. (16 October).

Daum, Meghan. (2019b) *The Problem with Everything: My Journey Through The New Culture Wars*. New York: Gallery Books.

Davies, Gareth. (2109) 'Rape convictions at record low, as CPS launces review to examine "myths and stereotypes" about sexual violence.' *The Telegraph*. (12 September).

Davis, Allison. (2019) '*The Wild Ride at Babe.Net* The Aziz Ansari controversy was just the beginning of the trouble for the website.' *The Cut*.

Delingpole, James. (2018) 'Jordan Peterson v Cathy Newman—Best SJW Takedown Evah!' *Breitbart*.

Delmar, Rosalind. "What is Feminism?" in Mitchell and Oakley, 8—33.

Deneuve, Catherine et al. 'Nous défendons une liberté d'importune indispensable à la liberté sexuelle.' *Le Monde*.

Department of Justice and Equality. (2018) 'Minister Flanagan brings landmark Domestic Violence Act into operation.' Available at http://www.justice.ie/en/JELR/Pages/PR19000001.

Dineen, Tana. (1999) *Manufacturing Victims*. London: Little, Brown Book Group.

Dinsmore, Emily. (2018) 'Je suis Catherine.' *Spiked*. (11 January).

Ditum, Sarah. (2018) 'After rape trials, is the court of public opinion now trumping the law?' *The Guardian*. (15 April).

Diver, Tony. (2018) 'Oxford University extends exam times for women's benefit.' *The Telegraph*. (1 February).

Donagan, Moira. (2018) 'How #MeToo revealed the central rift within feminism today.' *The Guardian*. (11 May).

Epstein, Angela. (2016) 'Durham rape case: name and shame the bogus victims.' *The Telegraph*. (13 January).

Evans, Martin. (2017) 'Police should refer to complainants and not "victims" when investigating rape cases, senior legal figures suggest.' *The Telegraph*. (20 December).

Evans, Martin. (2019) 'Nick: Operation Midland report into Carl Beech's bogus VIP paedophile ring claims published for the first time.' *The Telegraph*. (4 October).

Evers, Williamson M. (2019) 'California Wants to Teach Your Kids that Capitalism is Racist.' *Independent Institute*.

Farrell, Warren. (1993) *The Myth of Male Power: Why Men are the Disposable Sex*. New York: Simon & Schuster.

Fenwick, Kirby. (2018) 'Football clubs can end toxic masculinity, but first they need to talk about it.' *The Guardian*. (22 June).

Feuer, Lewis S. (2010/1975) *Ideology and the Ideologists*. London: Transaction Publishers.

Fiamengo, Janice. (ed.) (2018) *Sons of Feminism*, 2ⁿᵈ ed. Ottawa: Little Nightingale Press.

Fine, Cordelia. (2011) *Delusions of Gender: The Real Science behind Sex Differences*. London: Icon Books.

Firsht, Naomi. (2019) 'I'm a pay-gap denier and proud of it.' *Spiked*. (6 April).

Foges, Clare. (2017) 'The women who give feminism a bad name.' *The Times*. (24 March).

Friedersdorf, Conor. (2018) 'What One Professor's Case for Hating Men Missed.' *The Atlantic*. (11 June).

Friedman, Jaclyn. (2017) Tweet. Available at https://twitter.com/jaclynf/status/866817553720594432?lang=en.

Frostrup, Mariella. (2019) 'I want another baby but maternity leave would stall my career.' *The Guardian*. (15 September).

Furness, Hannah. (2018) 'Royal Opera House tenor rejects "in your face" sexual violence against women on stage.' *The Telegraph*. (3 January).

Francis, Richard C. (2011) *Epigenetics: How Environment Shapes our Genes*. New York: W. W. Norton & Company.

Fry & Laurie (A Bit of). (No date) 'Pre-Coital Agreement.' Available at https://www.youtube.com/watch?v=DxFU_fIUawM.

Gat, Azar. (2006) *War in Human Civilization*. Oxford: Oxford University Press.

Gentleman, Amelia. (2018) '"I'm beyond anger"—why the great pay gap reveal is an explosive moment for gender equality.' *The Guardian*. (28 February).

Gilder, George. (1987/1973) *Men and Marriage*. Gretna, Louisiana: Pelican Publishing.

Gillette. (2019) 'We Believe: The Best Men Can Be.' Available at https://www.youtube.com/watch?v=koPmuEyP3a0.

Gittos, Luke. (2015) *Why Rape Culture is a Dangerous Myth: From Steubenville to Ched Evans*. London: Societas (Imprint Academic).

Goldin, Claudia & Cecilia Rouse. (2000) 'Orchestrating Impartiality: The Impact of "Blind" Auditions on Female Musicians.' *American Economic Review*, Vol. 90, No. 4, 715-41.

Goldman, Bruce. (2017) 'Two Minds.' *Stanford Medicine* (Wu Tsai Neuroscience Institute).

Gray, Yvette et al. (2017) 'Female traffic light signals to go up at pedestrian crossing as Committee for Melbourne tackles "unconscious bias".' *ABC News*. (7 March).

Greenberg, David M., Varun Warrier et al. (2018) 'Testing the Emphatizing-Systemizing theory of sex differences and the Extreme Male Brain theory of autism in half a million people.' *Proceedings of the National Academy of Sciences of the United States of America*.

Greenberg, Zoe. (2018) 'What Happens to #MeToo When a Feminist Is the Accused?' *The New York Times*. (13 August).

Greer, Edward. (2000) 'The Truth behind Legal Dominance Feminism's Two Percent False Rape Claim Figure.' *Loyola Los Angeles Law Review*, Vol. 33, No. 3, 947-972.

Greer, Germaine. (1985) *Sex and Destiny: The Politics of Human Fertility*. Picador: London.

Greer, Germaine. (2019) *On Rape*. London: Bloomsbury.

Griffiths, Sian and Julie Henry. (2017) 'Oxford "takeaway" exam to help women get firsts.' *The Sunday Times*. (11 June).

Hakim, Catherine. (2011) *Honey Money: The Power of Erotic Capital*. London: Allen Lane.

Hakim, Catherine. (2015) *Supply and Desire: Sexuality and the Sex Industry in the 21ˢᵗ Century*. London: IEA.

Hall, Sir Matthew. (1736) *History of the Pleas of the Crown*. London.

Halliday, Josh. (2018) 'National Trust branded "ridiculous" for covering up paintings of men.' *The Guardian*. (6 November).

Hannun, Marya. (2014) '"Baby It's Cold Outside" was once an anthem for progressive women. What happened?; The complicated origins of a pilloried song.' *The Washington Post*. (19 December).

Harvard Medical School. (2010). 'Mars vs. Venus: The gender gap in health.' *Harvard Health Publishing*.

Hayden, Jade. (no date) 'Ashley Judd has accused film producer Harvey Weinstein of sexual harassment.' *Her*. Available at https://www.her.ie/news/ashley-judd-accused-film-producer-harvey-weinstein-sexual-harasment-368147.

Hayles, Katherine N. (1992) 'Gender Encoding in Fluid Mechanics: Masculine Channels and Feminine Flows.' *differences*, Vol. 4, No. 2, 16-44.

Heidt, Brianna. (2018) 'Parents Sue After Son Is Falsely Accused of Sexual Assault by "Mean Girls" at High School.' *Townhall*. Available at https://townhall.com/tipsheet/briannaheldt/2018/10/10/parents-sue-after-son-is-falsely-accused-of-sexual-assault-by-mean-girls-at-high-school-n2527344.

Hemingway, Mollie. (2014) 'It's Time to Push Back against the Feminist Bullies.' *The Federalist*.

Hemingway, Mollie and Carrie Severino. (2019) *Justice on Trial: The Kavanaugh Confirmation and the Future of the Supreme Court*. New York: Regnery Publishing.

Henderson, Michelle. (2019) '"Like someone flicked a switch": the premenstrual disorder that upturns women's lives.' *The Guardian*. (15 September).

Henriques, Sir Richard. (2016) *An Independent Review of the Metropolitan Police Service's handling of non-recent sexual offence investigations alleged against persons of public prominence*.

Hewson, Barbara. (2013) 'Believe the victim: a recipe for injustice.' *Spiked*. (11 November).

Higgins, Julia. (2018) 'Gender Stereotypes are still pervasive in our culture.' *The Guardian*. (2 March).

Higgins, Paul. (2017) 'Arrest warrant for woman who made false rape claim.' *The Belfast Telegraph*. (13 November).

High Court. (2011) *Assange vs Swedish Prosecution Authority*.

Hiscox, Michael J., Tara Oliver, Michael Ridgway, Lilia Arcos-Holzinger, Alastair Warren and Andrea Willis. 'Going blind to see more clearly: unconscious bias in Australian Public Service (APS) shortlisting processes. Available at https://behaviouraleconomics.pmc.gov.au/sites/default/files/projects/unconscious-bias.pdf

HMCPSI/HMIC. (2017) 'Making it Fair: A Joint Inspection of the Disclosure of Unused Material in Volume Crown Court Cases.' (17 July).

Holland, Tom. (2019). *Dominium: The Making of the Western Mind*. London: Little, Brown.

Horton, Helena. (2018) 'Chess contest offers free tickets to women, amid "long hard struggle' to address gender gap.' *The Telegraph*. (15 November).

Hoyle, Carolyn, Naomi-Ellen Speechley & Ros Burnett. (2016) *The Impact of being Wrongly Accused of Abuse in Occupations of Trust: Victim's Voices*. Centre for Criminology, University of Oxford.

Huxley, Aldous. (1952) *The Devils of Loudun*. London: Chatto and Windus.

Hymas, Charles. (2019) 'Alleged rapists' lawyers could be asked for lines of inquiry into their victims by prosecutors.' *The Telegraph*. (17 October).

Hynes, James. (2002) *The Lecturer's Tale*. London: Picador.

ITV. (2018) 'Tesco facing £4 billion bill over equal pay legal challenge.' Available at https://www.youtube.com/watch?v=Uyfu2ic80VY.

Johnson, Boris. (2014) 'Dr Matt Taylor's shirt made me cry, too—with rage at his abusers.' *The Telegraph*. (16 November.)

Johnson, Jamie. (2018) '"Shocking lack of female entrepreneurs" as it emerges just a fifth of British businesses are run by a woman.' *The Telegraph*. (21 September).

Jones, Dylan. (2016) *Manxiety*. London: Biteback Publishing.

Jones, Rupert. (2018) 'Gender pay gap means women work 67 days a year for free, says TUC.' *The Guardian*. (8 March).

Joyce, Peter. (2016) *Dry Ice: The True Story of a False Rape Complaint*. The Copy Press.

Judicial College. (2018) 'Equal Treatment Bench Book'.

Kaminer, Wendy. (2018) 'The dangers of vigilante feminism.' *Spiked*. (29 January).

Kandel, Jason. (2013) NBC. 'Woman Who Falsely Accused Brian Banks of Rape Ordered to Pay $2,6M.'

Kantor, Jodi & Megan Twohey. (2019) *She Said: Breaking the Sexual Harassment Story that helped ignite a Movement.'* London: Penguin.

Kilpatrick, Chris. (2013) 'Rape lie woman Natasha Foster cried wolf after ex-lover's snub,' *Belfast Telegraph*. (23 November).

Kimball, Roger. (1993) 'Sex in the twilight zone: Catherine MacKinnon's crusade.' *The New Criterion*. (October).

King, Alexandra. (2016) 'Couple rewrites "Baby It's Cold Outside" to emphasize importance of consent." CNN.

Kipnis, Laura. (2018) *Unwanted Advances: Sexual Paranoia Comes to Campus*. London: Verso.

Kirkham, Alli. (2015) 'How Do I Know If I've Been Raped?' *Everyday Feminism*. Available at https://everydayfeminism.com/2015/07/how-to-know-if-ive-been-raped/.

Knapton, Sarah. (2018) 'Women really are more empathetic and men more analytical, biggest ever study shows.' *The Telegraph*. (12 November).

Knoedler, J. R and N. M. Shah. (2018) 'Molecular mechanisms underlying sexual differentiation of the nervous system.' *Current Opinion in Neurobiology*. Vol. 53, pp. 192-97.

Kuby, Gabrielle. (2015/2012) *The Global Sexual Revolution: Destruction of Freedom in the Name of Freedom* (trans. James Patrick Kirchner). Kettering, Ohio: Lifesite.

Le, Paul and Cheryl E. Matias. (2018) 'Towards a truer multicultural science education: how whiteness impacts science education.' *Cultural Studies of Science Education*.

Lebow, Richard Ned. (2018) 'Warning: Telling a Lame Joke in an Elevator can Endanger Your Career.' *Quillette*. (23 November).

Lewinsky, Monica. (2018) 'Monica Lewinsky: Emerging from "The House of Gaslight" in the Age of #MeToo.' *Vanity Fair*. (February.)

Lewis, Bob. (2017) *The Feminist Lie: It Was Never about Equality*. Place: CreateSpace Independent Publishing Platform.

Lewis, Helen. (2019) 'She Said by Jodi Kantor and Megan Twohey review – the inside story of Weinstein and #MeToo.' *The Guardian*. (18 September).

Liddle, Ron. (2019) We've made morons of our police force.' *The Spectator*. (September)

Lloyd, Peter. (2016) *Stand by Your Manhood: An Essential Guide for Modern Men*. London: Biteback Publishing.

Lockwood, Michael. (2019) 'Operation Midland made mistakes, but the presumption of innocence must prevail. *The Guardian*. (8 October).

Lucey, Anne. (2018) 'Woman found guilty of making false report of rape gets suspended sentence.' *The Irish Independent*. (13 March).

Lyndon, Neil. (1993) *No More Sex War: The Failures of Feminism*. London: Mandarin Paperbacks.

MacDonald, Heather. (2018) 'Sarah Jeong is a Boring, Typical Product of the American Academy.' *National Review*. (August).

Malik, Nesrine. (2017) 'Now sexual harassment is a campaign against men? Get real.' *The Guardian*. (9 November).

Mamet, David. (2012) *The Secret Knowledge: On the Dismantling of American Culture*. New York: Sentinel.

Mangan, Katherine. (2018) 'Dispute Over "Lingerie" Comment Persists, as Society Rejects Professor's Appeal.' *The Chronicle of Higher Education*. (14 November).

Mansfield, Declan. (2018) 'The feminist two-step.' *The Spectator*. (February).

Mansell, Keeley. (2017) Menopause Managers Guide – PG50.

Mansfield, Harvey C. (2006) *Manliness*. New Haven, Connecticut: Yale University Press.

Mangan, Katherine. (2018) 'NYU Scholar Accused of Harassment Assails Rush to Judgment as Sign of "Sexual paranoia".' *The Chronicle of Higher Education*. (17 August).

Math and Social Justice. (no date) 'Math and Social Justice: A Collaborative MTBoS Site.' Available at https://sites.google.com/site/mathandsocialjustice/curriculum-resources.

Matthewson-Grand, Alisha. (2018) 'The World Chess championship is thrilling. But where are the women?' *The Guardian*. (20 November).

Mayer, Jane. (2019) 'The Case of Al Franken.' New Yorker Magazine. (29 July).

McCartney, Jenny. (2018) 'The new feminist war: your young women vs old women.' *The Spectator*. (January).

McDermott, Roe. (2018) 'Everything you want to know about consent but were afraid to ask.' *The Irish Times*. (7 April).

MacGiolla, Erik and Petri Kajonius. (2018) 'Sex differences in personality are larger in gender equal countries: replicating and extending a surprising finding.' *International Journal of Psychology*.

McGoogan, Cara. (2017) 'What can we learn from other countries when it comes to rape convictions?' *The Telegraph*. (22 December).

Meikle, James. (2014) 'Rosetta scientist Dr Matt Taylor apologises for "offensive" shirt.' *The Guardian*. (14 November)

Mendick, Robert. (2018) 'Police wrongly pursued retired fire chief rather than investigate blackmail claim against fantasist who accused him of rape.' *The Telegraph*. (10 February).

Merkin, Daphne. (2018) 'Publicly, We Say #MeToo. Privately, We Have Misgivings.' *The New York Times*. (5 January).

Miles, Rosalind. (2001 [1988]) *Who Cooked the Last Supper? The Women's History of the World*. New York: Three Rivers Press.

Mill, John Stuart. (1861) *Considerations on Representative Government*, in Mill 1991, 205-470.

Mill, John Stuart. (1965-1991) *Collected Works of John Stuart Mill*, 33 vols. ed. J. Robson. Toronto: University of Toronto Press.

Mitchell, Juliet and Ann Oakley. (1986) *What is Feminism?* Oxford: Blackwell.

Mitchell, Susan. (2017) 'Dangers of #MeToo mean #ImOut' *The Sunday Business Post*. (5 November).

Moore, Suzanne. (2018) 'Of course girls feel miserable. They can't move freely in the world.' *The Guardian*. (27 January).

Moran, Caitlin. (2011) *How to be a Woman*. London: Ebury Press.

Morris, Steven. (2011) 'False rape complaint case that split a small community.' *The Guardian*. (28 January).

Morrissey, Belinda. (2003) *When Women Kill: Questions of Agency and Subjectivity*. London: Routledge.

Mott, Carrie and Daniel Cockayne. (2017) 'Citation matters: mobilizing the politics of citation toward a practice of "conscientious engagement".' *Gender, Place & Culture*, Vol. 24, No. 7, 954-73.

Moutet, Anne-Elisabeth. (2019) 'My problem with the #MeToo movement.'

New Zealand Herald. (13 January).

Moxon, Steve. (2008) *The Woman Racket: The New Science Explaining How the Sexes Relate at Work, at Play and in Society.* Exeter: Imprint Academic.

Murray, Douglas. (2018) 'Cathy Newman's catastrophic interview with Jordan Peterson.' *The Spectator.* (December).

Murphy, Simon and Vikram Dodd. (2019) 'Met police agreed to say they believed VIP abuse claims—report.' *The Guardian.* (4 October).

Murphy, Trish. (2018) 'A woman tricked me to become pregnant and I am devastated.' *The Irish Times.* (17 January).

Myers, Fraser. (2018) 'After Toronto: a moral panic about men.' *Spiked.* (1 May).

Nathanson, Paul & Katherine K. Young. (2001) *Spreading Misandry: The Teaching of Contempt for Men in Popular Culture.* Montreal & Kingston: McGill-Queen's University Press.

Nathanson, Paul & Katherine K. Young. (2006) *Legalizing Misandry: From Public Shame to Systemic Discrimination against Men.* Montreal & Kingston: McGill-Queen's University Press.

Nathanson, Paul & Katherine K. Young. (2015) *Replacing Misandry: A Revolutionary history of Men.* Montreal & Kingston: McGill-Queen's University Press.

Nathanson, Paul and Katherine K. Young. (2015) *Replacing Misandry: A Revolutionary History of Men.* Montreal: McGill-Queen's University Press.

New York Times. (2018) 'Statements in Response to Criticism of the Hiring of Sarah Jeong to the Editorial Board in Opinion.' *The New York Times.* (2 August).

Newman, Cathy. (2019) 'Sally Challen: If we'd had a helpline for abused women, my husband would still be alive.' *The Telegraph.* (23 September).

O'Beirne, Kate. (2006) *Women Who Make the World Worse.* London: Sentinel.

O'Connell, Jennifer. (2018) '"Rape is a crime. But a persistent or clumsy come-on is not a crime".' *The Irish Times.* (9 January).

O'Halloran, Kate. (2018) 'Forbes rich list shows sport fails to respect women - let alone pay them properly' *The Guardian.* (6 June).

O'Hanlon, Eilis. (2019) 'Why are men more wary of women now?' *The Irish Independent.* (1 September).

O'Neill, Brendan. (2018) 'The misogyny of #MeToo.' *Spiked.* (11 January).

O'Neill, Brendan. (2019) 'Sally Challen is no hero.' *Spiked.* (8 June).

O'Toole, Emer. (2017) 'How should a woman respond when a man we like [*sic*] is accused of harassment?' *The Guardian.* (13 November).

Office for National Statistics. (2017) 'Homicide in England and Wales: Year

Ending March 2017.'

Oppenheim, Maya. (2019) '"Historic victory for women": Greece introduces new definition of rape after initial proposal sparked backlash.' *The Independent*. (6 June).

Paglia, Camille. (1991/1990) *Sexual Personae: Art and Decadence from Nefertiti to Emily Dickinson*. New York: Vintage Books.

Paglia, Camille. (1992) *Sex, Art, and American Culture*. New York: Vintage Books.

Paglia, Camille. (2017) *Free Women Free Men: Sex * Gender * Feminism*. New York: Pantheon Books.

Parkinson, Cyril Northcote. (1958) *The Evolution of Political Thought*. Boston: Houghton Mifflin Company.

Pascal, Julia. (2018) 'Women are being excluded from the stage. It's time for quotas.' *The Guardian*. (24 April).

Patai, Daphne. (1998) *Heterophobia: Sexual Harassment and the Future of Feminism*. Lanham, Maryland: Rowman & Littlefield.

Penman, Jim. (2015) *Biohistory*. Newcastle upon Tyne: Cambridge Scholars Publishing.

Perrins, Laura. (2013) 'Did you know the legal definition of rape and "consent" is changing? Here's How.' *The Telegraph*. (19 September).

Persio, Sofia Lotto. (2018) 'Man Wins $390,000 in Gender Discrimination lawsuit after Female Colleague Gets Promotion He Was More Qualified for.' *Newsweek*. (27 October).

Pessah, Tom. (2017) 'Men who are silent after #MeToo: it's time to speak up.' *The Guardian*. (20 October).

Phillips, Kristine. (2019) 'Complaint: California lawmaker who led #MeToo push invited staffer to play spin the bottle.' *The Washington Post*. (19 February).

Pilkington, Ed. (2018) 'New York Review of Books editor departs amid outrage over essay.' *The Guardian*. (19 September).

Proudman, Charlotte. (2017) 'Why does police mishandling of evidence only make headlines in rape cases?' *The Guardian*. (21 December).

Pulliam, Mark. (2019) 'Capra Meets Kafka: Political Intrigue Too Bizarre for Fiction.' *Law & Liberty*.

Purdy, Herbert. (2016) *Their Angry Creed: The Shocking History of Feminism and How It is Destroying our Way of Life*. LPS Publishing.

Ramaswamy, Chitra. (2018) 'Why are we so desperate to believe men in rape cases?' *The Guardian*. (24 September).

Reynolds, Emily. (2018) 'How men can show solidarity with the #MeToo movement.' *The Guardian.* (23 February).

Reynolds, Emily. (2018a) 'Universities are home to a rape epidemic. Here's what they can do.' *The Guardian.* (2 March).

Reynolds, Glenn Harlan. (2015) 'A war on college men' *USA Today.* (14 September)

Revolt Sexual Assault. (2018) Available at https://revoltsexualassault.com/research/.

Riley, Charlotte. (2019) 'How to play Patriarchy Chicken: why I refuse to move out of the way for men.' *NewStatesmanAmerica.* (22 February).

Riley, Donna. (2017) 'Rigor/Us: Building Boundaries and Disciplining Diversity with Standards of Merit.' *Engineering Studies*, Vol. 9, No. 3, 249-265.

Roberts, John Morris. (1993) *History of the World.* London: BCA.

Roberts, John Morris. (1997 [1996]) *The Penguin History of Europe.* London: Penguin Books.

Roberts, Yvonne, Afua Hirsch and Hannah Jane Parkinson. (2018) 'Reading Germaine: three generations respond to On Rape.' *The Observer.* (9 September).

Robertson, Noah. (2019) 'Meet America's top-ranked female chess player: A teenager.' *The Christian Science Monitor.* (6 September).

Robins, Jon. (2018) *Guilty Until Proven Innocent.* London: Biteback Publishing.

Ruddick, Graham. (2018) 'C4 calls in security experts after presenter suffers online abuse.' *The Guardian.* (19 January).

Rudgard, Olivia. (2017) 'Domestic abuse figures to spike as new law causes reversal of downward trend.' *The Telegraph.* (23 November).

Rudgard, Olivia. (2017a) 'Feminist theory could help treat anorexia, study suggests.' *The Telegraph.* (13 November).

R. v. Blackwell [2006] EWCA 2815.

Sailer, Steve. (2018) 'Sarah Jeong on the UVA Gang Rape on Broken Glass Hoax "I Believe Jackie".' *The Unz Review.*

Savino, John O. and Brent E. Turvey (eds) (2005) *Rape Investigation Handbook.* Amsterdam: Elsevier Academic Press.

Sawer, Patrick. (2018) 'Wimbledon's "working mothers" complain about match schedules because they miss their children.' *The Telegraph.* (3 July).

Sawer, Patrick. (2019) 'Drink driver spared jail and given another chance by judge because she is a woman.' *The Telegraph.* (12 April).

Schilller, Robin and Margaret Schelkowski. (2018) 'Irish woman traumatised by "violent" fiancé when she killed him—claim.' *Irish Independent.*

(24 October).

Schow, Ashe. (2015) 'Rep. Jared Polis did not misspeak, he just doesn't like the backlash' *Washington Examiner*. (16 September).

Seydoux, Léa. (2017) 'Léa Seydoux says Harvey Weinstein tried to sexually assault her.' *The Guardian*. (11 October).

Sharp, Andrew. (ed.) (1998) *The English Levellers*. Cambridge: Cambridge University Press.

Shaw, Andy. (2018) '7 easy steps to becoming a male feminist.' *Spectator Life*. (25 April).

Shaw, Julia. (2016) *The Memory Illusion: Remembering, Forgetting, and the Science of False Memory*. London: Random House.

Shriver, Lionel. (2018) 'What's wrong with hearing #MeToo men's side of the story?' *The Spectator*. (September).

Sigilitto, Serena. (2019) 'Rejecting Toxic Masculinity isn't an attack on Men.' *Public Discourse*.

Slawson, Nicola. (2018) 'Julia Gillard warns of backlash from gender equality critics.' *The Guardian*. (5 April).

Smethers, Sam. (2019) 'Here's the date when women will "stop being paid" in 2019 – no change there then.' *The Telegraph*. (29 October).

Solnit, Rebecca. (2018) 'The Brett Kavanaugh case shows that we still blame women for the sins of men.' *The Guardian*. (21 September).

Sommers, Christina Hoff. (1995/1994) *Who Stole Feminism?: How Women have Betrayed Women*. New York: Simon & Schuster.

Sommers, Christina Hoff. (2015/2000) *The War against Boys: How Misguided Policies are Harming our Young Men*, new rev. ed. New York: Simon & Shuster.

Sommers, Christina Hoff. (2017) '"Feminism has been hijacked".' *Spiked*. (29 December).

Sommers, Christina Hoff. (2019) 'Blind Spots in the "Blind Audition" Study.' *Wall Street Journal*. (20 October 2019)

Sowell, Thomas. (2018) *Discrimination and Disparities*. New York: Basic Books.

Squires, Nick. (2018) 'Italy gives world-famous opera Carmen a defiant new ending in stand against violence to women.' *The Telegraph*. (2 January).

Starr, Sonja. (2012) 'Estimating Gender Disparities in Federal Criminal Cases.' *Law & Economics Working Papers*, Paper 57.

Stoet, Gijsbert and David C. Geary. (2018) 'The Gender-Equality Paradox in Science, Technology, Engineering, and Mathematics Education. *Psychological Science*, 29, 581-593.

Su, Rong, James Rounds & Patrick Ian Armstrong. (2009) 'Men and Things, Women and People: A Meta-Analysis of Sex Differences in Interests,' *Psychological Bulletin*, Vol. 135 No. 6, 859-884.

Summers, Hannah. (2017) 'Rape victims to be spared ordeal of cross-examination in court.' *The Guardian*. (19 March).

Sweney, Mark. (2018) 'Sexist and body-shaming ads could be banned under new rule.' *The Guardian*. (17 May).

Symons, Donald. (1981) *The Evolution of Human Sexuality*. Oxford: Oxford University Press.

Taki. (2017) 'What was the New York Times's real motive for exposing Weinstein?' *The Spectator*. (14 October).

Tate, J. P. (2014) *Feminism is Sexism*. [No publisher or place of publication specified].

Taylor, Diane. (2019) 'Lady Hale: at least half of UK judiciary should be female.' *The Guardian*. (24 March).

Thomas, David. (1993) *Not Guilty: In Defence of the Modern Man*. Weidenfeld & Nicolson: London.

Thornhill, Randy and Craig T. Palmer. (2000) *A Natural History of Rape*. Cambridge, Massachusetts: MIT Press.

Thorpe, Vanessa. (2018) 'Cambridge marks women's equality struggle—with a two-storey vulva.' *The Guardian*. (6 October).

Thurston, E. Temple. (1939/1910) *The City of Beautiful Nonsense*. London: Penguin.

Tiger, Lionel. (1999) *The Decline of Males: The First Look at an Unexpected New World for Men and Women*. New York: St Martin's Griffin.

Title IX For All. Website. Available at http://www.titleixforall.com/.

Tomassi, Rollo. (2013) *The Rational Male*. CreateSpace Independent Publishing Platform.

Topping, Alexandra. (2018) 'Scrap juries in rape trials, Labour MP suggests.' *The Guardian*. (21 November).

Turner, Camilla. '(2017) 'Oxford University blasted for "insulting decision to allow students to sit exams at home as it implies women are the "weaker sex".' *The Telegraph*. (11 June).

Turner, Camilla. (2018) 'Oxford University set to feminise curriculum by requesting inclusion of women on reading lists.' *The Telegraph*. (14 March).

Turvey, Brent, John Savino, Aurelio Mares. (2017) *False Allegations: Investigative and Forensic Issues in Fraudulent Reports of Crime*. Academic Press.

Tuttle, Lisa. (1986) *Encyclopedia of Feminism*. New York: Facts on File

Publications.

Twitter. (23 February 2019) 'Eye on Anti-Semitism.' Available at https://twitter.com/AntisemitismEye/status/1099321644861009920.

United States Department Of Justice Archives. (2012) 'An Updated Definition of Rape.' Available at https://www.justice.gov/archives/opa/blog/updated-definition-rape.

Valenti, Jessica. (2014) 'Who is Jackie? Rolling Stone's rape story is about a person – and I believe her.' *The Guardian*. (8 December).

Valenti, Jessica. (2015) "It wasn't Jackie's job to get the details of her rape correct. It was Rolling Stone's.' *The Guardian*. (6 April).

Various. (2019) 'Falling rape convictions putting people at risk of "serial attackers", Victims' Commissioner Vera Baird warns.' *The Telegraph*. (28 August).

Verkaik, Robert. (2018) 'To drain the swamp of men-only clubs there must be a public register of members.' *The Guardian*. (27 January).

Vine, Sarah. (2015) 'Crazy law could make nagging your other half illegal.' *Mail Online*. (30 December).

Wade, Lisa. (2017) 'The Big Picture: Confronting Manhood after Trump.' *Public Books*.

Wade, Nicholas. (2014) *A Troublesome Inheritance: Genes, Race and Human History*. New York: The Penguin Press.

Wasserman, Elizabeth. (2015) 'Rise of the Femsplainers.' *National Post*.

Walker, Rebecca. (1992) 'Becoming the Third Wave.' *Ms*, Vol. 2 No. 4, 39 ff.

Wallace, Tim. (2018) 'Instant gender pay gap for young workers as women choose lower-wage apprenticeships than men.' *The Telegraph*. (16 September).

Walter, Suzanne Danuta. (2018) 'Why can't we hate men?' *The Washington Post*. (8 June)

Ward, Victoria. (2019) 'Police Watchdog accused of "gross negligence" for ignoring "explosive" report into disastrous Carl Beech investigation. *The Telegraph*. (8 September).

Watson, Leon. (2019) '"Queen of chess" says it's hard to imagine women competing at the same level as men.' *The Telegraph*. (12 October)

Way, Katie. (2018) 'I went on a date with Aziz Ansari. It turned into the worst night of my life.' *Babe*. Available at https://babe.net/2018/01/13/aziz-ansari-28355.

West, Lindy. (2014) 'Rolling Stone threw a rape victim to the misogynist horde.' *The Guardian*. (8 April).

Whipp, Glenn. (2017) 'Kate Winslet didn't thank Harvey Weinstein when she won the Oscar. Here's why.' *Los Angeles Times*. (14 October).

Whipple, Tom. (2018) 'Patriarchy paradox: how equality reinforces stereotypes.' *The Times*. (15 September).

Wilson, Edward O. (1978) *On Human Nature*. Cambridge, Massachusetts: Harvard University Press.

Winton, Tim. (2018) 'About the boys: how toxic masculinity is shackling men to misogyny.' *The Guardia*n. (9 April).

Wolff, Michael. (2015) 'At Rolling Stone, "Rape Culture" stopped questions.' *USA Today*. (9 April).

Wong, Julia Carrie. (2018) '#MeToo leaders say Asia Argento abuse claim should not discredit movement.' *The Guardian*. (20 August).

Wootton, David (ed.) (2003 [1986]) *Divine Right and Democracy: An Anthology of Political Writing in Stuart England*. Indianapolis, Indiana: Hackett Publishing Company, 2003.

Wright, Tiffany. (201) 'Assault is not a feeling. The Aziz Ansari story shows why language matters. *The Guardian*. (17 January).

YouTube. (2012) 'Affirmative Action.' Available at https://www.youtube.com/watch?v=q8JEybbei60.

Young, Katherine K. and Paul Nathanson. (2010) *Sanctifying Misandry: Goddess Ideology and the Fall of Man*. Montreal: McGill-Queen's University Press.

Young, Toby. (2019) 'The unending war against masculinity and men.' *The Spectator*. (12 January).